Dedication

To my mother and the memory of my father.

Acknowledgements

I wish to thank the following who have given so generously of their time and effort to help in either lending their paper dolls or sending information without which this book could not have been possible: Betsy Addison, Norene Allen, Grace Battjes, Carol Carey, Sharon Carter, Virginia Crossley, Judy Curtis, Zelda Cushner, Jenny Elmore, Rosalie Eppert, Barbara Ferguson, Kassey Ferguson, Patti Fertel, Bonnie Fuson, Jeannine Gliwski, Betty Gohmert, Shirley Hedge, Pam Hunter, Marilyn Johnson, Genie Kalb, Joan Carol Kaltschmidt, Louise Kaufman, Mary Kelley, Francine Kirsch, Verna Kubin, Judy LeJeune, Louise Leek, Edith Linn, Rosemary McBurnett, Joyce McClelland, Katharine McIntire, Ted Menten, Cynthia Musser, Wanda Myers, Van Dyke Pearson, Grayce Piemontesi, Maurine Popp, Nancy Reilly, Peggy Jo Rosamond, Richard Rusnock, Audrey Sepponen, Betsy Slap, Estelle Spyes, Elsie Stevens, Jane Sugg, Emma Terry, Suzanne Tessey, Fran Van Vynckt, Jean Vandiver, Anne Wallach, Verlee Waterman, Ruth Garfinkel West, Ann Wilmer, Jean Woodcock and Wynn Yusas.

My appreciation also goes to the following who so graciously helped me with my project: Peter Lowe, George Chartier, Cheryl Bryson, June Butcher, Hugh Wiberg, David Atkinson, Marybeth Biddiscombe, J. Parker Scott, Clifford Loveheim, Virginia McEnerney, Jane Hughes and Susan Maher. Also, my thanks to Patsy Powers and Joe Daole at the Toy Museum of Atlanta, Mary Thomas Justice and Sylvia MacNeil at the Yesteryears Doll Museum in Sandwich, Mass., and Beatrice Parsons and Helen Woughter at the Detroit Public Schools Children's Museum.

All photographs by the author unless otherwise noted.

All paper dolls from the author's collection unless otherwise noted

Introduction

In the first *Collector's Guide to Paper Dolls*, three major companies were covered that produced paper dolls in this century. This Collector's Guide is a continuation that features paper dolls produced by many other companies in quantities ranging from substantial amounts to just a very few. Over one hundred companies are covered. In keeping with the intent to not overlook any of the paper doll sets published by these companies, every attempt was made to identify all of their paper dolls published from the turn of the century to the present. Some paper doll sets could not be obtained for photographing; nevertheless all known sets are identified.

Price Guide

The prices in this book are based on mint, uncut original paper dolls. Cut sets are usually half the price, providing all the dolls and outfits are included and the pieces are in very good condition. Otherwise the price decreases accordingly. Some of the older paper dolls covered in this book were produced in die cut form (packaged with the dolls and outfits already cut). In these cases the price shown is for a die cut set in mint condition with all costumes and accessories.

The paper dolls pictured are copyrighted by the company in whose section they appear, unless otherwise stated.

A Collector's Guide To
Paper Dolls
Second Series

By

Mary Young

COLLECTOR BOOKS
A Division of Schroeder Publishing Co., Inc.

Other Books By The Author

Paper Dolls And Their Artists-Book I
Paper Dolls And Their Artists-Book II
A Collector's Guide To Paper Dolls-Saalfield, Lowe and Merrill

The current values in this book should be used only as a guide. They are not intended to set prices, which vary from one section of the country to another. Auction prices as well as dealer prices vary greatly and are affected by condition as well as demand. Neither the Author nor the Publisher assumes responsibility for any losses that might be incurred as a result of consulting this guide.

Additional copies of this book may be ordered from:

Collector Books
P.O. Box 3009
Paducah, KY 42001

@$9.95 Add $1.00 for postage and handling.

Copyright: Mary Young, 1984
ISBN: 0-89145-245-1

This book or any part thereof may not be reproduced without the written consent of the Author and Publisher.

A.T. Co.

No information has been found to indicate what the initials A.T. Co. stand for.

There were two different styles of *Our Favorite Dolls*. The one style has the boy in short hair and the girl in long hair parted in the center. The dolls pictured came with outfits reading "A.T. Co." on their back. This set has also been found to say "A.T. Co." on the back of the dolls. The folder pictured came with these two A.T. Co. dolls and is not marked with the company name.

The second style of *Our Favorite Dolls* has the boy in long hair and the girl in long hair with bangs. This pair was published by Selchow and Righter and also by the Amlico Co. They are pictured in their own sections in this book. Notice that the boy dolls are the same from the neck down and likewise for the girl dolls. Both Selchow and Righter and the Amlico Co. put their company name on their folders. The A.T. Co. folder pictured is green, brown and white. The Selchow and Righter folder is yellow, brown and white, and the Amlico folder is yellow, purple (grape) and white.

Each doll came with five costumes and hats for a total of ten outfits for the pair. The ten outfits came in six sets all of which are described on the back of each A.T. Co. outfit and sometimes on the back of the dolls. The following description is quoted exactly as it is written on the dolls and outfits. "Set No. 1 consists of Girl Doll, Girl's Turquoise Blue Dress, with Hat to match. Set No. 2 consists of One Girl's Pink Dress, with Hat to match. One Girl's Plaid Dress, with Hat to match. Set No. 3 consists of One Girl's Old Rose figured Dress, Apron filled with Flowers, and hat to match. One Girl's Royal Blue Defender Sailor Dress, with hat to match. Set No. 4 consists of Boy Doll, Red Newport Sailor Suit with Cap to match. Set No. 5 consists of One Boy's Suit American Guard, Army Blue Uniform, with Cap to match. One Boy's Suit, Scotch Highland costume, complete, with Cap to match. Set No. 6 consists of One Boy's Suit, Zouave Uniform, with Cap to match. One Boy's Suit, Prince Charles costume, complete, with Cap to match."

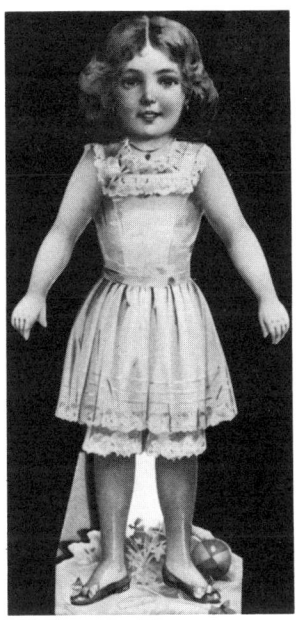 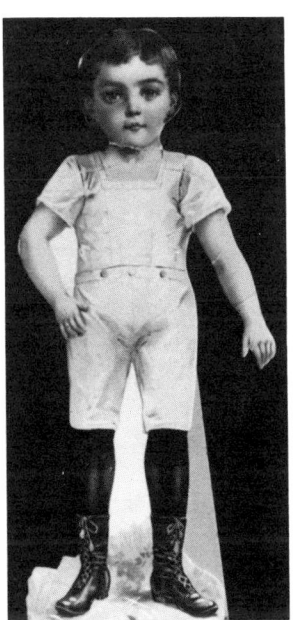 

OUR FAVORITE DOLLS. $50.00

Courtesy of Virginia Crossley

The Abingdon Press

China 1931 (not pictured)
Indian 1924 (not pictured)

TWINS TRAVELOGUES-Japan 1923

Courtesy of Jane Sugg

Advance Games, Inc.

466 *A DRESS A DAY*. $15.00

Courtesy of Virginia Crossley

Aldon Industries, Inc.

Courtesy of Virginia Crossley

NEW JUDY. $7.00

Courtesy of Jane Sugg

NEW LAURIE. $7.00

201 *SUSIE, JUDY, LAURA AND ANNIE*. $7.00

101 *LAURA AND ANNIE*
102 *ANNETTE* (Disney)
103 Walt Disney's Formed Plastic Cut-outs. Two sheets of cut-outs, Donald and Daisy Duck on one sheet, Disney Stand-ups on the other.
201 *SUSIE, JUDY, LAURA AND ANNIE* (pictured)
203 *ANNETTE, CINDERELLA, SNOW WHITE AND ZORRO*
The following sets did not have numbers or the numbers were not available.
NEW JUDY (pictured)
NEW LAURIE (pictured)
NEW SUSIE
MICKEY MOUSE AND HIS PALS

SLEEPING BEAUTY
CINDERELLA
ZORRO
DARLENE
POPEYE THIMBLE THEATER
PETER PAN
TINKER BELL
ALICE IN WONDERLAND
MIGHTY MOUSE
HECKLE AND JECKLE
MY FAIR LADY

American Colortype Company

Most of the paper dolls printed by American Colortype were done in the early 1900's through the first World War. Many of their dolls were also printed with advertising for various companies. Bakeries especially used these paper dolls to advertise their bakery goods on the backs of the dolls.

In 1927 six books of paper dolls were printed by the American Colortype Co. and were completely different from their earlier paper dolls. They came in two sets of three books each, two dolls to a book. Set #1 contained books #25, 26 and 27 and they were marked "copyright A.C. Co." On the next set of three books, #101, 102 and 103, the company name is spelled out completely, "c. American Colortype Co."

Folder For Set #1

#25 *MARIE* 1927. $17.50. *PATSY ANN* (back cover)

Courtesy of Virginia Crossley

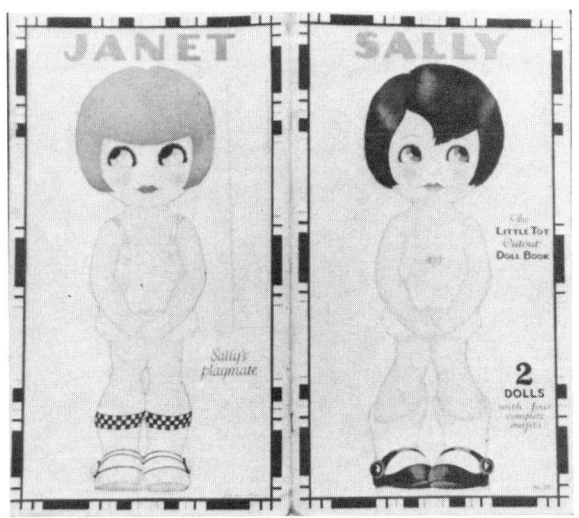

Courtesy of Jane Sugg

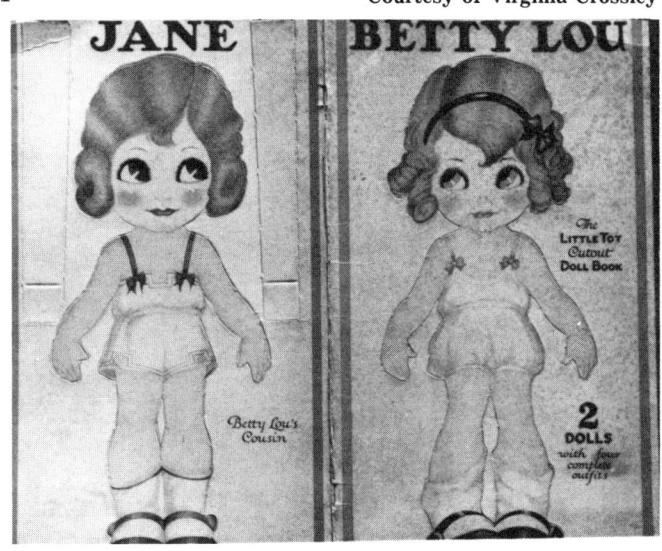

#26 *BETTY LOU* 1927. $17.50. *JANE* (back cover)

#101 *SALLY* 1927. $17.50. *JANET* (back cover)

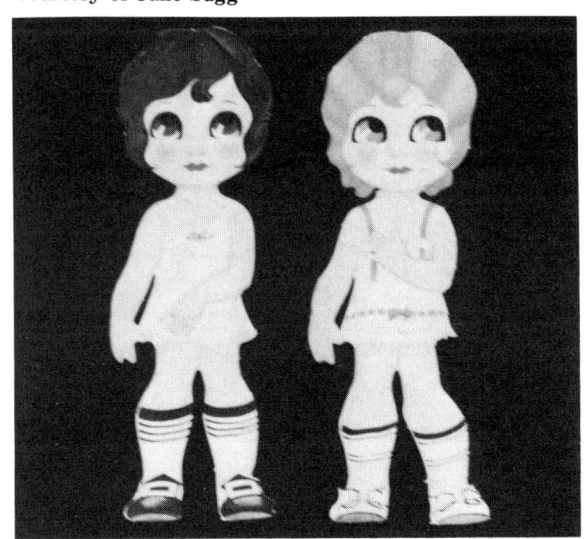

#102 *MARGY* (left) *MILDRED* 1927. $17.50

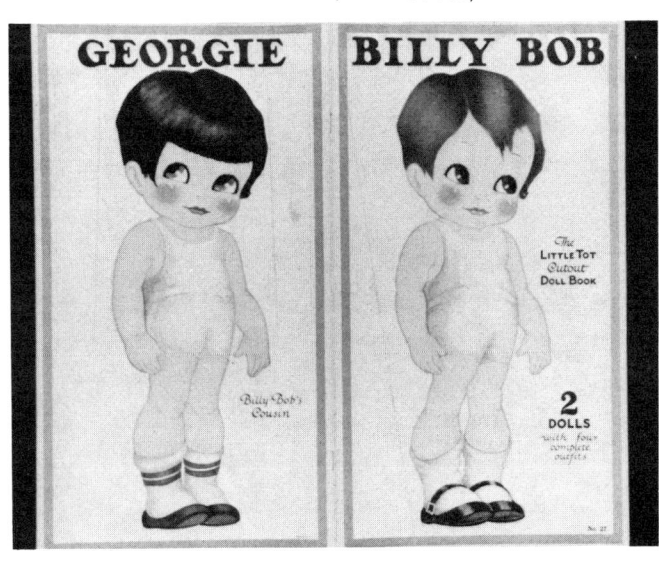

#27 *BILLY BOB* 1927. $17.50
GEORGIE (back cover)

Courtesy of Virginia Crossley

#103 *JIMMY* 1927. $17.50. *JACK* (back cover)

The following paper dolls were found intact in a salesman's sample case and provide invaluable information as to the name and stock number of each doll. All American Colortype paper dolls listed with a 600 number are 6½″ tall.

All courtesy of Rosalie Eppert.

Left to right; 601-Henry, 602-Pearl, 603 Martha. $8.00 each.

604-Nancy, 605-Ruth, 606-Anna. $8.00 each.

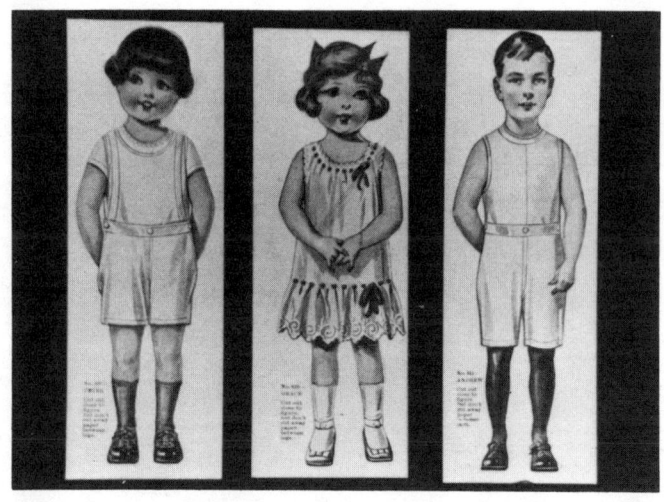

Left to right; 607-Peter, 610-Grace, 611-Andrew. $8.00 each.

612-David, 613-Jack, 615-Catherine. $8.00 each.

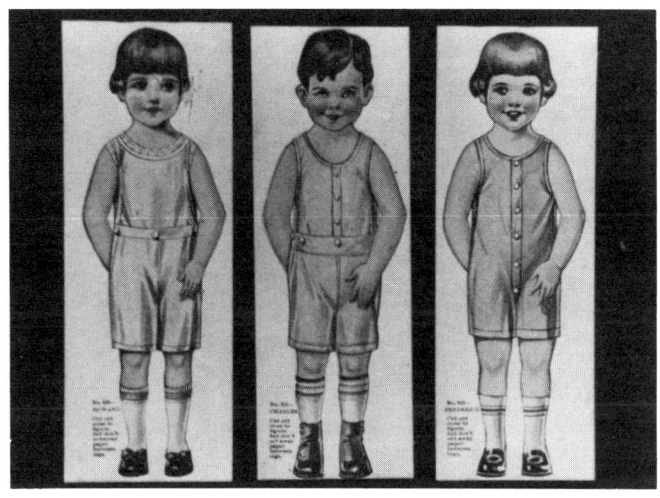

Left to right; 616-Betty, 617-Gladys, 619-Arthur. $8.00 each.

620-Howard, 621-Charles, 623-Frederick. $8.00 each.

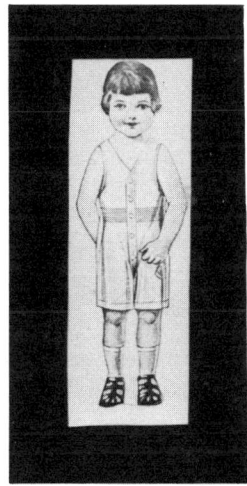

622 *WILLIAM*. $8.00

Courtesy of Jane Sugg

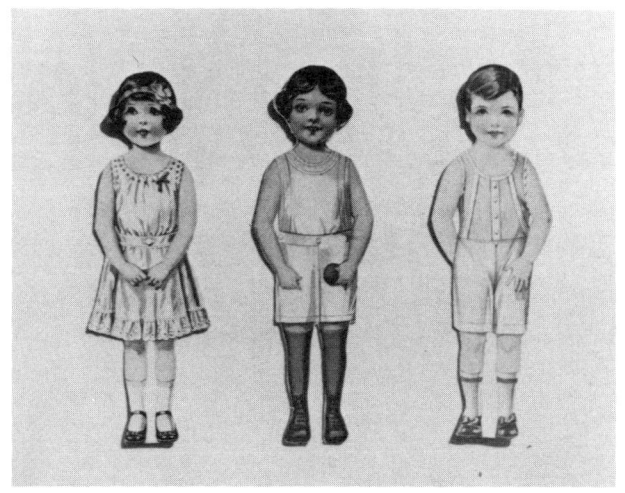

6½" dolls, names and numbers are not available.

Courtesy of Virginia Crossley

624 *LITTLE BETTY GAD-ABOUT*. $25.00 Envelope and outfit sheets #909, 910 and 911.

LITTLE MISS UP-TO-DATE. $25.00
Since #625 *Little Miss-Up-To-Date* was not available, the #727 set is shown which is identical but larger. The sheets #728, 729 and 730 are shown which are also identical to the smaller sheets #912, 913 and 914.

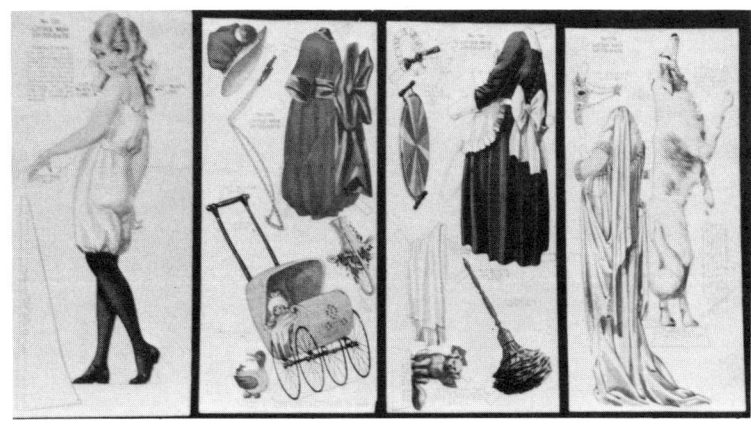

Courtesy of Rosalie Eppert

Courtesy of Rosalie Eppert
626 *LITTLE ALICE BUSY BEE*. $25.00
Outfit sheets #915, 916 and 917.

Courtesy of Rosalie Eppert
627 *LITTLE WILLIE WIDE-AWAKE*. $25.00
Outfit sheets #918, 919 and 920.

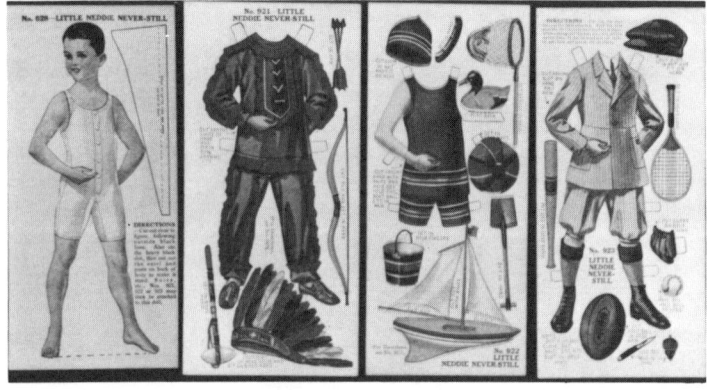

Courtesy of Rosalie Eppert
628 *LITTLE NEDDIE NEVER-STILL*. $25.00
Outfit sheets #921, 922 and 923.

Courtesy of Rosalie Eppert
629 *LITTLE POLLY DRESS-UP*. $25.00
Outfit sheets #924, 925 and 926.

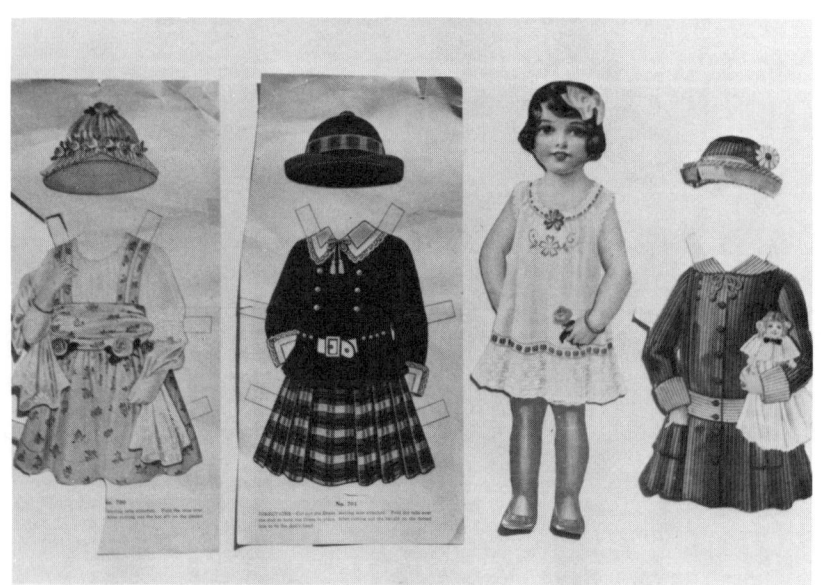

13″ Doll with outfits #700, 701 and 702. $30.00

Courtesy of Virginia Crossley
13″ Doll named *CORINNE* with outfit #703.
$30.00

Courtesy of Rosalie Eppert

OUR SAMMY, box and 13" doll. $35.00

Courtesy of Rosalie Eppert

13" Doll with outfits, left to right-#713, 714 and 717. $30.00

13" Doll with outfits, left to right-#715, 716 and 717.

Courtesy of Rosalie Eppert

Courtesy of Rosalie Eppert

The above doll and her outfits were used to advertise Bond Bread. There are no identifying numbers on the sheets. $20.00

All 800 numbers are outfits for the 6½" dolls. The outfit's number is given under each picture. For the outfit's caption consult the list of American Colortype paper dolls. Outfits $4.00 each.

All outfits on this page courtesy of Rosalie Eppert

12

All outfits pictured are courtesy of Rosalie Eppert

858	859	860	861	863	865	866	867	868
869	872	874	875	876	877	878	879	880
881	883	884	885	886	888	889	890	892
893	900	901	902	903	904	907	908

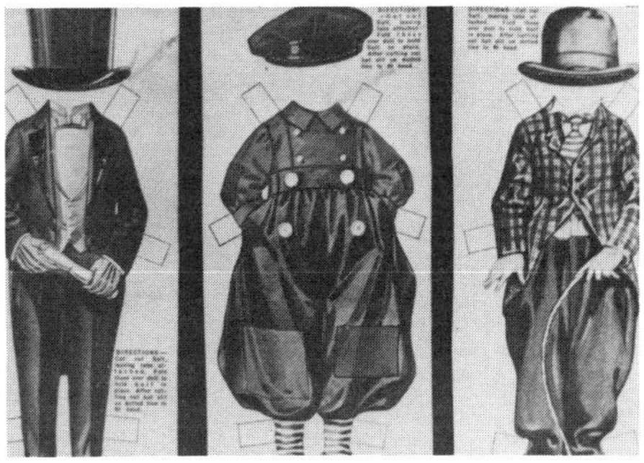

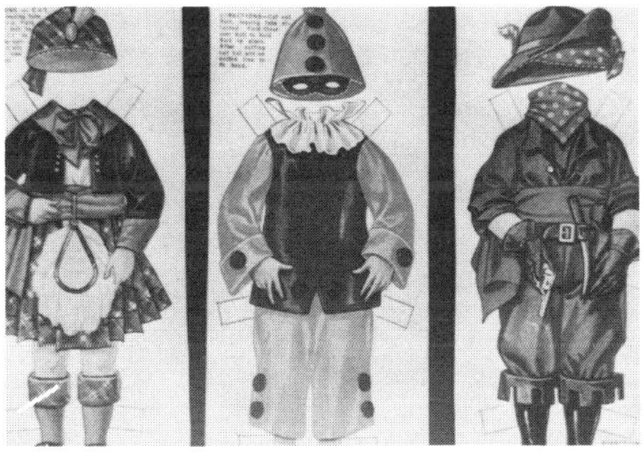

The number is not available for the Newsboy outfit or the baseball player outfit

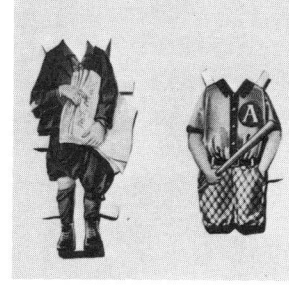

Notice that the outfit #829 Party Dress, is the same as one of those pictured with the Bond Bread set. The difference is that the doll's arms have been added to #829. $4.00

Courtesy of Suzanne Tessey

829   870

DOLLY'S HOME. $50.00
DOLLY'S HOME is a house for paper dolls and was sold by The Fair Store in Chicago. The house came with two paper dolls and fifteen outfits. Pictured on the outside of the large envelope are fifteen Colortype dolls, each wearing a different Colortype outfit.

Courtesy of Rosalie Eppert

LITTLE DARLING DRESSING DOLLS. $40.00
LITTLE DARLING DRESSING DOLLS on the right came with six dolls. The two boys are shown, they are William #622 and Charles #621. There were four girls in the set also. They are Pearl #602, Grace #610, Catherine #615 and Betty #616.

Courtesy of Jane Sugg

LITTLE DARLING DRESSING DOLLS (four doll set, missing one boy doll). $30.00

PRETTY KITTY. $40.00
Courtesy of Richard Rusnock

CHUBBY CUBBY. $40.00
Courtesy of Rosalie Eppert

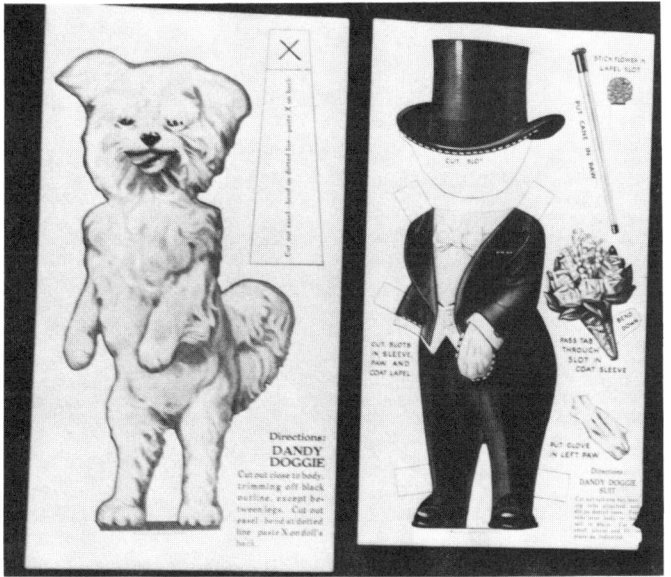

DANDY DOGGIE and one outfit. $40.00
Courtesy of Rosalie Eppert

Courtesy of Rosalie Eppert

LITTLE KITTY CUT-UP AND HER PLAYMATES. $45.00

LITTLE KITTY CUT-UP AND HER PLAYMATES is a small box set containing *PRETTY KITTY, CHUBBY CUBBY,* and *DANDY DOGGIE* in miniature. They range in size from 4¾" for *CHUBBY CUBBY* to 5¼" for *DANDY DOGGIE.* The outfits for the three dolls are the same as in the larger sets pictured.

The following is a list of all the American Colortype paper dolls and outfits known to the author at the time of this writing. Some numbers have not been identified and are left blank so the reader can fill these in as the dolls or outfits are found in the future.

25 *MARIE AND PATSY ANN* 1927
26 *BETTY LOU AND JANE* 1927
27 *BILLY BOB AND GEORGIE* 1927
101 *JANET AND SALLY* 1927
102 *MARGY AND MILDRED* 1927
103 *JIMMY AND JACK* 1927
All 600 numbrs are 6½" dolls
600
601 *HENRY*
602 *PEARL*
603 *MARTHA*
604 *NANCY*
605 *RUTH*
606 *ANNA*

607 *PETER*
608
609
610 *GRACE*
611 *ANDREW*
612 *DAVID*
613 *JACK*
614
615 *CATHERINE*
616 *BETTY*
617 *GLADYS*
618
619 *ARTHUR*
620 *HOWARD*

621 *CHARLES*
622 *WILLIAM*
623 *FREDERICK*
624 *LITTLE BETTY GAD-ABOUT*
625 *LITTLE MISS UP-TO-DATE*
626 *LITTLE ALICE BUSY-BEE*
627 *LITTLE WILLIE WIDE-AWAKE*
628 *LITTLE NEDDIE NEVER-STILL*
629 *LITTLE POLLY DRESS-UP*

Numbers 700 to 717 are outfits for the 13" dolls.
700 *DRESS*
701 *DRESS*
702 *COAT*

703 *COAT*
704 *SUIT* (not pictured)
705 *DRESS* (not pictured)
706 *SAILOR SUIT* (not pictured)
707 *SOLDIER SUIT* (not pictured)
708 *COAT* (not pictured)
709
710 *OUR JACKIE* (for picture see #900)
711 *COLONIAL DRUMMER* (for picture see #901)
712 *OUR SAMMY* (for picture see #902)
713 *MISS LIBERTY*
714 *ARMY NURSE*
715 *MISS COLUMBIA*
716 *MISS PATRIOT*
717 *GLORY ON PARADE*
718
719 *LITTLE BETTY GAD-ABOUT 13″ DOLL* (for picture see #624)
720 *OUTFIT FOR LITTLE BETTY GAD-ABOUT*
721 *OUTFIT FOR LITTLE BETTY GAD-ABOUT*
722 *OUTFIT FOR LITTLE BETTY GAD-ABOUT*
723 *LITTLE WILLIE WIDE-AWAKE 13″ DOLL* (for picture see #627)
724 *OUTFIT FOR LITTLE WILLIE WIDE-AWAKE*
725 *OUTFIT FOR LITTLE WILLIE WIDE-AWAKE*
726 *OUTFIT FOR LITTLE WILLIE WIDE-AWAKE*
727 *LITTLE MISS UP-TO-DATE 13″ DOLL* (for picture see #625)
728 *OUTFIT FOR LITTLE MISS UP-TO-DATE*
729 *OUTFIT FOR LITTLE MISS UP-TO-DATE*
730 *OUTFIT FOR LITTLE MISS UP-TO-DATE*
731 *LITTLE POLLY DRESS-UP 13″ DOLL* (for picture, see #629)
732 *OUTFIT FOR LITTLE POLLY DRESS-UP*
733 *OUTFIT FOR LITTLE POLLY DRESS-UP*
734 *OUTFIT FOR LITTLE POLLY DRESS-UP*
735 *LITTLE NEDDIE NEVER-STILL 13″ DOLL* (for picture, see #628)
736 *OUTFIT FOR LITTLE NEDDIE NEVER-STILL*
737 *OUTFIT FOR LITTLE NEDDIE NEVER-STILL*
738 *OUTFIT FOR LITTLE NEDDIE NEVER-STILL*
739 *LITTLE ALICE BUSY-BEE 13″ DOLL* (for picture, see #626)
740 *OUTFIT FOR LITTLE ALICE BUSY-BEE*
741 *OUTFIT FOR LITTLE ALICE BUSY-BEE*
742 *OUTFIT FOR LITTLE ALICE BUSY-BEE*

All 800 numbers are outfits for the 6½″ dolls
800 *MORNING SUIT*
801 *SUMMER BOY*
802 *LITTLE BOY BLUE*
803 *HOUSE DRESS*
804 *SCOTCH LASSIE*
805 *COWBOY GIRL*
806 *PINK TEA DRESS*
807 *CALICO GIRL*
808 *PLAYTIME DRESS*
809
810 *SAILOR GIRL*
811 *PLAID DRESS*
812
813 *SCHOOL DAYS*
814 *OUTING DRESS*
815
816 *MOTHER HUBBARD*
817
818 *SWEATER GIRL*
819 *SEASHORE GIRL*
820 *AUTOMOBILE GIRL*
821 *SIOUX INDIAN*
822 *SCOUT*
823 *BOY SCOUT*
823-X *AVIATOR*
824 *CAPTAIN*
825
826 *CATCHER*
827
828
829 *PARTY DRESS*
830
831 *AFTERNOON DRESS*
832
833
834 *SNOW GIRL*
835 *WINTER GIRL*
836 *BATHING GIRL*

837
838 *GIRL FROM THE WEST*
839 *COWBOY*
840
841 *CADET*
842 *SAILOR*
843 *OUTING SUIT*
844
845 *SCHOOL DAYS*
846
847 *SOLDIER*
847-X *MARINE*
848 *CAPTAIN*
849 *BATTER*
850 *MESSENGER*
851 *BAKER*
852
853 *KNIGHT*
854
855
856 *TURK*
857 *OLIVER TWIST*
858 *JOCKEY*
859 *FARMER*
860 *SKATER*
861 *BEAU BRUMMEL*
862
863 *HOLLANDER*
864
865 *GUESS WHO?*
866 *RIDING SUIT*
867 *ON THE BEACH*
868 *CAVALIER*
869 *SCOTCH LAD*
870 *YAMA-YAMA*
871
872 *DOMINO*
873
874 *BANDIT*
875 *SPANIARD*
876 *GEISHA GIRL*
877 *POCOHONTAS*
878 *RAINY WEATHER*
879 *JOCKEY*
880 *ON PARADE*
881 *WINTER GIRL*
882
883 *WEDDING BELLS*
884 *MISS NORMANDIE*
885 *SURF GIRL*
886 *FLOWER GIRL*
887
888 *GOLF GIRL*
889 *TEA PARTY DRESS*
890 *ROB ROY*
891
892 *HOLLAND GIRL*
893 *MORNING GLORY*
894
895
896
897
898
899

All 900 numbers are outfits for the 6½″ dolls
900 *OUR JACKIE*
901 *COLONIAL DRUMMER*
902 *OUR SAMMY*
903 *MISS LIBERTY*
904 *ARMY NURSE* (for picture, see #714)
904 *RED CROSS NURSE*
905 *MISS COLUMBIA* (for picture see #715)
906 *MISS PATRIOT* (for picture see #716)
907 *GLORY ON PARADE*
908 *MISS KNITTING*
909 *LITTLE BETTY GAD-ABOUT OUTFIT TO FIT DOLL #624*
910 *LITTLE BETTY GAD-ABOUT OUTFIT TO FIT DOLL #624*
911 *LITTLE BETTY GAD-ABOUT OUTFIT TO FIT DOLL#624*

912 *LITTLE MISS UP-TO-DATE OUTFIT TO FIT DOLL #625*
913 *LITTLE MISS UP-TO-DATE OUTFIT TO FIT DOLL #625*
914 *LITTLE MISS UP-TO-DATE OUTFIT TO FIT DOLL #625*
915 *LITTLE ALICE BUSY-BEE OUTFIT TO FIT DOLL #626*
916 *LITTLE ALICE BUSY-BEE OUTFIT TO FIT DOLL #626*
917 *LITTLE ALICE BUSY-BEE OUTFIT TO FIT DOLL #626*
918 *LITTLE WILLIE WIDE-AWAKE OUTFIT TO FIT DOLL #627*
919 *LITTLE WILLIE WIDE-AWAKE OUTFIT TO FIT DOLL #627*
920 *LITTLE WILLIE WIDE-AWAKE OUTFIT TO FIT DOLL #627*
921 *LITTLE NEDDIE NEVER-STILL OUTFIT TO FIT DOLL #628*
922 *LITTLE NEDDIE NEVER-STILL OUTFIT TO FIT DOLL #628*
923 *LITTLE NEDDIE NEVER-STILL OUTFIT TO FIT DOLL #628*
924 *LITTLE POLLY DRESS-UP OUTFIT TO FIT DOLL #629*
925 *LITTLE POLLY DRESS-UP OUTFIT TO FIT DOLL #629*
926 *LITTLE POLLY DRESS-UP OUTFIT TO FIT DOLL #629*

The following paper dolls by American Colortype did not have a number.
LITTLE DARLING DRESSING DOLLS-Box
CHUBBY CUBBY-Envelope
DANDY DOGGIE-Envelope
LITTLE KITTY CUT-UP AND HER PLAYMATES-Box(Chubby Cubby, Dandy Doggie and Pretty Kitty in Miniature)
OUR SAMMY DRESSING DOLL-Box with outfits #710, 711 and 712
PRETTY KITTY-Envelope
MY FAVORITE DRESING DOLLS-Richard (not pictured) outfits are #706, 707 & 708
DOLLY'S HOME-Doll house for paper dolls sold by the Fair Store in Chicago. The house came with two American Colortype paper dolls and 15 dresses and hats. On the envelope are pictured 15 American Colortype paper dolls.

American Toy Works

The American Toy Works was founded in 1896. In 1931 their address was 7&8 Chatham Square, N.Y. The paper dolls pictured were not dated.

The American Toy Works participated in the American Toy Fair from 1932 to 1936. At that time they produced toy money sets, paint sets, sewing and embroidery sets, paper doll outfits, Santa Claus surprise packages, ring toss, duck pins, hammer and nail sets, chalk & slate sets, clay sets, tapestry sets and garden sets.

102 *PAPER DOLL OUTFIT*. $20.00

Courtesy of Audrey Sepponen

417 *MODERNE SEWING FOR LITTLE GIRLS*. $10.00

903 *LITTLE FOLKS CREPE PAPER DOLL OUTFIT.*
$25.00

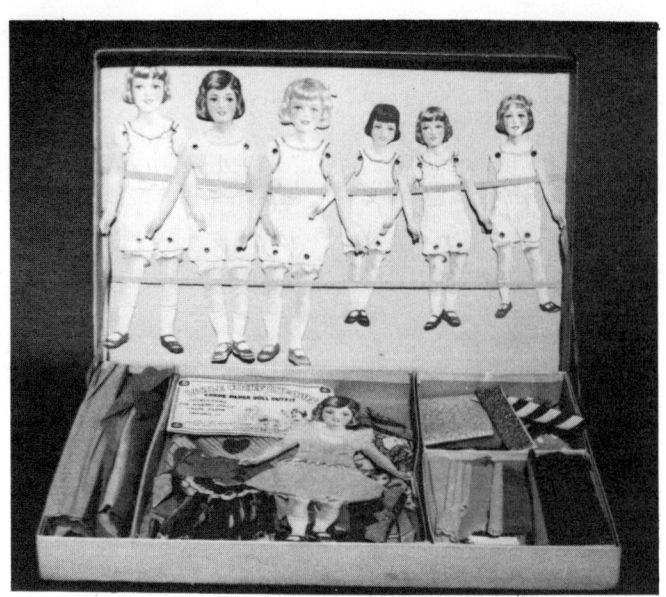

Inside of hinged box #903

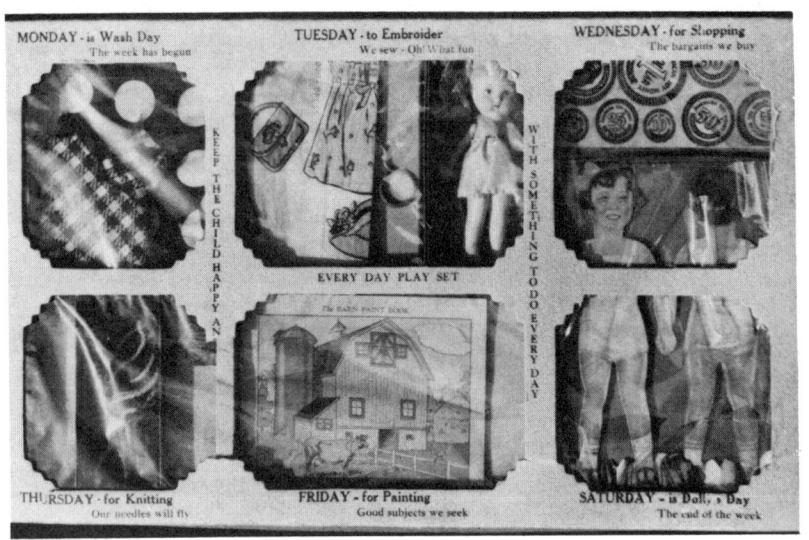

1000 *EVERY DAY PLAY SET*. $15.00
The *EVERY DAY PLAY SET* pictured includes two paper dolls, each with a front and back. Their feet have shoes that fold to make stands. The outfits for the paper dolls are of crepe paper.

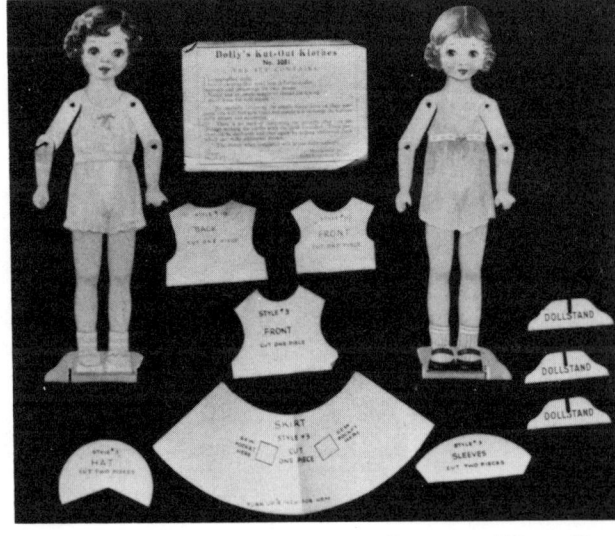

3081 *DOLLY'S KUT-OUT KLOTHES*. $10.00

Courtesy of Betsy Slap

901 *LITTLE FOLKS CREPE PAPER DOLL OUTFIT*-2 jointed dolls (not pictured)
3083 *MAKE DOLLY'S WARDROBE* (not pictured)

Amlico Publishing Company

OUR FAVORITE DOLLS-no date, but research has shown that they were being sold as late as 1907.

Pictured is the 16½″ girl and her folder. A 17″ boy was also published. Please see the Selchow and Righter and A.T. Co.'s sections for further information on these dolls.

OUR FAVORITE DOLLS. $50.00

Courtesy of Kassey Ferguson

Animated Book Company

Courtesy of Joyce McClelland

HELLO, I'M ADELINE 1944. $18.00
A spiral paper doll storybook, plus words and music to ten songs.

Art Award Company

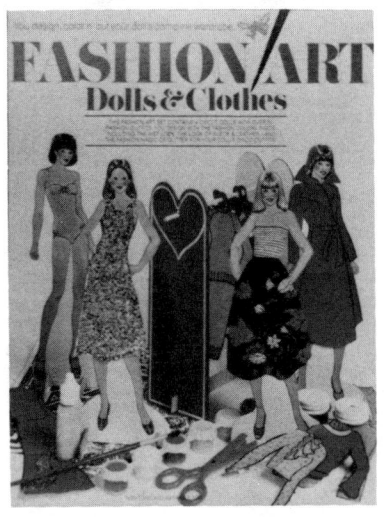

6000 *FASHION ART DOLLS*. $4.00

Artcraft Paper Products

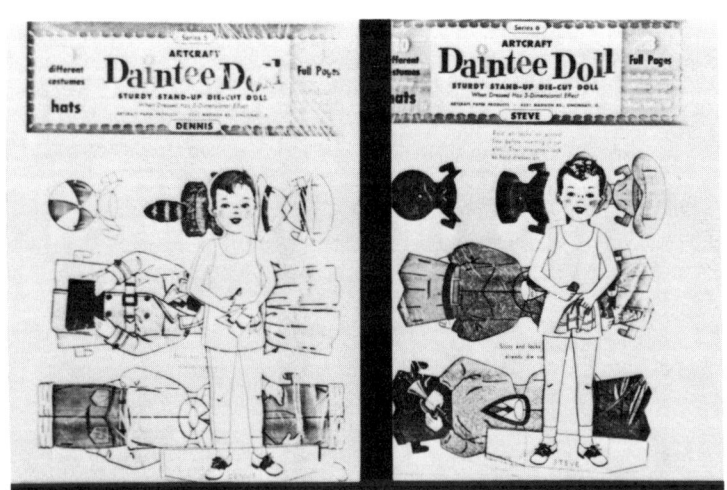

Courtesy of Jane Sugg

Courtesy of Virginia Crossley
SERIES 5-DENNIS, SERIES 6-STEVE. $6.00 each

STOCK MED-2 ROSETTA FROM MEXICO. $12.00

STOCK MED-3 CHRISTINA FROM SWEDEN. $12.00

Courtesy of Jane Sugg

STOCK MED-1 KATRINE FROM HOLLAND. $12.00

Athena Publishing Company

The Athena Publishing Co. was founded in 1972 by Johana Gast Anderton. Johana's start in the publishing business was brought about when she compiled a little book on depression glass called *The Glass Rainbow* in 1969. The book was printed by a local printing company and the first printing of 500 copies quickly sold out. The book was reprinted eight more times (in much larger quantities) before Johana finally let it go out of print. About this time Johana's early love of dolls surfaced. She began to think of compiling a book about modern dolls and the result was *Twentieth Century Dolls, From Bisque To Vinyl.* The book was published by Trojan Press, Inc. of North Kansas City, Mo. It was reprinted twice by this Company. Problems arose, however, and Johana decided to set up her own company (Athena) in 1972. The Company produced a number of books besides her own. Of particuliar interest to the paper doll collector is the *Collectors Art Series*. The first book in this series was *The Antique French Dolls Coloring Book* published in 1974. The books that followed were paper doll books, and they are listed below.

Eventually, the numerous tasks of running a publishing company began to take their toll on Johana, and her health became affected. Because of this, part of her publishing business was sold to American Broadcasting Company of New York. Later, Wallace Homestead Book Co. began publishing her doll books.

During Johana's working years at Athena, she used the pseudonym Jay Richards.

THE ANTIQUE FRENCH DOLLS COLORING BOOK 1974 (not pictured)
ANTIQUE GERMAN BISQUE PAPER DOLLS 1980 (not pictured)
DOLLS OF THE 1930'S 1976 (not pictured)

THE ANTIQUE FRENCH DOLL PAPER DOLLS ©
1975 Peggy Jo Rosamond And Athena Publishing Co.
Currently available

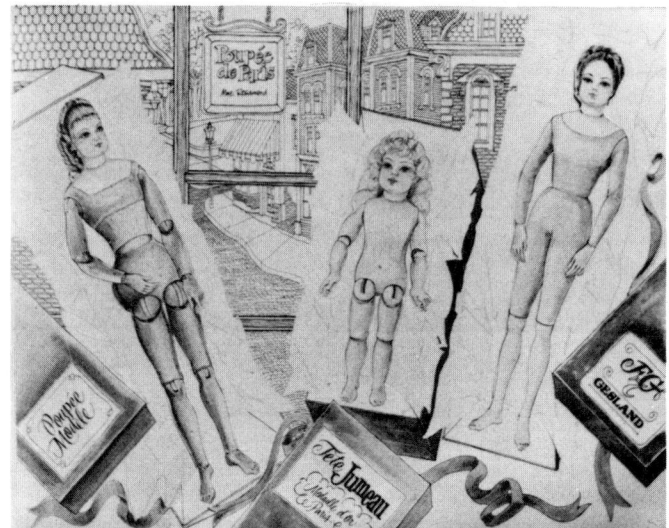

THE ANTIQUE FRENCH DOLL PAPER DOLLS Inside page of dolls

THE ANTIQUE DOLLS GO TO A PAPER DOLL WEDDING © *1976 Peggy Jo Rosamond And Athena Publishing Co.* Currently available

THE ANTIQUE DOLLS GO TO A PAPER DOLL WEDDING, Inside page

Avalon Industries, Inc.

Formerly Standard Toykraft

Avalon industries, formerly known as Standard Toykraft, was founded by brothers Nathan and Louis Ullman. They began as box manufacturers for toy companies in Long Island City. In 1887, after extensive research, Standard Toykraft began manufacturing toys of their own. Their first products were crayon/watercolor sets and stitchery sets.

Just prior to World War I, a young European engineer, Soloman Luber, joined the firm. With the advent of Mr. Luber the company began to grow and prosper. Eventually Mr. Luber acquired control of Standard Toykraft which became Avalon Industries, Inc. The company is still owned by members of the Luber family.

Bibliography: *Avalon...A Century of Creativity.* Ed Weiss and Ellen Kaplan

Paper dolls through the mid 1960's are marked "Standard Toykraft" on the boxes. By the late 1960's the name Avalon appears and from then on the boxes have either Avalon Industries, Inc.-Standard Toykraft Div. or Avalon Industries, Inc.-Toykraft Division. Notice the Toykraft is spelled with a "k" until the late 1960's when it was changed to "Toycraft".

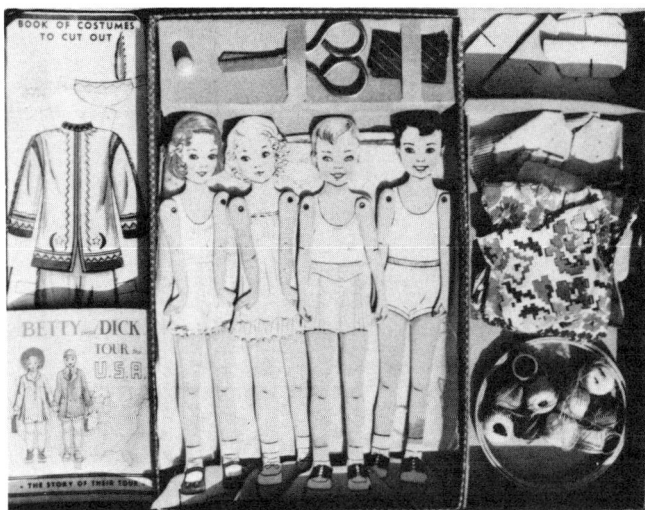

D100 contents inside box

D100 *BETTY AND DICK TOUR THE U.S.A.* 1940
Standard Toykraft. $17.50

Three sizes of dolls 10″, 8¼″ and 6¼″. Left to Right- Jane, Betty, Dick and Tom (top row)
BETTY AND DICK TOUR THE U.S.A. #D100 is a large 17″ x 13″ box set. Included in the set are both cloth clothes for the child to sew, and paper clothes to cut out. Some cloth towels and handkerchiefs are also included to be embroidered. Dick and Betty are 10″ tall and are jointed at the shoulders. The set shown also included dolls of Jane and Tom. It is debatable whether they belong to this set or not. The little booklet enclosed tells of Betty and Dick's tour of Chicago, Hollywood and Hawaii etc. but no mention is made of Jane and Tom. Set #D10 has exactly the same cover as #D100 but is smaller, only 11″ x 8″ with dolls 6¼″ tall. The clothes are the same but reduced in size. Medium sized dolls of 8¼″ tall have also been found, so presumably there was a medium size box set also. It is possible there were sets called "Jane and Tom Tour the U.S.A." also, or maybe they toured Europe, or it could be Jane and Tom were just an added feature in the Betty and Dick sets.

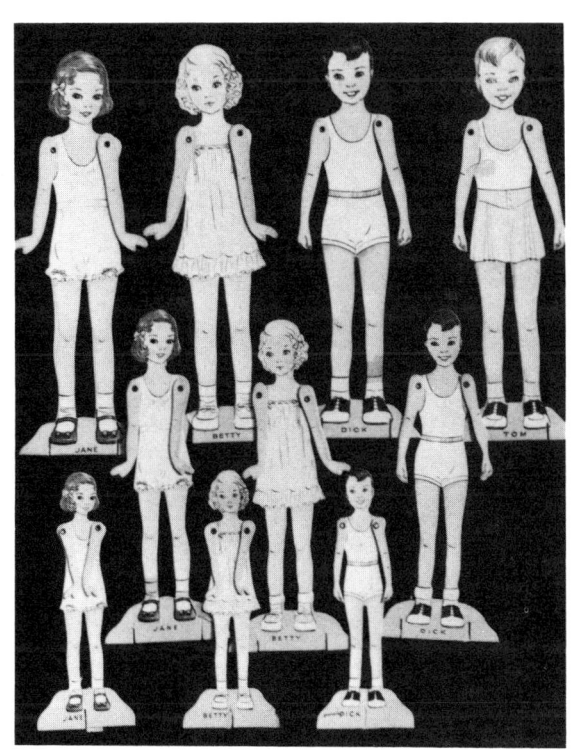

Courtesy of Audrey Sepponen

401 *BETSY McCALL'S FASHION SHOP* 1959. $15.00
© The McCall Publishing Co. reprinted by permission of The McCall Publishing Co.

Courtesy of Audrey Sepponen

301 PETTICOAT JUNCTION
© Wayfilms. $18.00

701-1 *LINDA THE BALLERINA*. $4.00

Courtesy of Virginia Crossley

701-2 *TEENA THE TEENAGER*. $4.00

Courtesy of Audrey Sepponen

401 *MY FAIR LADY*. $18.00
© Columbia Broadcasting System, Inc.

Courtesy of Virginia Crossley

701-2 *DEBBIE*. $4.00

701-3 *SANDRA THE BRIDE*. $4.00

Courtesy of Virginia Crossley

701-3 *CONNIE*. $4.00

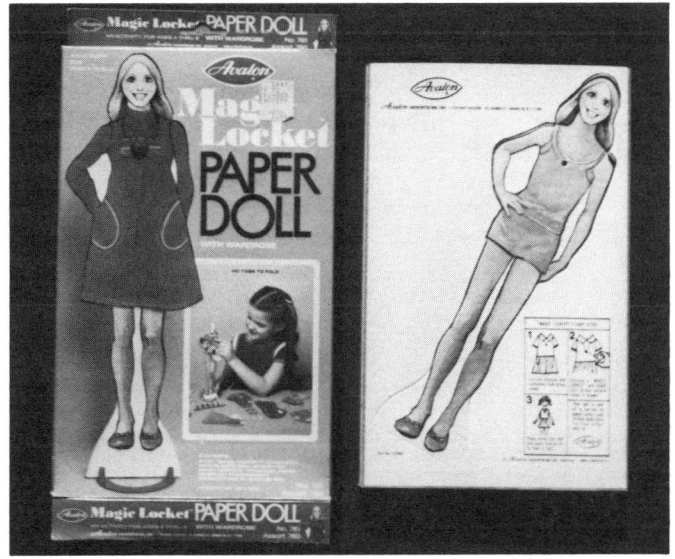

761 *MAGIC LOCKET PAPER DOLL* 1978. Currently available

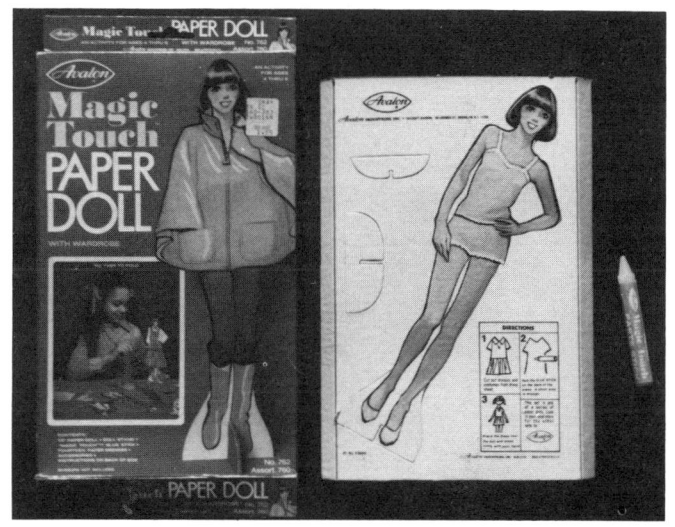

762 *MAGIC TOUCH PAPER DOLL* 1978. Currently available

Courtesy of Audrey Sepponen

801 *BETSY McCALL DRESS'N PLAY* 1963 © The McCall Publishing Co. $12.00
Reprinted by permission of The McCall Publishing Co.

Courtesy of Virginia Crossley

801-1 *LINDA THE BALLERINA* 1969. $4.00

191 *FASHION DESIGN CENTER* 1979 (picture not available)
601 *GIDGET* 1965 (picture not available)
701-1 *SUSIE MAGIC LOCKET PAPER DOLL* (picture not available)
801-2 *TEENA THE TEENAGER* 1969 (picture not available, see #701-2)
801-3 *SANDRA THE BRIDE* 1969 (picture not available, see #701-3)

811 *MARGIE*. $18.00

Bellerophon Books

QUEEN ELIZABETH I © *Bellerophon Books* 1972
Currently available

ROYAL FAMILY PAPER DOLLS © *Bellerophon Books* 1982 Currently available

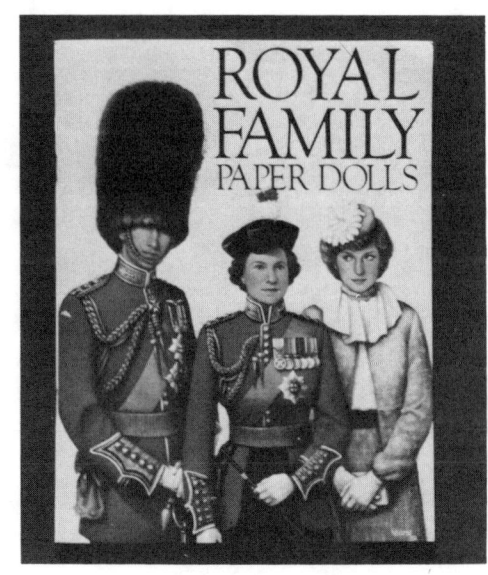

Other paper doll coloring books:
HENRY VIII AND HIS WIVES, Paper Dolls to Color 1972
GREAT WOMEN PAPER DOLLS 1974
INFAMOUS WOMEN PAPER DOLLS 1976

Blaise Publishing Company

TOMMIE LEE (not pictured)
LITTLE SISTER (not pictured)

1000 *CLEOPATRA* 1963. $15.00

Courtesy of Virginia Crossley

1001 *MARK ANTONY* 1963. $15.00

Courtesy of Virginia Crossley

Gertrude Breed

RAY-N-BO JOY-N-TED DOLLS
(not pictured)

DANCING PRISCILLA 1927. $17.50

Courtesy of Joyce McClelland

Courtesy of Jane Sugg

BABY JANE 1927. $17.50

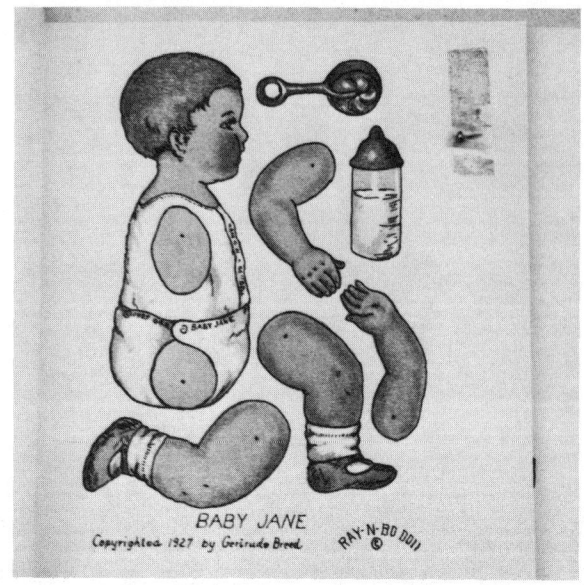

BABY JANE

Burton Playthings, Inc.

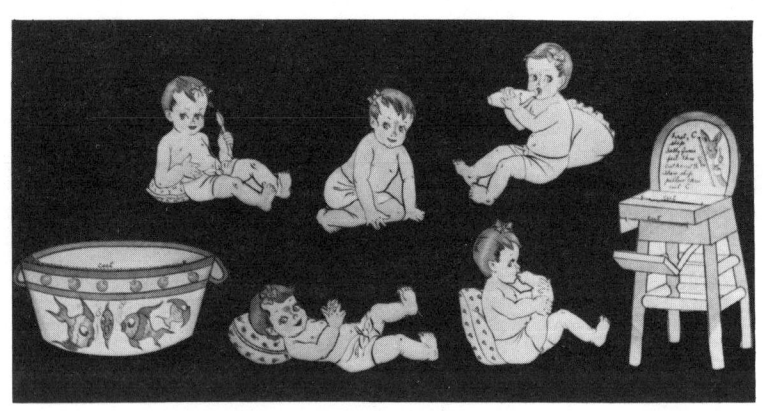

275 *YOUR OWN QUINTUPLETS 1935.* $25.00
In the picture of the Quintuplets, the dolls in the top row are left to right-Peggy Ann, Betty Lou, Sally Jane. Bottom row, left to right-Mary Joan and Rose Marie.

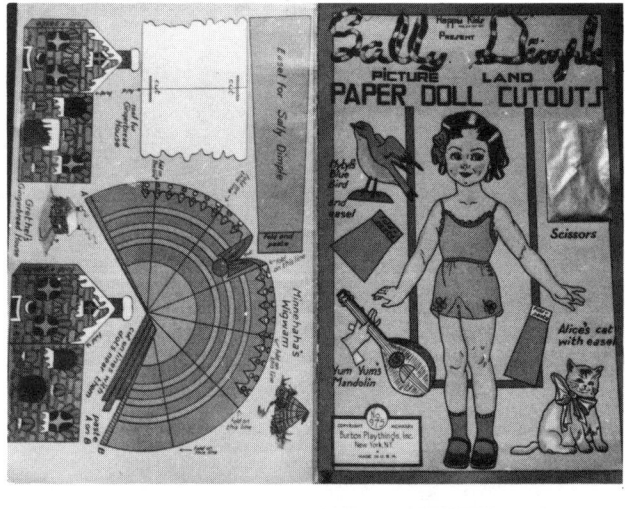

Courtesy of Audrey Sepponen

975 *SALLY DIMPLE 1935.* $22.50

875 DOTTY AND DANNY ON PARADE 1935. $22.50

Courtesy of Joyce McClelland

C and M Publishing Company

Courtesy of Judy LeJeune
WESTERN GAL, PAT. $5.00

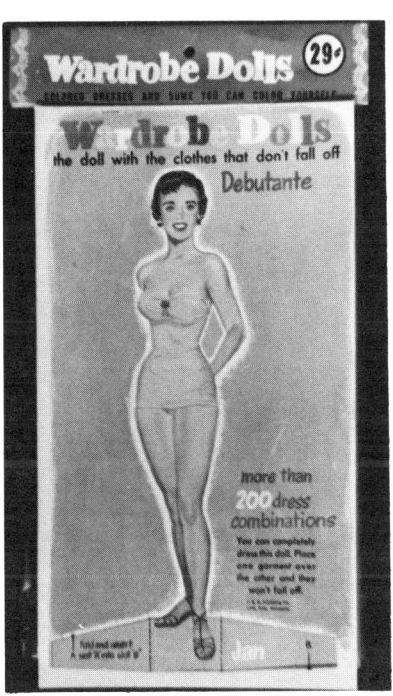

Courtesy of Judy LeJeune
DEBUTANTE, JAN. $5.00

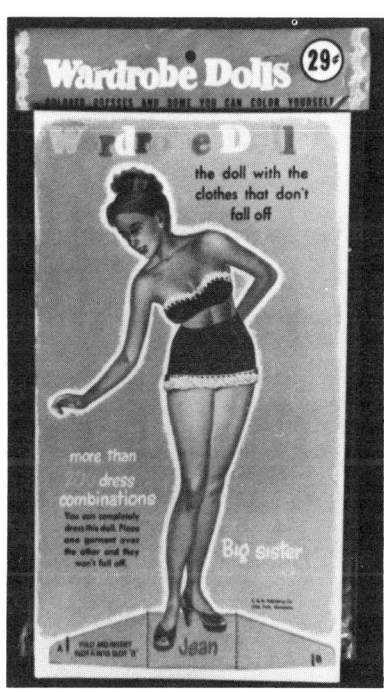

Courtesy of Wynn Yusas
BIG SISTER, JEAN. $5.00

Wardrobe Dolls-*LITTLE SISTER* (not pictured)
Wardrobe Dolls-*SPORTS GAL* (not pictured)
Wardrobe Dolls-*MISS TEENS* (not pictured)

CARDINAL GAMES

HAPPI TIME DRESSMAKER KIT. $15.00

HAPPI TIME DRESSMAKERS KIT pictured has no identification of any kind as to publisher, date or number. Since the three dolls in the set so closely resemble Betty in the Sewing Set the chances are very strong that Cardinal Games produced this set also. Happi Time is a logo Sears uses on many of their toy items so this box set may have been manufactured by Cardinal Games and sold by Sears.

Courtesy of Wanda Myers

501 SEWING SET, DOLLS TO DRESS $10.00

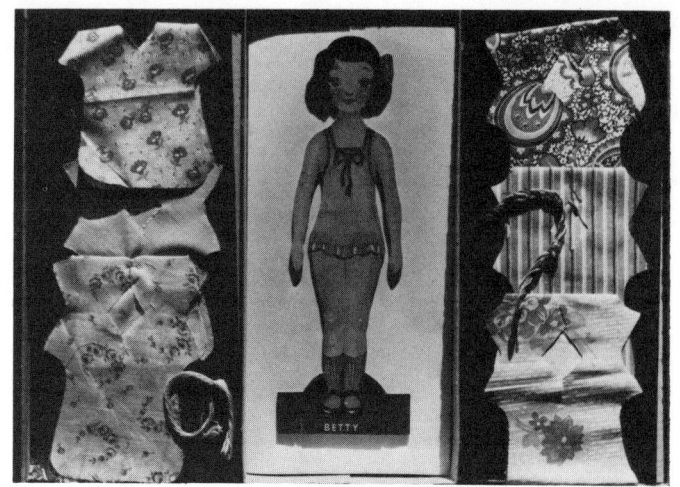

Inside Contents of Box 501

Carol Toys and Novelties

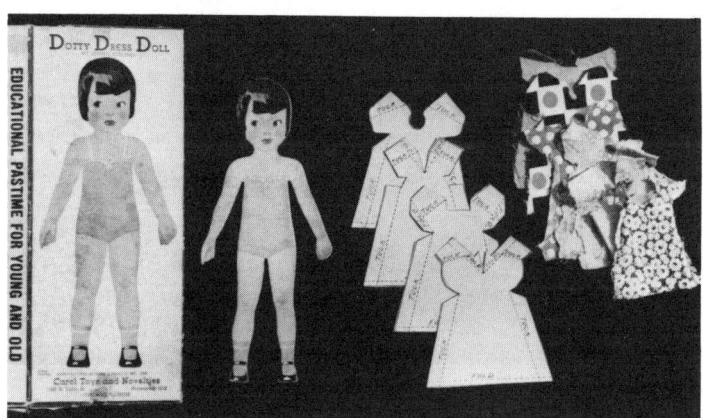

DOTTY DRESS DOLL. $15.00
Statuette doll with paper patterns and cloth clothes. Box set. Additional information on box says "Manufactured by Gaul and Ingalls, Inc. for Carol Toys and Novelties." No date.

Central Committee on United Study of Foreign Missions

Courtesy of Louise Leek

CHILDREN OF THE WAR ZONE 1916. $15.00
A set of ten paper dolls with costumes.

Courtesy of Louise Leek

CHILDREN OF THE WAR ZONE 1916

Child Art Productions

Not pictured

AMY 1977
DENIM DOLLS 1977
FASHION PARADE DOLL BOOK 1977
LITTLE LADIES 1977

Childrens Press, Inc.

R1000 NURSERY RHYMES 1950. $3.50
Record/coloring book with page of paper dolls

R1001 NURSERY GAMES 1950. $3.50
Record/coloring book with page of paper dolls

R1002 NURSERY LULLABIES 1950. $3.50
Record/coloring book with page of paper dolls

Courtesy of Audrey Sepponen

3000 AROUND THE WORLD WITH BOB AND BARBARA 1946. $15.00

Courtesy of Audrey Sepponen

3001 COUNTRY WEEK END WITH KATHY AND JILL 1946. $15.00

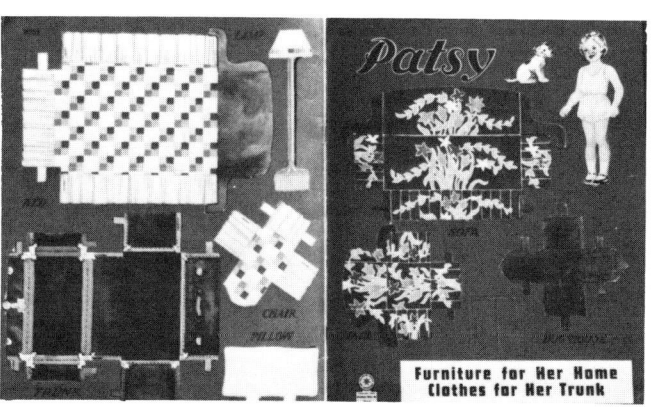

Courtesy of Virginia Crossley

3002 PATSY 1946. $15.00

3003 MOTHER AND DAUGHTER (for picture of this book see Lilja #914)

Children's World Publishing Company

Courtesy of Audrey Sepponen

101 MISS AIRLANES. $15.00 Pat Kennelly of TWA no date

Courtesy of Virginia Crossley

MAGNA MAGIC SUE 1954. $6.50 No number

Colorforms®

Colorforms® was founded in 1952 by Harry Kislevitz in the basement of his home. The first Colorforms® were simply thin flat pieces of shiny plastic cut into the basic shapes. The child would then create pictures with the shapes on a special playboard included in the set. The plastic pieces would peel right off when the child wanted to change the picture. In a short while these basic sets gave way to more elaborate play sets. The plastic pieces took the form of characters from stories and TV shows. Children could spend many happy hours creating scenes from their favorite TV shows or storybooks.

In 1957 the first "Dress-Up" sets appeared on the market, and they have continued to be popular all through the years. These sets contain costumes for a doll or dolls, and the costumes cling to the doll and easily peel off when a new outfit is wanted.

The following is a list of the known Colorforms® paper doll sets:

105 *JOHNNY DRESS-UP SET* 1957
117 *POPEYE THE WEATHERMAN DRESS-UP SET* 1957
150 *SLEEPING BEAUTY DRESS DESIGNER KIT* 1959
152 *DEBBIE REYNOLDS DRESS DESIGNER KIT* 1960
155 *SHARI LEWIS DRESS UP SET* 1963
160 *DALE EVANS WESTERN DRESS-UP SET* 1959
175 *BETSY McCALL'S GARDEN DRESS-UP SET* 1960
176 *MY BABY DRESS-UP KIT* 1964 (pictured)
182 *ANNETTE DRESS DESIGNER KIT* 1961
199 *MISS BALLERINA DRESS-UP SET* 1962
234 *BRIDE DRESS-UP SET* 1963
250 *TAMMY DRESS-UP SET* 1964
300 *MARY POPPINS DRESS-UP SET*
302 *MORK FROM ORK DRESS-UP SET* 1979
345 *CURLEY McDIMPLE* (circa 1972) *DRESS-UP KIT*
350 *LITTLE ORPHAN ANNIE DRESS-UP KIT* 1968
355 *JULIA DRESS-UP KIT* 1967
400 *MISS WEATHER DRESS-UP SET* 1966
408 *MISS NURSE DRESS-UP KIT* (circa 1972; pictured)
460 *TWIGGY DRESS-UP KIT* 1967
480 *RAGGEDY ANN DRESS-UP KIT* 1967
495 *LITTLE KIDDLES DRESS-UP KIT* 1968
525 *THE OLD FASHIONED DOLL* 1970 (pictured)
581 *SMILE DRESS-UP SET* 1971 (pictured)
583 *MISS AMERICA DRESS-UP SET* 1972
585 *MARY POPPINS DRESS-UP KIT*
587 *DAVID CASSIDY DRESS-UP SET* 1972
589 *LITTLE LULU DRESS-UP SET* 1974
597 *HOLLY HOBBIE DRESS-UP SET* 1975
604 *HEATHER DRESS-UP SET* 1976
616 *BALLERINA BARBIE DRESS-UP KIT* 1977

628 *BABY HOLLY HOBBIE DRESS-UP SET* 1978
639 *SINDY DRESS-UP SET* 1979
644 *MISS PIGGY DRESS-UP SET* 1980
647 *DARCI, COVER GIRL, DISCO DRESS-UP SET* 1980
653 *MONCHHICHI DRESS-UP SET* 1981
657 *WESTERN BARBIE DRESS-UP SET* 1982
752 *HOW'S THE WEATHER, LUCY? DRESS-UP SET* 1972
1933 *BETTY BOOP DRESS-UP SET* circa 1975
2117 *POPEYE THE WEATHERMAN DRESS-UP SET* 1963
2152 *DEBBIE REYNOLDS DRESS DESIGNER KIT* 1963
2155 *SHARI LEWIS DRESS-UP KIT* 1963
2160 *ROY ROGERS AND DALE EVANS WESTERN DRESS-UP SET* 1959
2175 *BETSY McCALL'S GARDEN DRESS-UP SET* 1960
2176 *MY BABY DRESS-UP SET* 1964
2199 *MISS BALLERINA DRESS-UP SET* 1962
2234 *BRIDE DRESS-UP SET* 1963
2301 *CRISSY DRESS-UP SET* 1970
2341 *DAWN DRESS-UP SET* 1970
2352 *BARBIE SPORT FASHION SET* 1975
2354 *DONNY AND MARIE DRESS-UP SET* 1977
2356 *SUPER STAR BARBIE DRESS-UP SET* 1978
2362 *SNOOPY HOW'S THE WEATHER? DRESS-UP SET* circa 1981
2363 *BARBIE AND BEAUTY DRESS-UP SET* 1981
2500 *TAMMY DRESS-UP SET*
4109 *HOLLY HOBBIE GENERAL STORE STAND-UP PLAY SET* (with costumes) 1976
4300 *MICKEY MOUSE PUPPETFORMS* 1972 (includes outfits)
4301 *POPEYE PUPPETFORMS* (includes outfits)
4307 *SNOOPY, YOU'RE A STAR* 1971 (includes outfits)
4310 *RAGGEDY ANN PUPPET SHOW* 1975 (includes outfits)
5550 *TINA THE TALKING PAPER DOLL* (pictured)

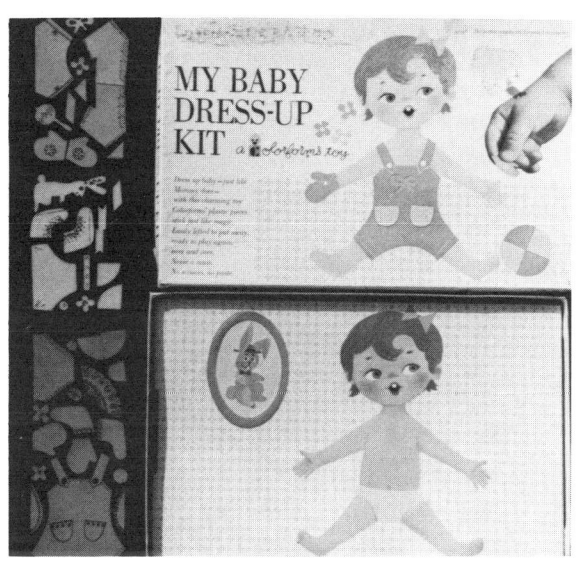

Courtesy of Rosalie Eppert

176 *MY BABY DRESS-UP KIT* 1964. $6.00

408 *MISS NURSE DRESS-UP KIT.* $3.00

525 *THE OLD FASHIONED DOLL* 1970. $3.00

5550 *TINA THE TALKING PAPER DOLL.* $10.00

581 *SMILE DRESS-UP SET* 1971. $3.00

Colorforms is a registered TM owned by Colorforms Ramsey, New Jersey.

David C. Cook Publishing Co.

Each of the nine sheets pictured measure 11¼" x 16¼". Each sheet contains a story from the Bible with paper dolls to act out the story. 1933. $18.00 for set of 9 sheets

Courtesy of Jenny Elmore

Robert J. Crombie Co.

AROUND THE WORLD WITH DOROTHY DOT 1910 Box set with 12 different sheets

Courtesy of Jane Sugg

Left, *CIRO OF CUBA*; Right, *LITTLE ISABELLA, BRAZIL*. $8.00 each sheet

Courtesy of Jane Sugg

Left, *ANTOINETTE, PARIS FRANCE*; Right, *HILDA OF NORWAY*. $8.00 each sheet

Current, Inc.

A Subsidiary of Looart Press

Looart Publishers was founded by Orin Loo in 1947. Earlier Mr. Loo had been a lithographic director at Hallmark Greeting Cards which he gave up when he joined the Army in World War II. When he returned from the war, he and his wife Miriam wanted to live in Colorado Springs but no print shop for greeting cards was to be found there. So, he decided to start his own company. This he did at the age of 38, together with an older brother. The first products of Looart Publishers were original Christmas cards. By 1948 Looart had a product line of 17 Christmas card designs. In 1950 Looart publishers developed a new idea in stationery, the POST-A-NOTE. Miriam Loo was convinced that the POST-A-NOTE was a sure seller and she started Current, Inc., a direct mail business designed to appeal to the fund raising groups.

By 1966 Current, Inc. had grown so large it necessitated a building of its own and a decision was made to purchase a building large enough to hold both Looart Publishers and Current, Inc. In 1967 Looart Publishers and Current merged as one company and became known as Looart Press. In 1980 Current became a subsidiary of Looart Press which allowed the parent company to enter into new business areas. In 1981 the first Current retail store was opened in Phoenix, Arizona as a new venture outside the direct mailing business.

Current's direct mail business has a mailing list of 7,000,000. Their business is one of the most automated in the country. The orders are processed in fast and efficient order even when as many as 75,000 orders are received in one week.

The Company's product line has expanded remarkably since the early fifties. They produce stationery, greeting cards, cookbooks, children's games and numerous paper items. Recently, craft and gift items have been added to the line. Three paper doll sets have been produced in recent years and are pictured here.

3216 *WHEN I GROW UP* 1980. $5.00
Clothes lace on the dolls

3204 *LACE-ME-UPS* 1979. $5.00
Dog and cat paper dolls with clothes that lace on

5607 *PLAYTIME PALS* 1982. $4.00
One doll, boy on one side, girl on the other. The outfits are of vinyl and peel off and on

The Dandyline Company

LITTLE SISTER 1918. $18.00

ELSIE DINSMORE 1917 (not pictured)
ELSIE DINSMORE 1918 (not pictured)

H. Davis Toy Corporation

The H. Davis Toy Corporation produced weaving looms, sewing cards, pot holder sets, lacing sets, flannel boards and other items besides the paper doll set pictured below.

Courtesy of Marilyn Johnson
242 *TOWN AND COUNTRY-TO DRESS AND EMBROIDER.* $15.00
The paper doll is of heavy cardboard and has a special surface that allows cloth clothes to cling to the doll.

Decalco Litho. Co.

DOLL CUT-OUTS SET #1 on top. $7.00 (lady and little girl)
SET #2 on bottom. $7.00 (lady and little girl)
Set #3 on bottom. $7.00 (two ladies)

Decro Plaks, Inc.

Decro Plaks, Inc. produced animated pin-up wall plaques, Mother Goose nursery plaques and animated T.V. cartoon plaques. Their only known paper doll is pictured.

LIFE SIZE DOLL. $15.00
No date-late 1950's or early 1960's

Courtesy of Audrey Sepponen

The DeJournette Mfg. Company

It was in the late 1930's when a paper doll company called The Paper Doll House was formed in Atlanta, Georgia. When the company expanded, it was renamed after their paper doll designer, Alma De Journette, and was incorporated in 1946. The company was sold in 1962 to Merry Manufacturing Company of Cincinnati. This company is covered later in this book.

The first paper doll was "Curly Top", a paper doll with "real" hair. She was patented in 1938 when the company was still known as The Paper Doll House. This paper doll and variations of the doll were sold for many years. In the 1950's the paper dolls had many added features that were not like your run-of-the-mill paper dolls. Some would come in a box that converted to a trunk or a house. Another would have paper clothes that were washable or have eyes that blink or, if a baby paper doll, come with a cloth diaper and bottle and actually drink water! The "real" hair feature was carried over to many of these later paper dolls as well.

Following the DeJournette list are pictures of the paper dolls. The pictures and list will give you some hint as to some of the ingenuity that went into the DeJournette paper doll sets to give them a certain quality of distinction.

The following is a list of all the known DeJournette paper dolls.

23 *WORLD'S FIRST PAPER DOLL TO DRINK* (not pictured; see #222)
R-30 *BLONDIE* (R-90)
35 *FROGGIE WENT A COURTING*
R-50 *HONEY BUN*
R-55 *SHOO-SHOO SHIRLEY*
60 *MOTHER DAUGHTER DOLLS*
65 *TRACY* (not pictured; see #711)
72 *CLAIRE*, same doll and outfits as Jill #711 but this doll is smaller and her hair has been shortened.

R-75 *MASQUERADE PARTY* (not pictured; this set has the same dolls and outfits as #2202)
R-80 *GINA* (800)
85 *BRIGHT EYES* The Winking Blinking Doll
90 *PENNY AND HER DOLLY*, "real" hair in a choice of three colors.
91 *GOLDILOCKS AND THE THREE BEARS*
P-100 *MY NAME IS MARIAN*
100 *BRIDE*, This doll is the same as #1350 but clothes are different.

150 *BOBBIE GIRLS* (set of twins)
198 *3 BIG DOLLS*, the dolls are the same as Gina #R-80. Each of the three dolls have a different hair color.
200 *HEIDI*-Pocket Book Doll
222 *LITTLEST DARLING*
300 *PAM* (not pictured; same as R-55 but Pam's shoes are attached with a chain).
500 *THE DOLLY TWINS*, dolls same as R-90
701 *7 DOLLS IN ONE*
711 *JILL*
777 *NEW BECKY*
800 *PLAYMATE*, 22″ tall
899 *CURLY TOP AND HER OWN LITTLE DOLLY TOPSEY* (not pictured) see R-90
899 *MISS CANDY AND HER DOLLY-WORLD'S LARGEST REAL HAIR DOLL* (not pictured)
901 *LITTLE RED RIDING HOOD*
903 *LITTLE BO PEEP*
911 *JAYNE* 1961 (not pictured) see #300 and #R-55)
1000 *GLENDORA* Paper Doll with Curly Locks
1350 *DOTTIE WITH THE SNAP-ON DRESSES*, doll same as #100 Bride, clothes different
1440 *HANSEL AND GRETEL*, box becomes Gingerbread House
2200 *MIMI THE FRENCH MODEL PAPER DOLL*
2201 *MISS HOLLY DAY*, box is fitted suitcase
2202 *SLEEPING BEAUTY AND PRINCE CHARMING*, box becomes four poster bed.
11-947 *BROWNIE PAPER DOLL*
11-950 *BROWNIE PAPER DOLL*
11-951 *GIRL SCOUT PAPER DOLL*
11-952 *GIRL SCOUT PAPER DOLL*
11-953 *BROWNIE PAPER DOLL*

The following paper dolls have no stock numbers:

BETSY BALLERINA, includes stage, scenery changes and stage settings.
BOBBIE TWINS (not pictured; same as #150 but new box cover and includes crayons and soap)
BROWNIE SCOUT PAPER DOLL
CURLY TOP, came with choice of three hair colors. Published by PAPER DOLL HOUSE
CURLY TOP 1947
CURLY TOP, with washable dresses
CURLY TOP DOLL AND COLOR SET
CURLY TOP DELUXE SET
GINGHAM GIRL
GINGHAM GIRL DOLL
GIRL SCOUT PAPER DOLL (not pictured)
MAMMY AND KINKY TOP
MY BABY (flat rubber doll with complete layette of paper outfits)
POKY HONTAS
PUBLISHER NAME NOT GIVEN:
FESTIVAL FUN, This box just reads "Atlanta, Georgia" which is where De-Journette was located. The doll is the early *Curly Top* doll with "real" hair. Jewish festival outfits, songs and handicrafts are included in the set.

R-30 *BLONDIE*. $6.00

35 *FROGGIE WENT A COURTING*. $8.00

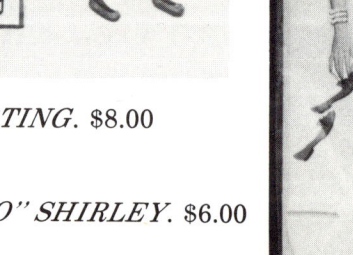

R-55 *"SHOO-SHOO" SHIRLEY*. $6.00

Courtesy of Audrey Sepponen

Courtesy of Audrey Sepponen

60 *MOTHER DAUGHTER DOLLS*. $6.00

R-50 *HONEY BUN*. $6.00

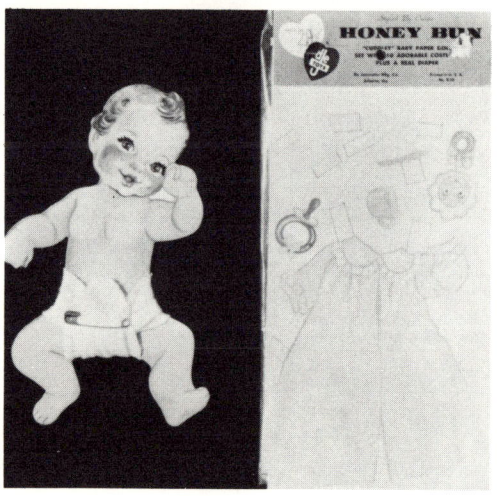

38

R-80 *GINA*. $5.00

Courtesy of Audrey Sepponen
85 *BRIGHT EYES*. $5.00

90 *PENNY AND HER DOLLY*. $6.00

72 *CLAIRE*. $10.00

91 *GOLDILOCKS AND THE THREE BEARS*. $6.00

Courtesy of Fran Van Vynckt
100 *BRIDE*. $8.00

P-100 *MY NAME IS MARIAN*. $8.00

Courtesy of Grayce Piemontesi

Courtesy of Virginia Crossley
150 *BOBBIE GIRLS*. $6.00

Courtesy of Audrey Sepponen
198 *3 BIG DOLLS*. $8.00

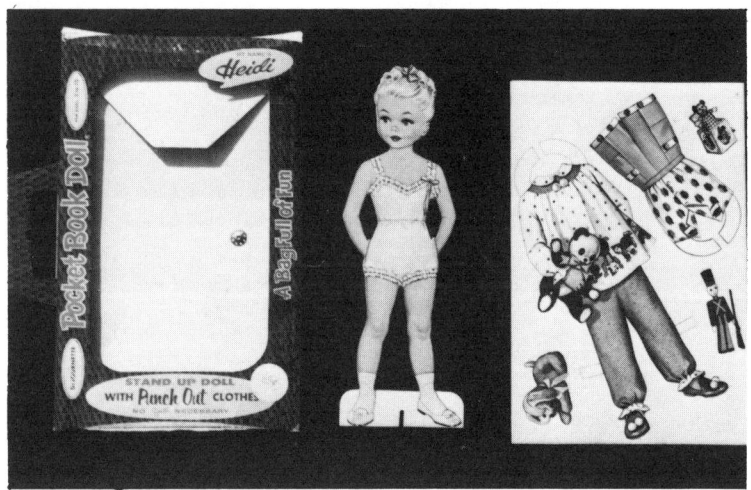

Courtesy of Virginia Crossley
200 *HEIDI*. $8.00

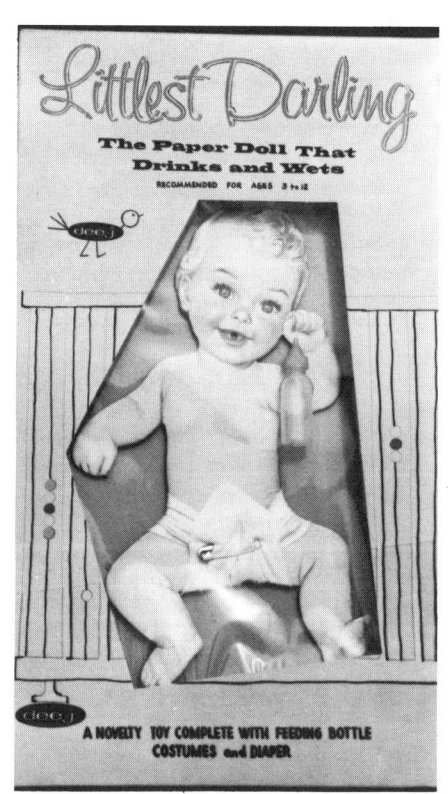

Courtesy of Virginia Crossley
222 *LITTLEST DARLING*. $8.00

500 *THE DOLLY TWINS*. $10.00

500 *THE DOLLY TWINS* Box contents

701 *7 DOLLS IN 1.* $10.00

777 *NEW! BECKY.* $12.00

Courtesy of Audrey Sepponen

Courtesy of Virginia Crossley

711 *JILL.* $12.00

Courtesy of Rosalie Eppert

800 *PLAYMATE.* $15.00

901 *LITTLE RED RIDING HOOD.* $10.00

Courtesy of Audrey Sepponen

Courtesy of Audrey Sepponen
1000 *GLENDORA*. $10.00

Courtesy of Audrey Sepponen
903 *LITTLE BO PEEP*. $10.00

Courtesy of Audrey Sepponen
1350 *DOTTIE WITH THE SNAP-ON DRESSES*. $12.00

Courtesy of Audrey Sepponen
1440 *HANSEL AND GRETEL*. $18.00

Courtesy of Audrey Sepponen
2200 *MIMI, THE FRENCH MODEL*. $20.00

Courtesy of Audrey Sepponen
2201 *MISS HOLLY DAY*. $18.00

2202 *SLEEPING BEAUTY AND PRINCE CHARMING* $20.00

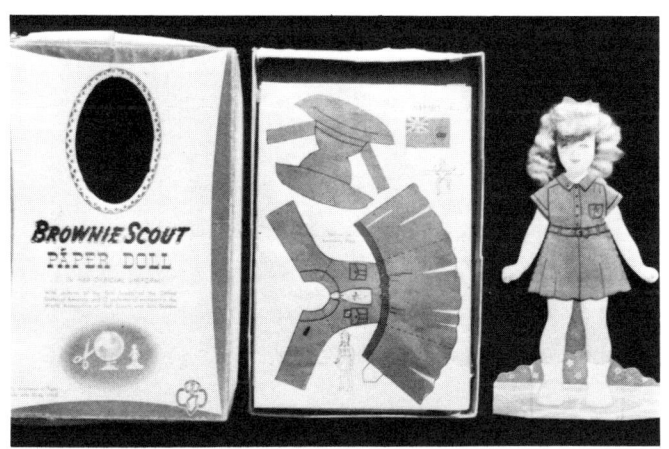 

BROWNIE SCOUT PAPER DOLL. $12.00
No stock number on box. Earliest Brownie paper doll. Doll is front-and-back style and the clothes wrap around the doll and fasten in back.

Courtesy of Marilyn Johnson
11-947 *BROWNIE PAPER DOLL.* $10.00
Doll is slightly changed in design from earliest Brownie and she now has brown shoes and socks. Still a front/back style doll, but clothes do not wrap around the doll.

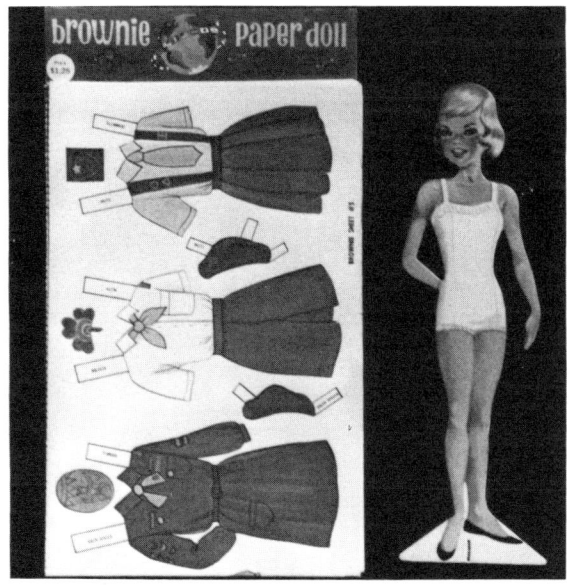 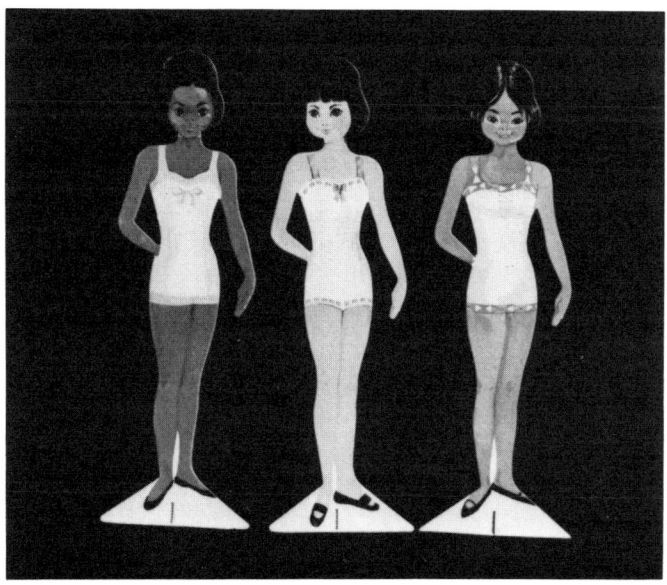

11-950 *BROWNIE PAPER DOLL.* $6.00
This doll was used for Brownie and Girl Scout sets #11-951, 11-952 and 11-953 but uniforms are different.

It is known that these three dolls came with either a Girl Scout or Brownie set, but the stock number is not available. These three dolls were also sold separately for 20 cents each.

CURLY TOP This is the original *CURLY TOP* put out by The Paper Doll House. Patented in 1938 and 1939. $10.00

Courtesy of Virginia Crossley

CURLY-TOP 1947. $8.00

CURLY-TOP. $8.00
Now the sets start to feature washable dresses

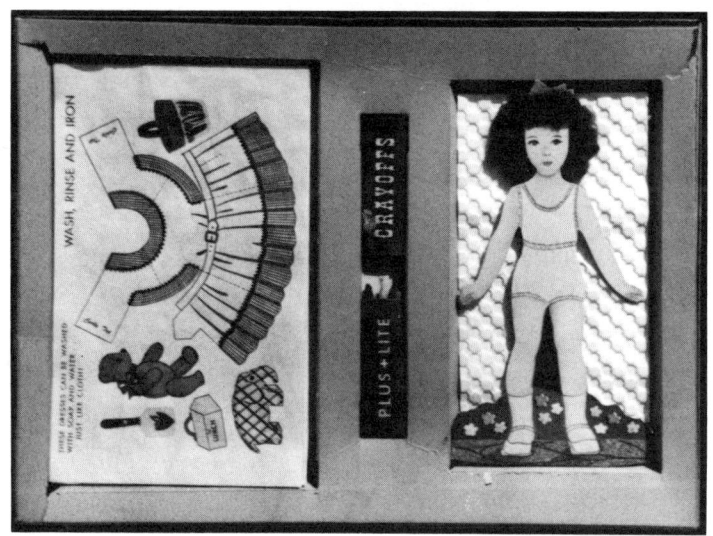

Shown here are the contents of the *CURLY-TOP DOLL AND COLOR SET.* $8.00

Courtesy of Virginia Crossley

CURLY-TOP DELUXE SET. $10.00
Includes three dolls each with different hair color

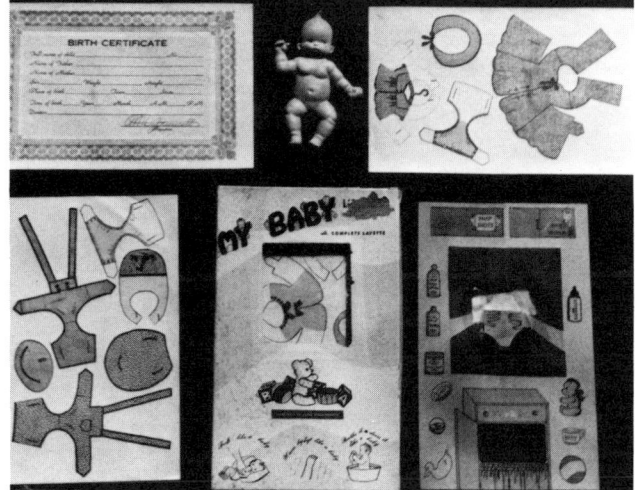

Courtesy of Betsy Slap

MY BABY. $15.00

BETSY BALLERINA. $25.00 — Courtesy of Audrey Sepponen

 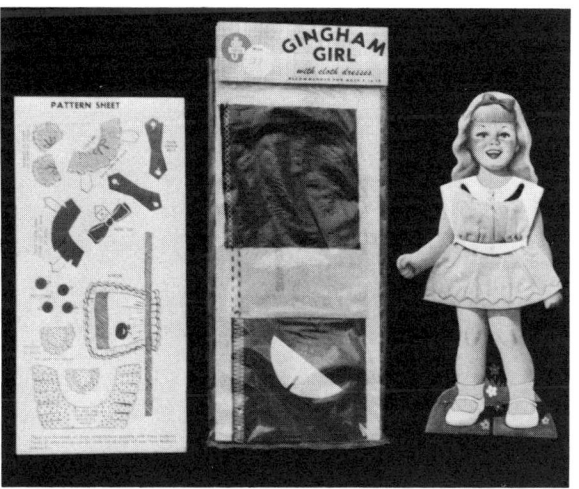

Courtesy of Shirley Hedge — *GINGHAM GIRL DOLL.* $8.00

Courtesy of Audrey Sepponen — *GINGHAM GIRL.* $8.00

Courtesy of Virginia Crossley

FESTIVAL FUN. $12.00
No publisher is given on this set but it is marked Atlanta, Ga. where DeJournette was located. The doll is the early Curly Top doll with "real" hair. The outfits are for Jewish festivals.

POKY-HONTAS. $10.00

Courtesy of Audrey Sepponen

45

Photo courtesy of Midwest Paper Dolls and Toys Quarterly

MAMMY AND KINKY-TOP. $25.00

Dennison Manufacturing Company

The Dennison Manufacturing Company is known world wide for its paper products. The Company was established in 1843 in the state of Maine. The first items produced by the Company were jewelry boxes. By the time of the Civil War the Company was producing shipping tags which became one of their mainstays. Late in the 19th century the firm moved to Boston and from there to Framingham, Massachusetts in the very early 1900's. Today every imaginable type of tag and gummed label is being manufactured by the Company plus school and office supplies. In recent years Dennison has acquired many companies which manufacture similar products.

Tissue and crepe paper were added to the product line in the late 1800's, and it was at this time that the Dennison paper dolls were introduced. Except for very early paper dolls and those from the 1950 era, the Dennison paper dolls were of the jointed type.

The Dennison Stationers Catalog of 1909 shows a paper doll outfit "No.8". It included two jointed dolls, crepe paper, tissue paper and other material used to design outfits for the dolls. Also featured is a doll house outfit "No. 18" which included (besides the doll house and furniture) two paper dolls and material for making paper clothes for the dolls. The Dennison jointed dolls could also be bought separately. In the 1907-1908 catalog there were eleven dolls available; two different sized babies, ballet dancers in three sizes, two different sized children, prima donnas in two sizes, one Indian and one African baby. Just two years later, in the 1909 catalog, there were only the two sizes of children available.

The following list includes all the known Dennison paper doll sets produced after 1900. A catalog date is to aid in dating but does not necessarily mean the set was new that year.

8 *PAPER DOLL OUTFIT* (shown as "Kit A" in 1905, no stock number in 1907-1908, and is called "No. 8 *PAPER DOL OUTFIT*" in 1909.)
11 *DESIGN-A-DOLL JOAN* circa 1950
11 *DESIGN-A-DOLL BETTE* circa 1950 (not pictured)
11 *DESIGN-A-DOLL NANCY* circa 1950 (not pictured)
16 *DENNISON'S DRESSED DOLL SET*, 9" doll and three dresses and hats
17 *DENNISON'S DRESSED DOLL SET*, 7" doll and three dresses and hats (not pictured)
18 *DOLL HOUSE OUTFIT* 1909 catalog (includes two paper dolls)
21 *DESIGN-A-DOLL CAROL AND BETTE* circa 1950 (not pictured)
21 *DESIGN-A-DOLL JOAN AND NANCY* circa 1950

31 *DENNISON'S CREPE AND TISSUE PAPER DOLL OUTFIT* 1913 catalog
33 *DENNISON'S CREPE AND TISSUE PAPER DOLL OUTFIT* 1922 catalog
34 *DENNISON'S DOLLS AND DRESSES* (advertised in 1916 magazine and 1922 catalog)
36 *CREPE PAPER DOLL OUTFIT* (some sets say *LITTLE TOT'S CREPE PAPER DOLL OUTFIT*)
37 *DENNISON'S DOLLS AND DRESSES*
38 *NANCY CREPE PAPER DOLL OUTFIT* (advertised in 1931 magazine ad)
512 *DRESS-A-DOLL, BUD AND BABS* circa 1950 (not pictured; see #513)
512 *DRESS-A-DOLL, PAT AND BUNNY* circa 1950
513 *DRESS-A-DOLL, BUD, BABS AND BUNNY* circa 1950

Courtesy of Betsy Addison

The set pictured is very similar to set No. 8 shown in the 1909 Dennison Catalog. The box cover has the same cut out window, however this box shown here was evidently sold at Christmas time as it has a Christmas holly print. The booklet shown next to the set was included in the box.

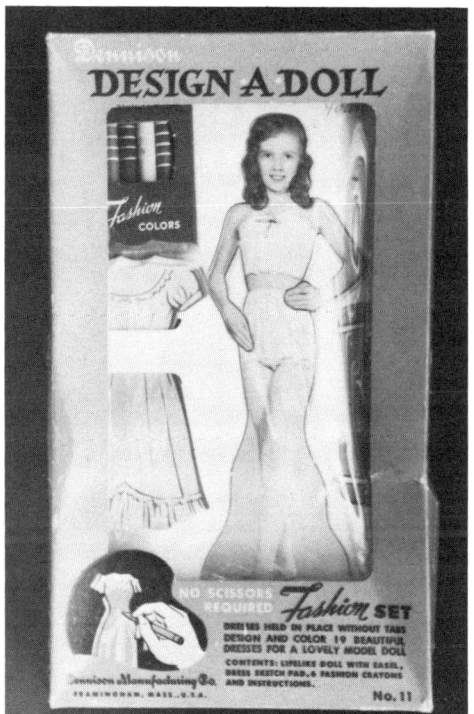

Courtesy of Marilyn Johnson

11 *DESIGN-A-DOLL JOAN.* $8.00 circa 1950

Courtesy of Rosalie Eppert

21 *DESIGN-A-DOLL, JOAN AND NANCY.* $10.00 circa 1950

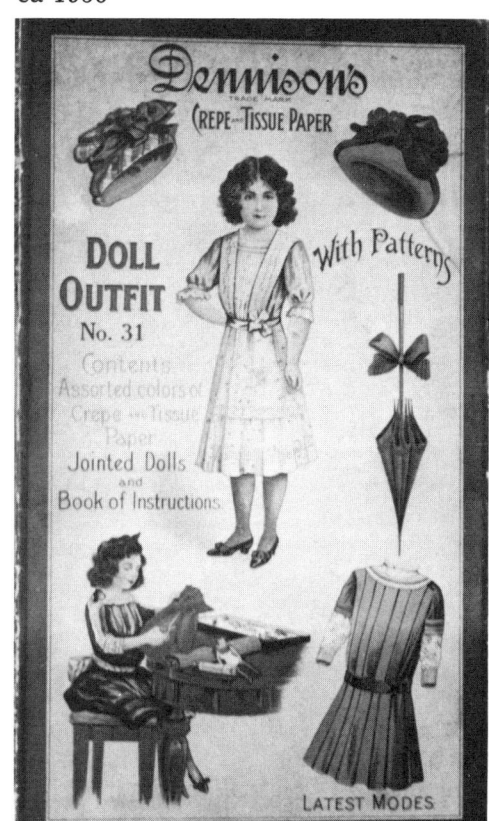

Courtesy of Atlanta Toy Museum

31 *DENNISON'S DOLL OUTFIT.* $55.00
No date, listed in 1913 catalog

33 *DENNISON'S CREPE AND TISSUE PAPER DOLL OUTFIT.* $35.00
No date, listed in 1922 catalog.

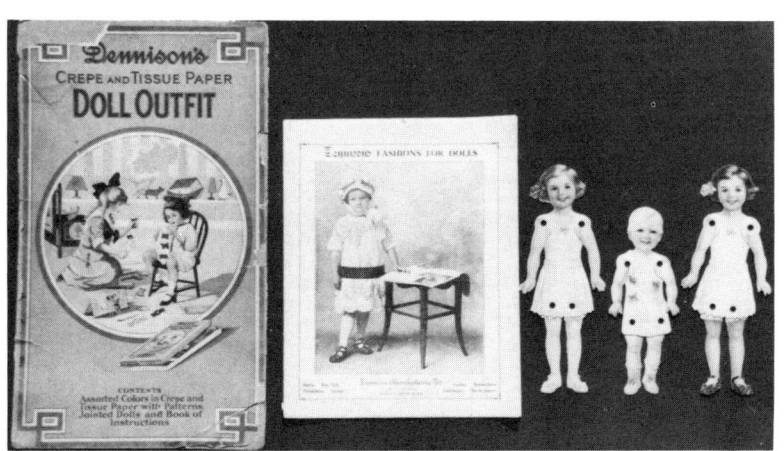

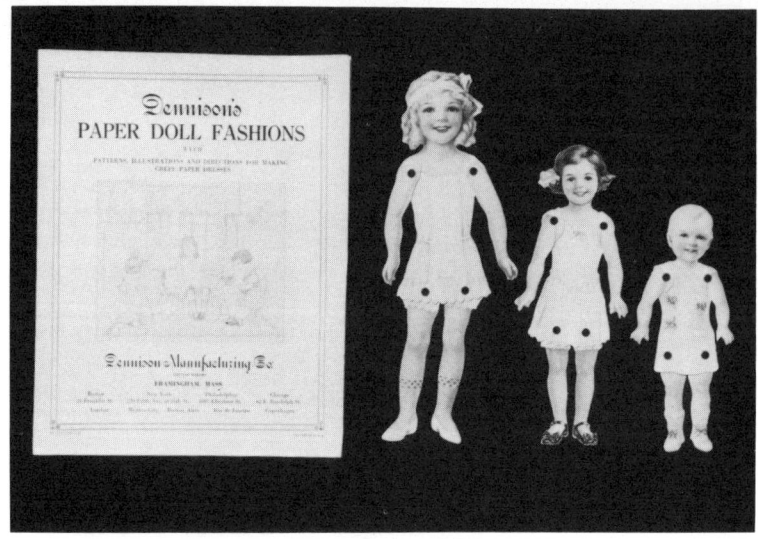

Courtesy of Edith Linn

34 *DENNISON'S DOLLS AND DRESSES*.
$35.00
Earliest known date is 1916 advertisement, also in 1922 catalog

34 *DENNISON'S DOLLS AND DRESSES*. The girl dolls came with either blond or brunette hair. The baby was either in a pink or blue outfit.

Courtesy of Audrey Sepponen
36 *CREPE PAPER DOLL OUTFIT*. $30.00

Courtesy of Rosalie Eppert
37 *DENNISON DOLLS AND DRESSES*. $30.00
The dolls in #36 & #37 were printed front & back

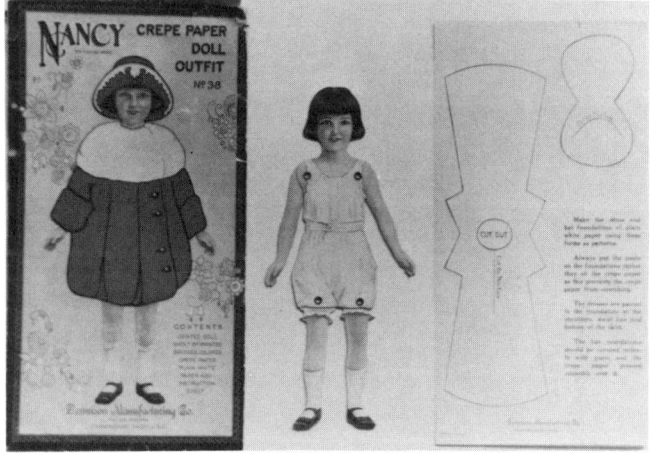

July 1931 ad in *HOME CIRCLE MAGAZINE* for paper doll *NANCY LEE* which is the same doll as Nancy #38

Courtesy of Rosalie Eppert
38 *NANCY CREPE PAPER DOLL OUTFIT*. $27.50
Notice that Nancy is the same doll as the middle doll in sets #36 and #37. Nancy was advertised in 1931, so sets #36 & #37 must be same era.

513 *DRESS-A-DOLL BUD, BABS AND BUNNY.*
$10.00 circa 1950

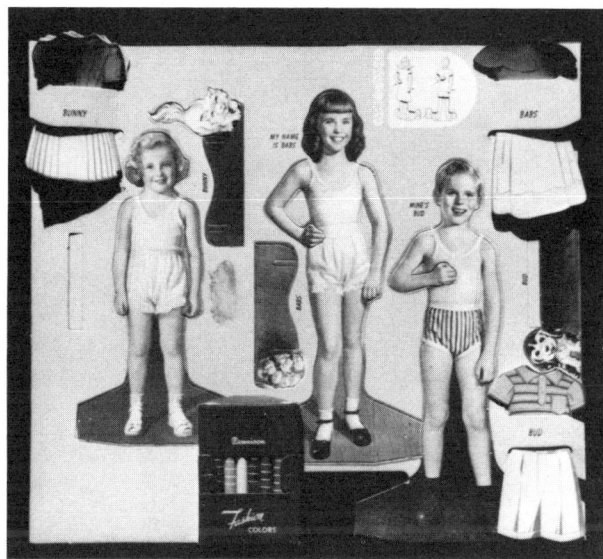

513 *DRESS-A-DOLL* Box contents

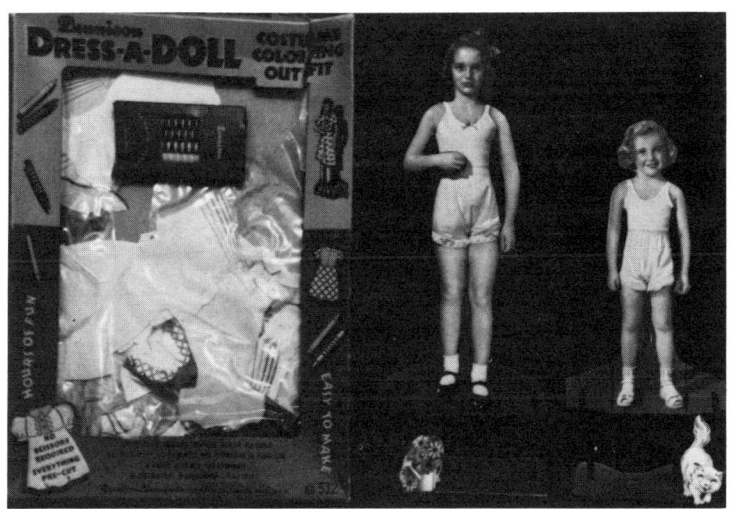

512 *DRESS-A-DOLL PAT AND BUNNY.* $8.00 circa 1950

Courtesy of Virginia Crossley

Determined Productions, Inc.

Wolfpit Enterprises, Inc. and Boucher Associates are subsidiaries of Determined Productions, Inc.

LISA YOUR PAPER DOLL PLAYMATE AND HER CLOTHES CLOSET © *1961.* (Large 20″ jointed doll) $10.00 Determined Productions, Inc.

Courtesy of Pam Hunter

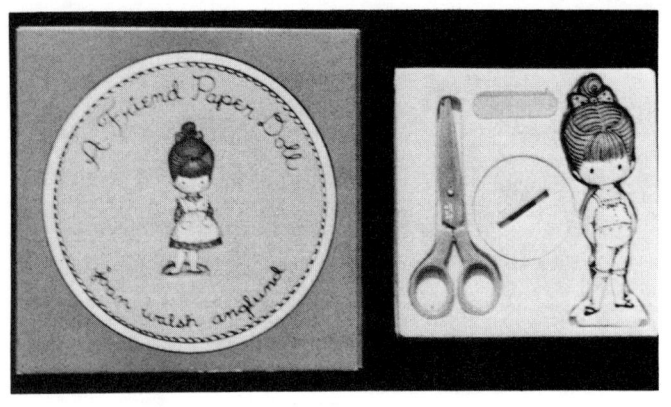

A FRIEND PAPER DOLL © 1967. $5.00
Boucher Associates

LOVE PAPER DOLL © 1975. $5.00
Wolfpit Enterprises, Inc.

S.S. HAPPINESS CREW STICKER DOLLS © 1981
Determined Productions Inc. World Rights reserved; currently available

S.S. HAPPINESS CREW STICKER DOLLS © 1981
Determined Productions, Inc. World rights reserved; currently available

SNOOPY PAPER DOLL Peanuts Character © 1958, 1965 United Feature Syndicate, Inc. (not pictured)

M.A. Donohue and Company

80A *BOB AND NAN.* $20.00

Courtesy of Virginia Crossley

80C *ANN AND JOE.* $20.00

81C *TED AND BOB.* $20.00

Courtesy of Rosalie Eppert

85B *TINY TIPTOE AND HER NEIGHBORS.* $40.00

TINY TIPTOE

TINY TIPTOE

TINY TIPTOE

TINY TIPTOE

TINY TIPTOE

TINY TIPTOE   TINY TIPTOE   TINY TIPTOE

Courtesy of Jane Sugg
671 *FAIRY FAVORITE* 1913. $30.00

Courtesy of Edith Linn
672 *THE NURSERY FAVORITE* 1913. $30.00

Courtesy of Virginia Crossley
675 *FAIRY-TALE AND FLOWER PAPER-DOLLS*
1913. $45.00 This book combines #671 and #672.

675 *FAIRY-TALE AND FLOWER*

675 *FAIRY-TALE AND FLOWER*

675 *FAIRY-TALE AND FLOWER*

675 *FAIRY-TALE AND FLOWER*

675 *FAIRY-TALE AND FLOWER*

675 *FAIRY-TALE AND FLOWER*

675 *FAIRY-TALE AND FLOWER*

675 *FAIRY-TALE AND FLOWER*

675 *FAIRY-TALE AND FLOWER*

675 *FAIRY-TALE AND FLOWER*

675 *FAIRY-TALE AND FLOWER*

675 *FAIRY-TALE AND FLOWER*

673 *BOB AND NAN* (not pictured) See #80A
674 *ANN AND JOE* (not pictured) See #80C

Dot and Peg Productions

Dot and Peg Productions was founded in 1941 by a sister team of Mrs. Dorothy Hedges (Dot) and Mrs. Margaret Lamb (Peg).

Dot designed the first paper dolls as a result of making handmade paper dolls for her two young daughters. Seeing the possibility of interesting other children, Dot asked Peg to collaborate with her in making a set for the public.

In the summer of 1941 Dot took the handmade paper doll sample of "Young American Designer" to New York and was led to the Good Housekeeping magazine editor. It was wartime and imported toys had stopped, so there was a big demand for original American toys. Good Housekeeping was promoting a department of the best American made toys of the year. The editor was so enthusiastic over "Young American Designer" that a contract was immediately signed. This was all done in a day's work and Dot returned home to Chattonooga informing Peg that they were in business! Orders began pouring in from all over the country. Marshall Field and Company alone bought 10,000 sets that first year.

The Christmas issue of Good Housekeeping that year not only gave "Young American Designer" the seal of approval but featured the set as the best American toy of the year. The set contained two paper dolls named "Peg" and "Dot", seven basic patterns and 18 sheets of "material" made of paper which resembled velvet, gingham, wool, tweed, prints, polka dots, etc. There were two gummed sheets that resembled fur and eight gummed sheets to trim the dresses. Real veiling was also included to trim the hats. Also included was an illustrated booklet of instructions plus wooden stands for the dolls, a pencil and even an automatic "hydraulic" (with sponge tip) that could be filled with water for moistening the gummed pieces.

This was the beginning of a 20 year business that progressed into other business ventures besides paper dolls. When paper became scarce near the end of the war they decided to produce a shell craft kit for making shell jewelry and ornaments. Their last paper doll set was produced in 1950 and then their toy line was discontinued as by this time they had entered into a new venture--manufacturing ladies scuffs and accessories. The scuffs were so elegant that all the large stores in the country were ordering in great quantities. Stores like Bonwits in New York, Marshall Field in Chicago and I. Magnin in California. Saks Fifth Avenue liked the scuffs so much they had their own label sewn in them. In addition to scuffs, bed jackets and sleepwear were also added to the line.

By 1962 Dot and Peg Productions had grown so large the sisters decided it was time to retire and sell their business, which they did.

THE YOUNG AMERICAN DESIGNER 1941. $18.00

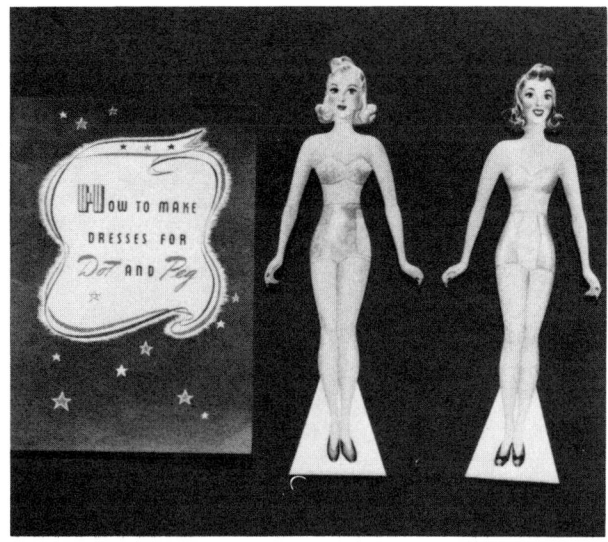

DOLLS FROM THE YOUNG AMERICAN DESIGNER

MOTHER AND DAUGHTER DRESSES 1943. $15.00

DOLLS FROM MOTHER AND DAUGHTER

Courtesy of Virginia Crossley

DOTTIE DRESS-UP 1950. $10.00

WEDDING BELLES 1945. $15.00

Courtesy of Virginia Crossley

DOVER PUBLICATIONS, INC.

Dover Publications was founded in 1941 by Hayward Cirker. Before this Mr. Cirker was a salesman at Crown Publishers.

The first books Mr. Cirker sold in 1941 were scholarly books that were remainders. The books were sold through the mail by catalog. In 1943 Dover published its first book which was a reprint of a German book of higher mathematical tables. This was followed by many scientific reprint books. Three years later books on art design were added to the line and in 1951 the first Dover paperbacks were published.

Books for juveniles began in 1960 with reprints of well known books such as L. Frank Baum's "Wizard of Oz" and Palmer Cox's "Brownies". In the late 1960's a series of activity books for children was started. Included were coloring books, construction books and paper doll books. These activity books were and are still very popular with children as well as the adult collector of paper toys and paper dolls.

The simple Dover mail order business of the 1940's has grown to such heights that their mailings now reach 500,000 people. There are now about 200 people working at Dover. Mr. Cirker's wife, Blanche, teamed up with her husband in the early years of the business, and the two are still the chief operating directors of the Company.

The following is a list of the Dover paper doll books:

23175-5 *ANTIQUE PAPER DOLLS, THE EDWARDIAN ERA* 1975 (pictured)
23176-3 *ANTIQUE PAPER DOLLS, 1915-1920* 1975 (pictured)
23453-3 *VICTORIAN FASHION PAPER DOLLS FROM HARPER'S BAZAAR,* 1867-1898 (pictured) 1977
23511-4 *FASHION PAPER DOLLS FROM "GODEY'S LADY'S BOOK"* 1840-1854 (pictured) 1977
23627-7 *ERTE FASHION PAPER DOLLS OF THE TWENTIES* 1978
23711-7 *DOLLY DINGLE PAPER DOLLS* 1978
23715-X *GLAMOROUS MOVIE STARS OF THE THIRTIES* 1978 (pictured)
23768-0 *RUDOLPH VALENTINO* 1979 (pictured)
23769-9 *MARILYN MONROE* 1979
23848-2 *MORE DOLLY DINGLE PAPER DOLLS* 1979
23955-1 *JOHN WAYNE* 1981
24045-2 *ANTIQUE ADVERTISING PAPER DOLLS* 1981
24089-4 *LETTIE LANE PAPER DOLLS* 1981
24093-2 *PAVLOVA AND NIJINSKY* 1981
24153-X *KATE GREENAWAY* 1981
24200-5 *MORE LETTIE LANE PAPER DOLLS* 1981
24207-2 *VIVIEN LEIGH* 1981
24268-4 *GREAT EMPRESSES AND QUEENS* 1982
24281-1 *PETER RABBIT PAPER DOLLS* 1982
24285-4 *CARMEN MIRANDA* 1982
24376-1 *FLOPSY, MOPSY AND COTTON-TAIL* 1982
24386-9 *CURIOUS GEORGE* 1982
24404-0 *JUDY GARLAND* 1982
24415-3 *GREAT FASHION DESIGNS OF THE BELLE EPOQUE* 1982
24415-6 *BETTY BONNET PAPER DOLLS* 1982

#23176-3   Currently available   #23175-5

#23453-3   Currently available   #23511-4

#23715-X   Currently available   #23768-0

E.P. Dutton and Company

Many of the E.P. Dutton paper dolls were imported from the color printing and publishing firm of Ernest Nister in Nurenburg, Germany. Dutton was the sole distributor in the U.S. of the internationally famous firm's products from the middle 1880's until the outbreak of World War I which ended the asociation. Dutton distributed the beautiful Nister calendars, cards, valentines and children's books besides the paper dolls during that time period.

1312 *DUTTON'S DOLLS FOR DRESSING, LITTLE BO-PEEP*. $35.00

Courtesy of Joan Carol Kaltschmidt

Courtesy of Maurine Popp
2739 *DOLLY DARLING*. $40.00

2739 *DOLLY DARLING*-inside page

2739 *DOLLY DARLING*-inside page

2739 *DOLLY DARLING*-inside page

Courtesy of Yesteryears Doll Museum — Courtesy of Midwest Paper Dolls and Toys Quarterly

4309 *PRETTY PAPER PETS*. $40.00   3159 *DAINTY DOLLIES AND THEIR DRESSES*. $40.00

1311 *DUTTON'S DOLLS FOR DRESSING, LITTLE RED RIDING HOOD* (not pictured)
3916 *LETTIE LANE'S GREAT GRANDPARENTS* (not pictured)
LETTIE LANE'S SISTER'S CHILDREN (not pictured)

The Lettie Lane paper dolls are different from those that appeared in the *Ladies Home Journal*. The Dutton Co. also carried in its line a series of "Model" books that were also published by the McLoughlin Publishing Co. Examples are *The Model Book of Trains*, *The Model Book of Soldiers*, and *The Animal Model Book*. See the McLoughlin section for a more complete list of these books.

Einson Freeman Company, Inc.

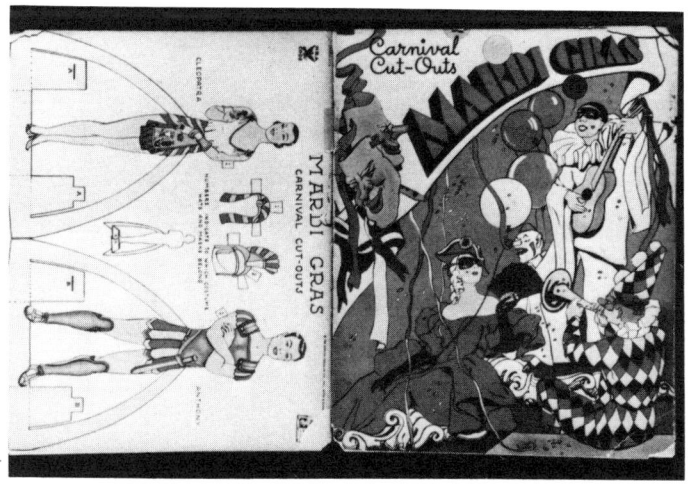 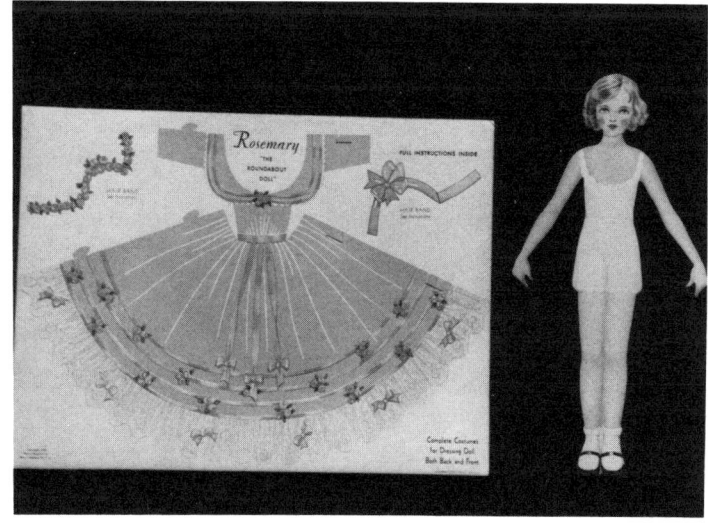

Courtesy of Carol Carey

432 *MARDI GRAS* 1935. $35.00

ROSEMARY THE ROUND ABOUT DOLL 1932. $25.00
No number (sold in glassine envelope)

59

Emmylou Specialties

Emmylou Specialties produced twelve different styles of cloth dresses to be sewn for a large cardboard doll that was jointed at the shoulders. The outfits came in envelopes for the price of 60 cents and the dolls were sold separately at 30 cents each. There were at least four different styles of dolls, either blonde or brunette. Two of the dolls are pictured here. In two known cases paper dresses were also included. The name of Karl Gut Litho. Co. appears on the paper outfit pages.

EMMYLOU SPECIALTIES

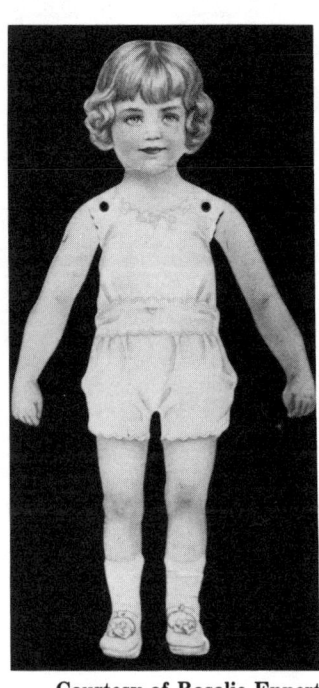

Courtesy of Rosalie Eppert
DOLL

Courtesy of Judy Curtis
EMMYLOU SPECIALTIES. $20.00

Fish-Lyman Company

In December 1922 the Fish-Lyman Company ran an ad in *Child Life* magazine on Margaret Evans Price paper dolls. The ad states there are 12″ paper dolls and 7″ paper dolls. The 12″ dolls are already cut out and mounted on cardboard, and the smaller dolls are to be cut out. The ad has an array of all the dolls in their different costumes. Actually there are four 12″ dolls and four small 7″ dolls, but each is pictured many times wearing a different costume (see illustration). Three of the 12″ dolls are pictured here (missing doll of boy) and the four smaller dolls are also pictured.

Three months later in March 1923 the company ran another ad for these paper dolls in *Child Life*. In this ad they state they will send a complete assortment of twelve 12″ dolls plus smaller dolls for a total of 34 possible combinations. Counting up all the dolls pictured in the earlier ad of December 1922 there are 34 pictured.

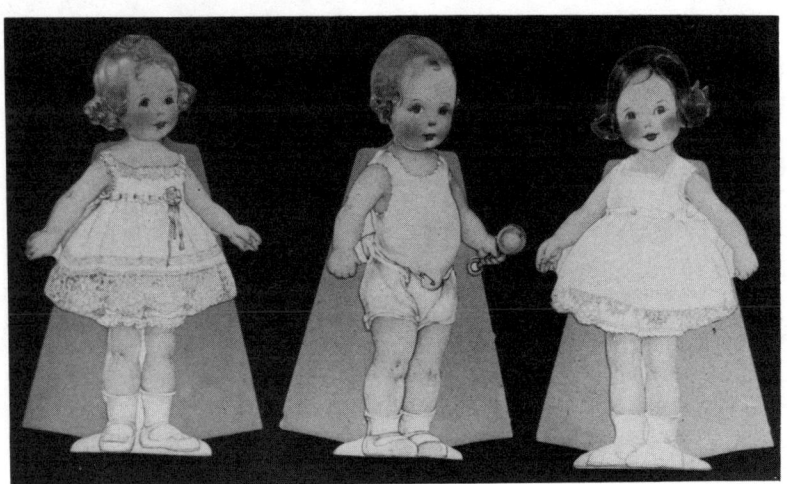

12″ dolls, one boy doll missing. $20.00 each doll with outfits

7" (approx.) dolls. $10.00 each doll with outfits

Child Life Ad, December 1922

Foster and Stewart Publishing Corporation

All pictures courtesy of Virginia Crossley

AFRICA   *ARABIA*   *AUSTRALIA*

CHINA   *INDIA*   *SWITZERLAND*   *FRANCE*

| JAPAN | HOLLAND/NETHERLANDS | RURAL MEXICO | ESKIMOS OF ALASKA |

OUR WORLD CUT-OUT OF THE MONTH 1946

GREECE (not pictured)
NORTH AMERICAN INDIANS (not pictured)
TURKEY (not pictured)

The fourteen sets listed contain paper dolls, outfits, animals and buildings. $10.00 each set

Foundation Desk Company, Inc.

THE JUVENILE ARTIST 1923-1924. A large book of activities for children including cutting, pasting and the four paper dolls pictured.

Courtesy of Jane Sugg

THE JUVENILE ARTIST 1923-1924. $15.00

THE JUVENILE ARTIST-Paper Doll Pages

Frann Paper Dolls

GRANDMOTHERS DOLLS 1955. $18.00

Courtesy of Emma Terry

NEW ORLEANS ANTE BELLUM PAPER DOLLS 1955 (not pictured)
LITTLE MISS (OLD) FASHION AND BABY SISTER This set was sold at F.A.O. Schwarz Toy Store and is the same set as *GRANDMOTHERS DOLLS*.)

THE BRIDE DOLL 1955. $18.00

Courtesy of Jane Sugg

Friendship Press

Courtesy of Zelda Cushner
FRIENDSHIP PAPER DOLLS. $25.00

FRIENDSHIP PAPER DOLLS

Samuel Gabriel Sons & Co.-Gabriel Industries, Inc.

New York City, New York

Samuel Gabriel Sons & Co. was established in 1907. In the 1930's the company was sold to American Colortype of Chicago who had been doing most of the printing for Sam Gabriel for many years.

In 1957 the Samuel Gabriel Division of American Colortype was sold to Jerome M. Fryer and Morton J. Levy of Levy and Fryer, Inc. a national sales representative business that had been formed in 1950. The name of Samuel Gabriel Sons & Co. was changed to Gabriel Industries, Inc.

In 1961 Levy and Fryer, Inc. merged into Gabriel and in 1965 Gym-Dandy Inc. and Hubley Mfg. Co. also merged into Gabriel. In the years to follow, many companies' toy lines were acquired; the chemistry and erector sets of A.C. Gilbert in 1967 and the Samsonite toy line in 1972. Kohner Bros., Inc., a manufacturer of toys and games, followed in 1975, and the Child Guidance line was acquired in 1978 from Questor Corporation. Also in 1978 Gabriel Industries merged with CBS Toys, a division of CBS, Inc. The next year, Gabriel Industries condensed and reorganized its products into four brand lines; Child Guidance,® , Gabriel® Toys and Games, Gym-Dandy® , and Wonder® . A wood gym line was added in 1981 under the brand name Creative Playthings® and in 1982 Ideal Toys was purchased.

Among the first paper dolls published by the company was a series called *DOLLY DEAR, DOLLY DELIGHT and DOLLY DARLING*. They were numbered #1, #2, and #3 respectively and dated 1911. A few of the early paper dolls came in envelopes. Later there were paper doll books, but the majority of the paper dolls came in boxed sets. The letter "D" that preceded the stock numbers stood for "Doll", and when a number was prefixed by the letter "T" the item was a toy. The 800 and 900 numbers did not use a letter preceding the numbers, and when the firm became known as Gabriel Industries, Inc., the letters were dropped altogether.

If a catalog date is included where the paper doll is pictured, this is only to aid in dating the paper doll and does not necessarily mean the paper doll was new in that catalog. Paper doll sets were often carried in the catalogs for many years. All the known paper dolls for Samuel Gabriel and Sons and Gabriel Industries are listed. The pictures will follow the list.

1 *DOLLY DEAR* 1911 (not pictured)
2 *DOLLY DELIGHT* 1911 (not pictured)
3 *DOLLY DARLING* 1911
D78 *MY DOLL JACK* (D134 Toddler Twins)
D79 *MY DOLL JILL* (D134 Toddler Twins)
D90 *MY DOLLY SERIES OF NEW DRESSING DOLLS-SISTER NAN*
D90 *MY DOLLY SERIES OF NEW DRESSING DOLLS-BROTHER BOB*
D90 *MY DOLLY SERIES OF NEW DRESSING DOLLS-COUSIN KATE*
D90 *BETSY McCALL BIGGEST PAPER DOLL*-32" doll
D92 *SWEETHEART DOLL-HELEN* (not pictured; see #876-doll of Helen)
D93 *POLLY PERT* (D135 Sisters)
D94 *SUZIE SWEET* (D135 Sisters)
D100 *DOLLY SHEETS TO CUT OUT*-4 sheets bound as a book (not pictured)
D100 *MY WARDROBE DOLLS* (D140)
D100 *SCHOOL MATES* 4 sheets and cover bound as a book
D104 *CLOTH DRESSES TO SEW FOR POLLY PET* (not pictured)
D104 *BEST OF FRIENDS* (not pictured; see #D117 Junior Fashions dolls of Rita and Irene)
D105 *PLAY PAPER DOLLS* (D115 Paper Doll Bazaar)
D106 *JUNIOR SHOP* (clothes from #D138 All My Dollies, dolls new)
D106 *DRESSES TO SEW FOR MARY ANN* (not pictured)
D107 *THE TWINNIES* (dolls same as #D133, clothes and box cover different)
D107 *BETTY JANE*
D108 *MARY ALICE*
D108 *CLOTH DRESSES TO SEW FOR MY TWIN DOLLS* (not pictured)
D109 *DOLL DRESSES TO COLOR* (4 dolls from #896 Fancy Dress Dolls)
D109 *DORIS DAINTY* (not pictured)
D111 *SWEET SUE DOLL* (not pictured)
D112 *MOVING EYE DOLLY BABY BETTY* 1920
D112 *MOVING EYE DOLLY TODDLING TOM* 1920
D113 *THE TWINNIES* 1921
D113 *LITTLE ORPHAN ANNIE* (includes doll of Sandy)
D114 *MY COMPLETE SEW-DRESS BOX*
D114 *OUR AMERICA* (#D117 Junior Fashions)
D115 *WINNIE WINKLE AND HER PARIS COSTUMES*
D115 THE "EVER NEW" DOLL (this same paper doll set was published under the title "Quick-Change Dolly" by Raphael Tuck & Sons)
D115 *PAPER DOLL BAZAAR*
115 *BALLERINA DOLLS* 1956 (not pictured)
D116 *FASHION MODEL*
D116 *DOLLIES A LA MODE*, a box set containing 6 dolls (not pictured)
D116 *TOTS AND TEENS* (not pictured)
116 "PONY TAIL" PAPER DOLL 1959
D117 *CAROL AND HER DRESSES*
D117 *JUNIOR FASHIONS* (The dolls are the same as D114 Our America)
D117 *DOLLIES AND THEIR WARDROBES* (not pictured)
117 *ANGEL FACE* (not pictured)
D118 *DOLLY ADORABLE*, doll body with 3 interchangeable heads (not pictured)

D118 *SCHOOL DAYS*
D118 *PAPER DOLL PLAY* (not pictured; contents same as #D118 *SCHOOL DAYS*)
D119 *DOLLYLAND*-Box with six dolls in envelopes. #1 Merry Marjorie, #2 Handsome Harold, #3 Graceful Gertrude, #4 Sweet Sallie, #5 Pretty Pauline, #6 Jolly Jack.
D119 *DOLLYLAND* 1920 box with 3 dolls-Grace, Edith and Mabel. Edith is pictured on the box cover. The dolls are from #877.
D119 *SEW-EASY DOLL*, paper doll with cloth clothes to sew.
D119 *SEW-EASY DOLL-DAINTY DOT* paper doll with 4 cloth outfits to sew.
D120 *SEW-EASY DOLLS*-2 paper dolls with 8 outfits to sew (not pictured)
D121 *FRANCES AND HER FROCKS*
D121 *FANNY AND HER FROCKS* the "Dainty Dolly" Series of Dressing Dolls (not pictured)
D121 *BABYLAND "PEGGY"* 1921
D121 *BABYLAND "BOBBY"* 1921
D122 *MOTHER AND DAUGHTER DOLLS* (not pictured)
D122 *WIDE AWAKE AND FAST ASLEEP DOLL-ALICE* (jointed at shoulders)
D122 *WIDE AWAKE AND FAST ASLEEP DOLL-DOROTHY* (jointed at shoulders) (not pictured)
D123 *HAPPY FACES DRESSING DOLLS*, 1 doll with 2 extra heads. (not pictured)
123 *LITTLE AUDREY WITH SWING OUT WARDROBE* 1960
D124 *MY DOLLY SHEETS TO CUT OUT*, 4 sheets and cover bound as a book (not pictured)
D125 *BETTY IS GOING AWAY TO BOARDING SCHOOL*
D126 *DOLLIES IN STYLE* (not pictured)
D126 *THE DIMPLE DOLL FAMILY*, 3 dolls from #876, not always the same three dolls.
D127 *SURPRISE DOLLIES* (not pictured)
D127 *THE WINKLE FAMILY*
D129 *TURN AND TURN ABOUT DOLLIES*, 2 12" doll bodies, 6 changeable heads.
130 *VICKI*-Velcro Paper Doll
D131 *SOLDIERS AND SAILORS*-4 sheets and cover bound as a book (not pictured)
D131 *QUARTET OF DOLLS*, 4 dolls from #D138 All My Dollies (not pictured)
D132 *WEDDING PARTY*, this is a smaller version of #D139 Bridal Party, same dolls.
D133 *THE TWINNIES*, same dolls as #D107, new clothes and box cover.
D134 *TODDLER TWINS*
D134 *THE YOUNGER SET* (not pictured)
D135 *SISTERS*
D135 *THE DEBUTANTES*
D137 *THE TWINS AND THEIR TROUSSEAU* (not pictured)
D137 *THE COSTUME PARTY* (issued with two different box covers, contents same)
D138 *ALL MY DOLLIES*

D138 *MY MAMMA DOLL*, 10" doll with crepe paper and patterns. (Doll cries when pressed) (not pictured)
D139 *BRIDAL PARTY*
D139 *DOLLS WITH WILLIAMSBURG COLONIAL DRESS* 1940 and 1955
D140 *DRESS OUR DOLLS*, dolls and clothes same as D100 My Wardrobe Dolls.
D141 *OUR HAPPY FAMILY* 1929, 4 sheets bound as a book
D144 *LET'S BUILD OUR CAMP* 1930, 6 sheets bound as a book. Log cabin, paper dolls.
T147 *LITTLE PET'S PLAY HOUSE*, a playhouse, furniture and paper dolls.
D149 *MY DOLLIES PASTIME CUTOUT SHEETS*, 4 sheets and cover bound as a book.
D172 *LITTLE AMERICANS FROM MANY LANDS* 1929
T199 *DOLL FURNITURE*, 8 sheets of furniture in box set (not pictured)
250 *LITTLE AUDREY*, 36" paper doll
300 *SHIRLEY TEMPLE* snap on paper doll 1958
301 *SHIRLEY TEMPLE* magnetic doll 1961
303 *SHIRLEY TEMPLE* magnetic doll, same doll as #301 except larger and new clothes
304 *SHIRLEY TEMPLE*, doll has "real" hair (not pictured)
305 *SHIRLEY TEMPLE*, 40" lifesize doll (not pictured)
826 *DOLLS AND CLOTHES TO CUT OUT AND PAINT* (not pictured)

867 *MY DOLLY'S CRAYON BOOK* 1917
876 *DAINTY DOLLIES* 1919
877 *MY BOOK OF DARLING DOLLIES* 1920
886 *SMART FASHIONS*, 4 dolls from #895
887 *MY BOOK OF DARLING DOLLS*, 6 dolls from #895
894 *TOWN AND COUNTRY*
895 *MODERN DOLLS A PLENTY*
896 *DOLLIES A'LA MODE*, dolls same as #895
896 *FANCY DRESS DOLLS*
963 *DRESS ME*

The following do not have numbers, or the number is not available:

MERRY MARJORY 1920 (not pictured)
SUSAN, her eyes can move and she has 3 outfits
DOLLY DELIGHT 1920, doll is Ruth from #877
DOLLY SHEET-JACK 1922, doll is from #877
DOLLY SHEET-RUTH 1922, doll is from #877

Courtesy of Sharon Carter
3 *DOLLY DARLING* 1911. $65.00

D78 *MY DOLL JACK* $15.00

D79 *MY DOLL JILL*. $15.00

D90 *COUSIN KATE*. $25.00
Cut set of the doll and two of her outfits

D90 *BROTHER BOB*. $25.00

D90 *SISTER NAN*. $25.00

Courtesy of Grayce Piemontesi

Courtesy of Rosalie Eppert

Reprinted by permission of the McCall Publishing Company

Courtesy of Jane Sugg

D90 *BETSY MCCALL, BIGGEST PAPER DOLL* © 1955 *Samuel Gabriel Sons And The McCall Corporation.* $18.00

D94 *SUZIE SWEET* $10.00

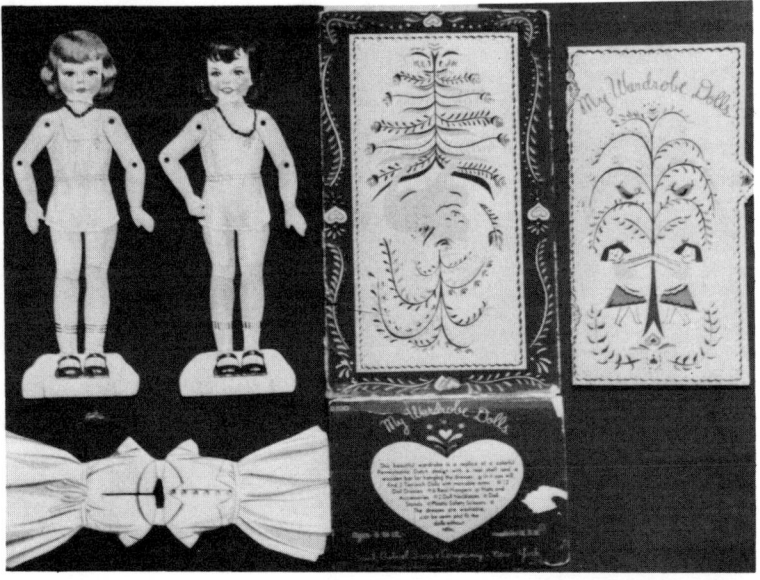

Courtesy of Shirley Hedge

Courtesy of Betsy Slap

D93 *POLLY PERT*. $10.00

D100 *MY WARDROBE DOLLS*. $20.00

Courtesy of Jane Sugg

D105 *PLAY PAPER DOLLS*. $18.00

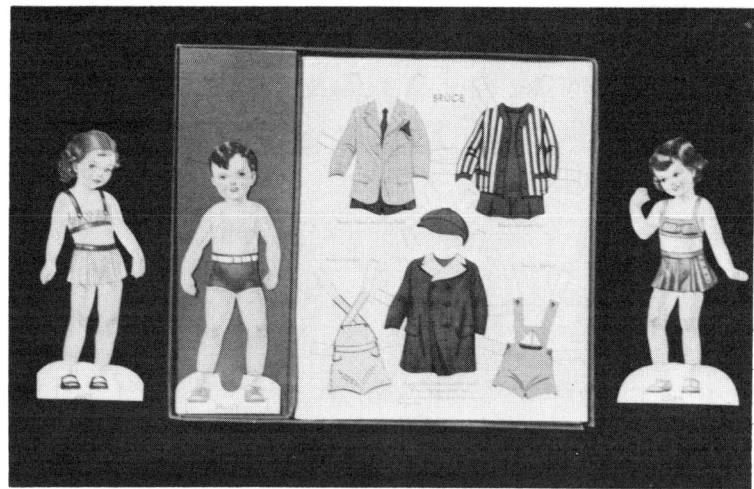
D105 Paper dolls and one page of clothes

Courtesy of Mary Kelley

D106 *JUNIOR SHOP*. $20.00

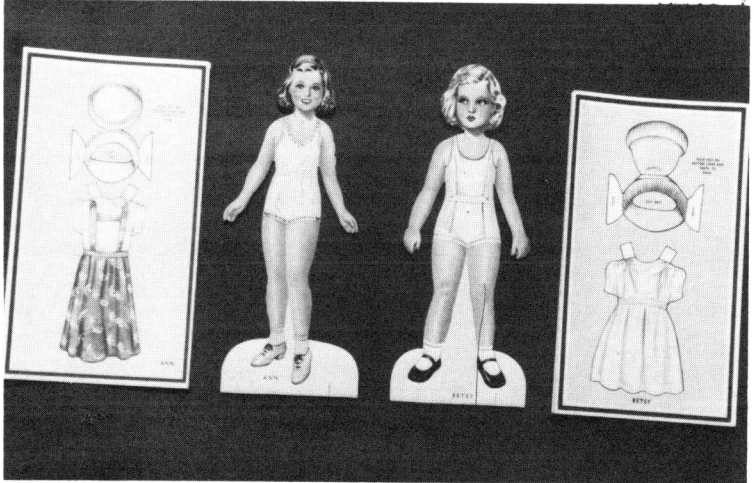
D106 *JUNIOR SHOP*-dolls and two outfits

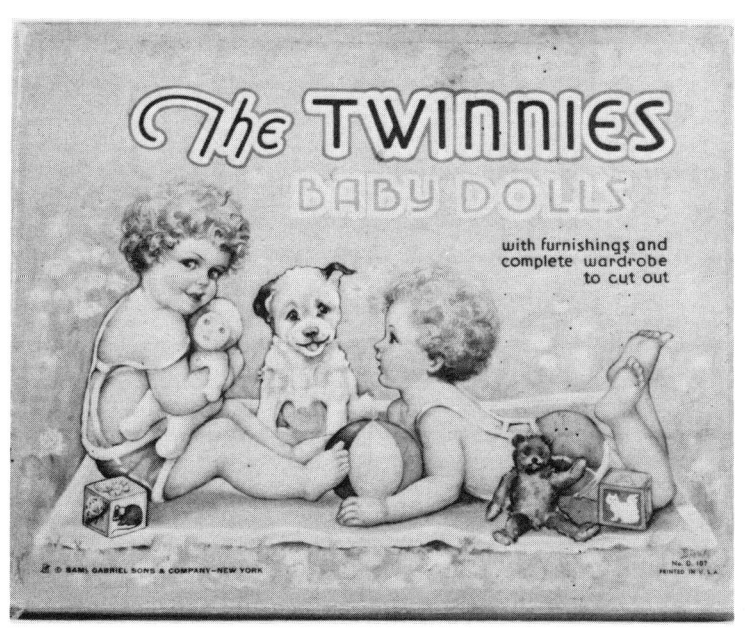

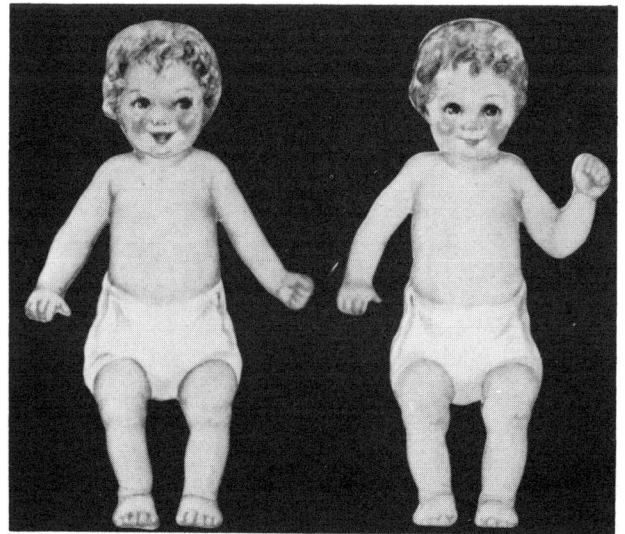
Photos by Robert Addison   Courtesy of Betsy Addison

D107 *THE TWINNIES*. $30.00
No date, listed in 1933 catalog.

Courtesy of Audrey Sepponen
D100 *SCHOOL MATES*. $18.00

Courtesy of Rosalie Eppert
D108 *MARY ALICE*. $20.00

Courtesy of Audrey Sepponen
D107 *BETTY JANE*. $20.00

D109 *DOLL DRESSES TO COLOR*. $15.00

D112 *MOVING EYE DOLLY--TODDLING TOM* 1920. $22.50

D112 *MOVING EYE DOLLY-BABY BETTY* 1920. $22.50

Courtesy of Jean Woodcock
D113 *LITTLE ORPHAN ANNIE*. $75.00

Courtesy of Betsy Addison, Photo by Robert Addison
D113 *THE TWINNIES* 1921. $35.00

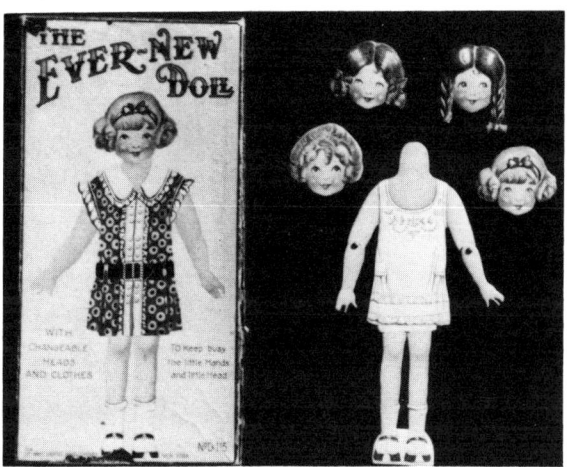

Courtesy of Betsy Slap
D115 *THE EVER-NEW DOLL*. $18.00

Courtesy of Mary Kelley
D114 *OUR AMERICA*. $25.00

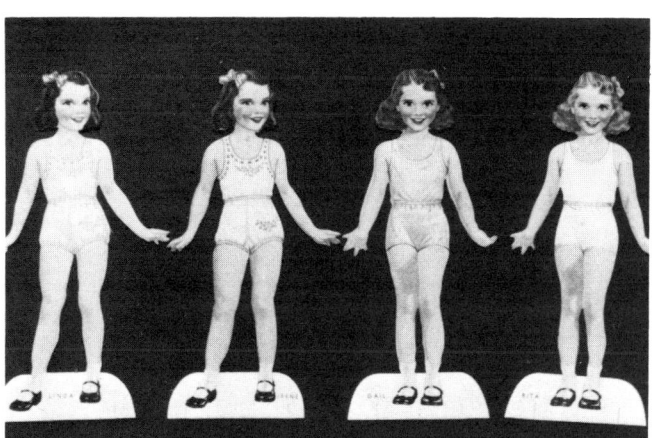

D114 *OUR AMERICA*, The four dolls from the set-Linda, Irene, Gail and Rita.

Courtesy of Audrey Sepponen
D114 *MY COMPLETE SEW-DRESS BOX*. $25.00

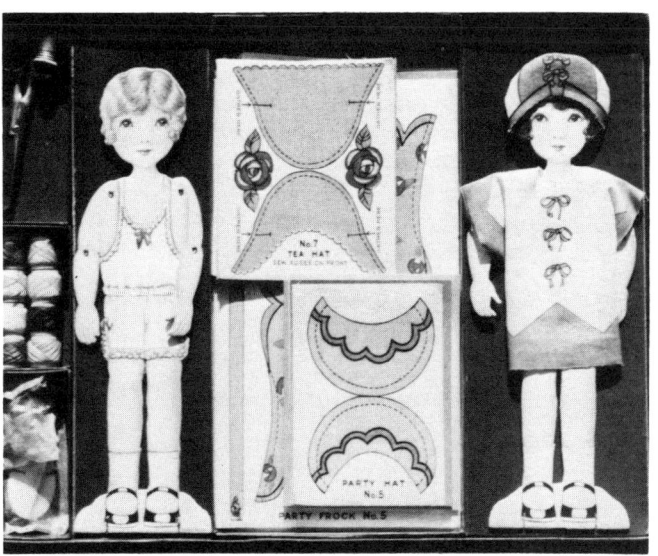

D114 *MY COMPLETE SEW-DRESS BOX*
Showing contents of box

D115 *PAPER DOLL BAZAAR.* $25.00

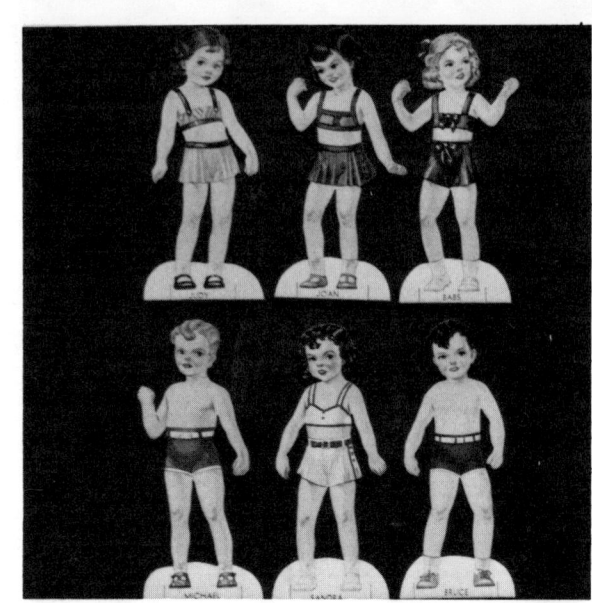

D115 Dolls from *PAPER DOLL BAZAAR*

Courtesy of Betsy Addison, Photo by Robert Addison

D115 *WINNIE WINKLE AND HER PARIS COSTUMES.* $60.00
No date, but appeared in 1933 catalog

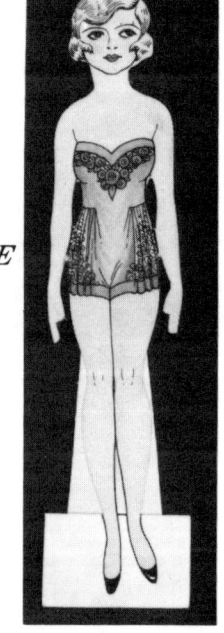

D115 *WINNIE WINKLE*

Courtesy of Rosalie Eppert

D116 *FASHION MODEL.* $15.00

D117 *CAROL AND HER DRESSES.* $18.00

Courtesy of Jane Sugg

70

Courtesy of Audrey Sepponen

116 *PONY TAIL*. $12.00

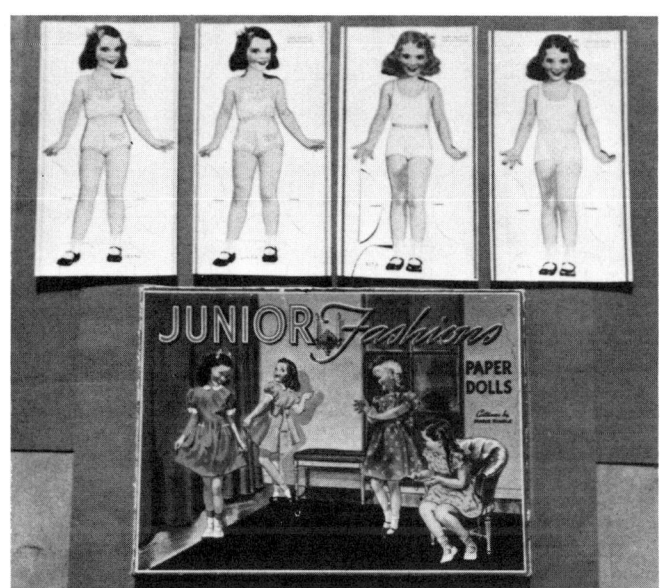

Courtesy of Audrey Sepponen

D117 *JUNIOR FASHIONS*. $25.00

D118 *SCHOOL DAYS*. $25.00

D118 Children and teacher from *SCHOOL DAYS*

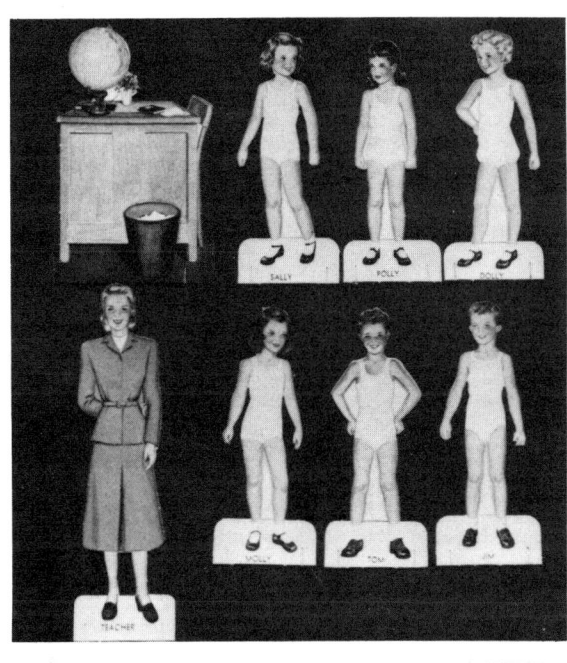

D119 *DOLLYLAND*. $60.00

The box and six envelopes are courtesy of Rosalie Eppert

D119 *DOLLYLAND-PRETTY PAULINE*
Envelope No. 5

71

D119 *DOLLYLAND-JOLLY JACK*
Envelope No. 6

D119 *DOLLYLAND-MERRY MARJORIE*
Envelope No. 1

D119 *DOLLYLAND-HANDSOME HAROLD*
Envelope No. 2

D119 *DOLLYLAND-GRACEFUL GERTRUDE*
Envelope No. 3

D119 *DOLLYLAND-SWEET SALLIE*
Envelope No. 4

Courtesy of Van Dyke Pearson

D119 *DOLLYLAND*, 1920. $30.00

D119 *SEW-EASY DOLL*. $12.00

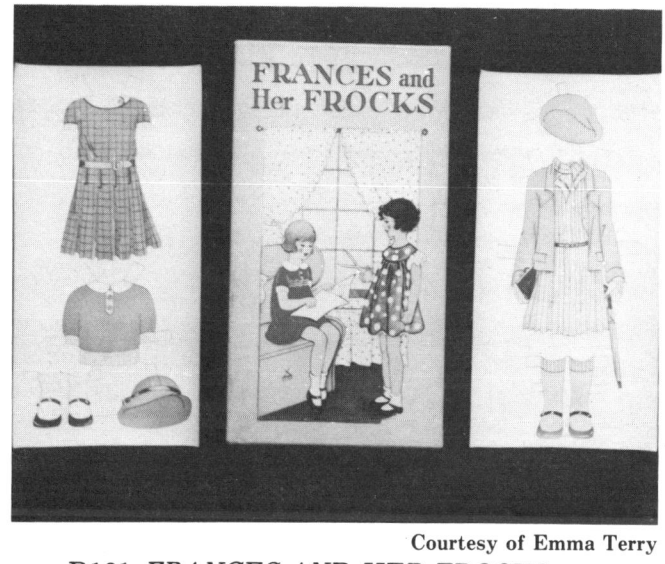

Courtesy of Emma Terry

D121 *FRANCES AND HER FROCKS*

Courtesy of Maurine Popp

D121 *BABYLAND-BOBBY*, 1921. $25.00

Courtesy of Nancy Reilly

D121 *BABYLAND-PEGGY*, 1921. $25.00

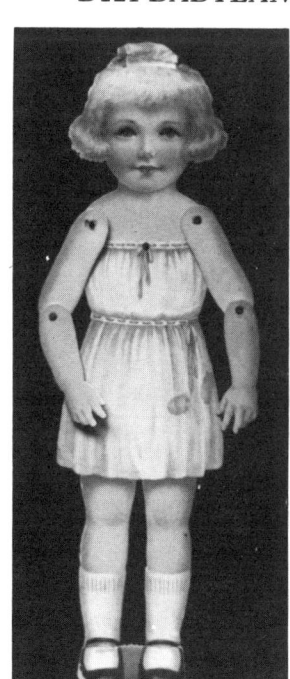

D122 *WIDE AWAKE AND FAST ASLEEP DOLL-ALICE*. $30.00

Courtesy of Grayce Piemontesi

D126 *THE DIMPLE DOLL FAMILY*. $25.00

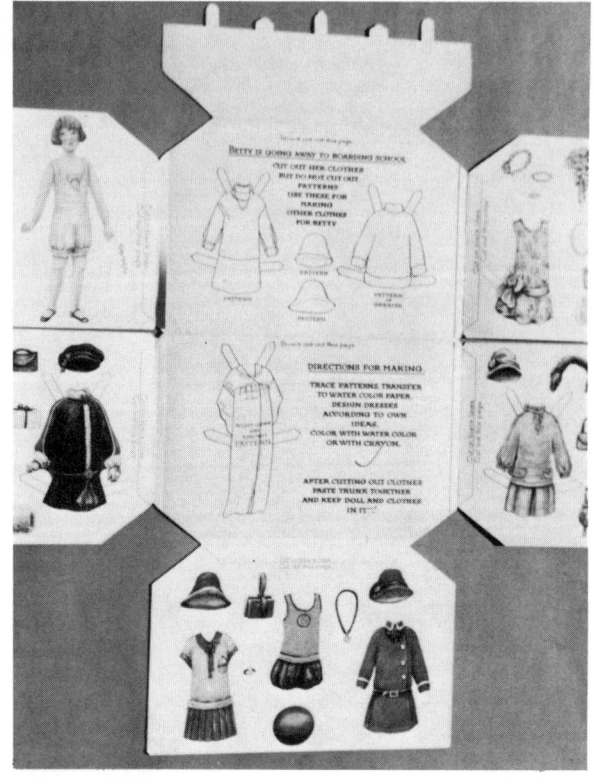

Courtesy of Audrey Sepponen

D125 *BETTY IS GOING AWAY TO BOARDING SCHOOL*. $40.00
No date but is listed in 1933 catalog

D125 Trunk unfolded to reveal the doll of Betty, her clothes and patterns.

D127 *THE WINKLE FAMILY*. $40.00

Courtesy of Richard Rusnock

Courtesy of Jean Woodcock

D129 *TURN AND TURN ABOUT DOLLIES*. $30.00

D127 *THE WINKLE FAMILY*   D127 *THE WINKLE FAMILY*

74

D132 *WEDDING PARTY*. $30.00

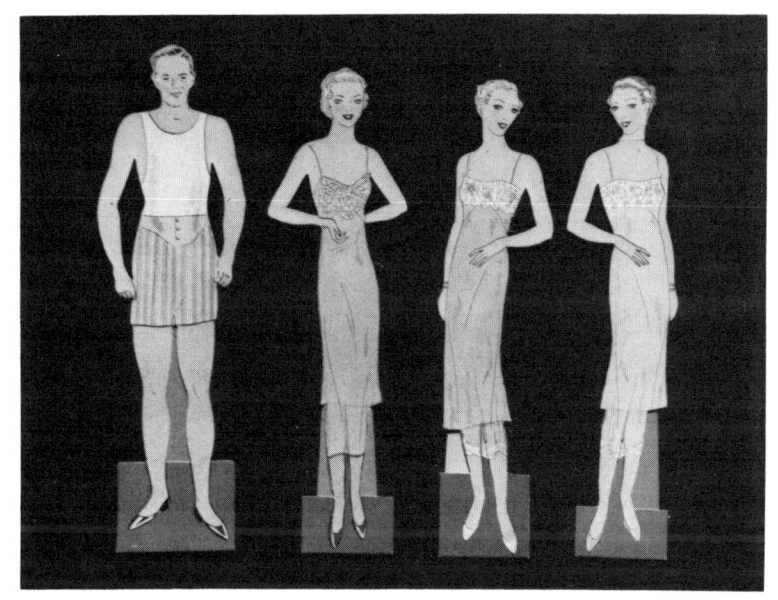

D132 *WEDDING PARTY*

130 *VICKI VELCRO® PAPER DOLL*. $10.00

Courtesy of Betsy Slap

D133 *THE TWINNIES*. $30.00
The dolls are the same as D107

Courtesy of Mary Kelley

D135 *THE DEBUTANTES*. $35.00

D135 *THE DEBUTANTES*

75

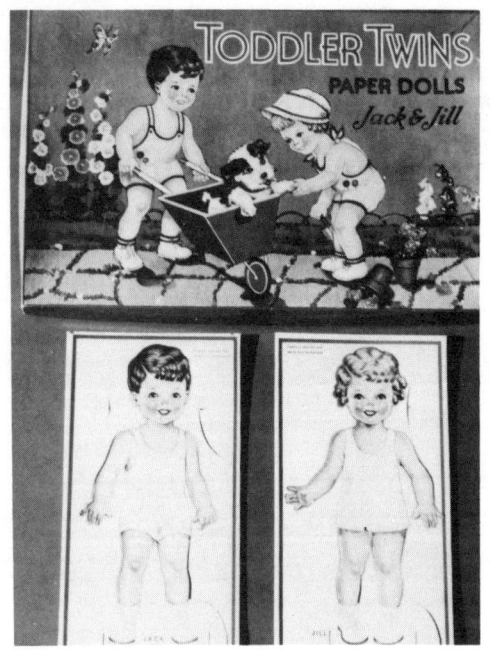

Courtesy of Audrey Sepponen
D134 *TODDLER TWINS*. $25.00

Courtesy of Audrey Sepponen
D135 *SISTERS*. $25.00

D138 *ALL MY DOLLIES*. $25.00

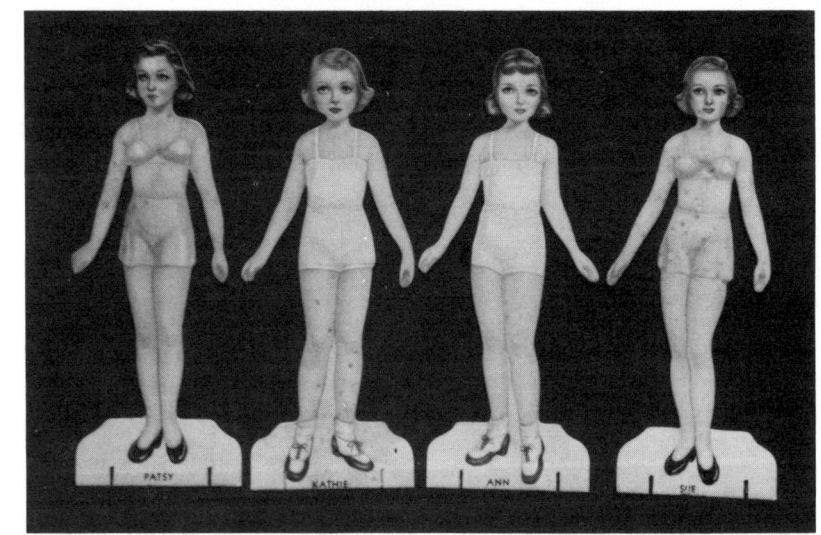

D138 *ALL MY DOLLIES*

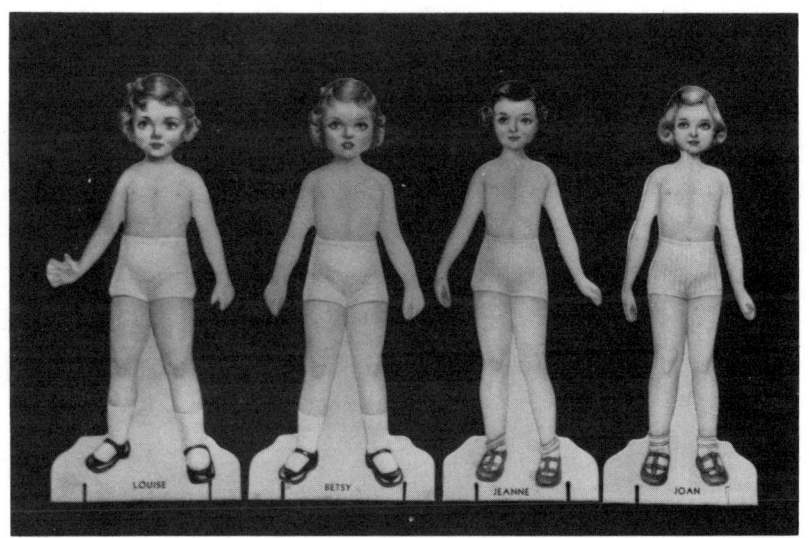

D138 *ALL MY DOLLIES*

76

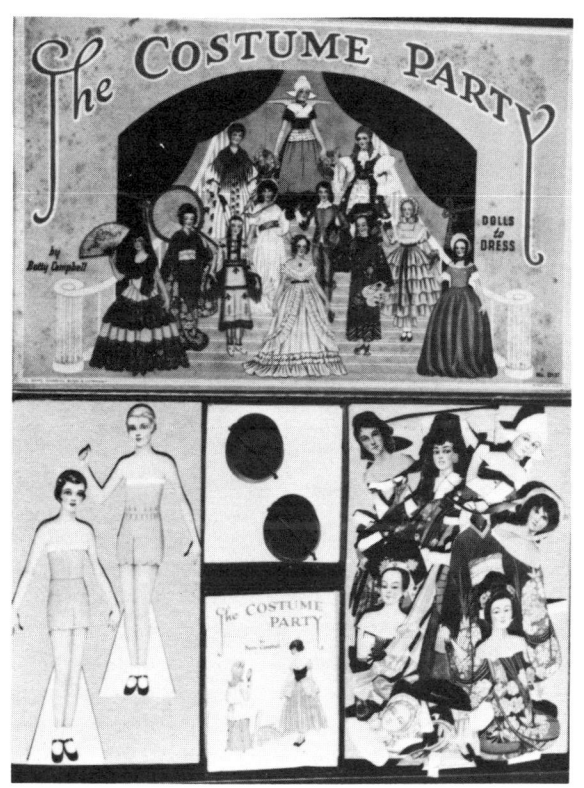

Photo courtesy of Richard Rusnock
D139 *BRIDAL PARTY.* $40.00

D137 *THE COSTUME PARTY* $40.00

D139 *BRIDAL PARTY*
Maid of Honor and Bridesmaid

D139 *BRIDAL PARTY*
Bride and groom

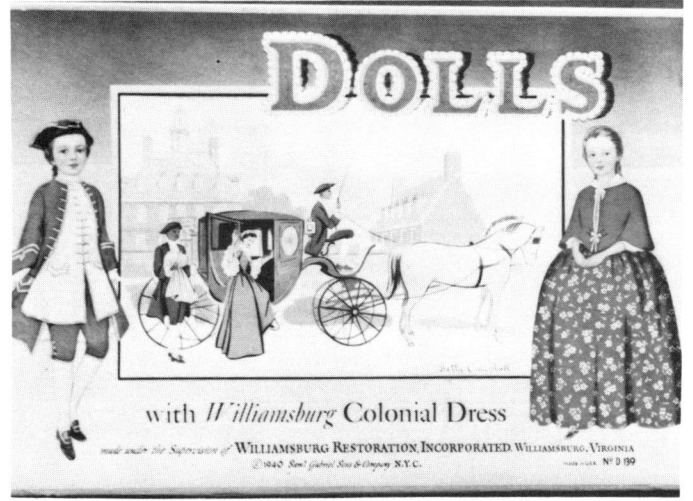

D139 *DOLLS WITH WILLIAMSBURG COLONIAL DRESS*, 1940. $20.00
(A reprint of the above set was done in 1955)

D141 *OUR HAPPY FAMILY*, 1929. $20.00

D141 *OUR HAPPY FAMILY-JEAN AND NANNY*

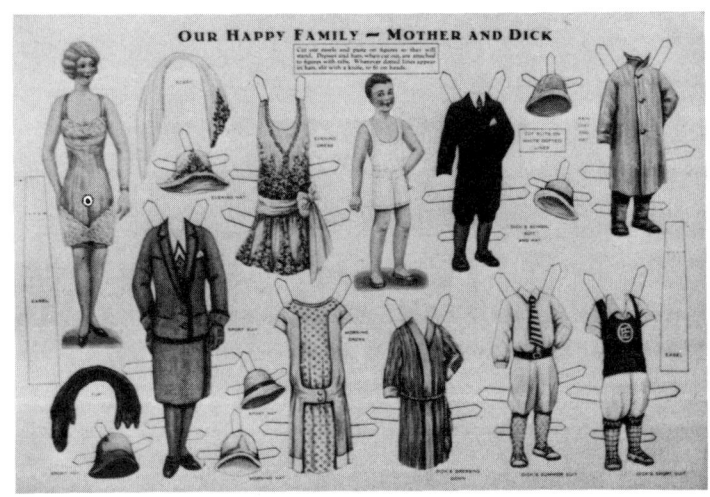

D141 *OUR HAPPY FAMILY-MOTHER AND DICK*

D141 *OUR HAPPY FAMILY - FATHER AND CHUBBY*

Courtesy of Betsy Slap

D144 *LET'S BUILD OUR CAMP*, 1930. $20.00

Page of paper dolls from *LET'S BUILD OUR CAMP*

D140 *DRESS OUR DOLLS*. $25.00

Photo by Elsie Stevens

D149 *MY DOLLIES PASTIME CUTOUT SHEETS*, 1920. $20.00

The above book contains eight dolls. There are four pages with two dolls on each page. Each doll has two outfits and two hats. The dolls are as follows: Elsie, Helen, Dorothy and Alice from #876 Dainty Dollies 1919. Cousin Kate, D90, Sister Nan, D90, Baby Betty, D112 and Toddling Tom, D112.

D172 *LITTLE AMERICANS FROM MANY LANDS*, 1929. $25.00
Box cover on left, Franz from Switzerland on right

T147 *LITTLE PET'S PLAY HOUSE*. $45.00

Courtesy of Grayce Piemontesi

D172 Selma from Sweden on left
Sonia from Russia on right

D172 Keith from Scotland on left
Cecile from France on right

D172 Mina and Hendrick from Holland

Courtesy of Van Dyke Pearson
D172 Carlotta from Germany   Matsue from Japan

D172 Eileen from Ireland on left
Sigrid from Norway on right

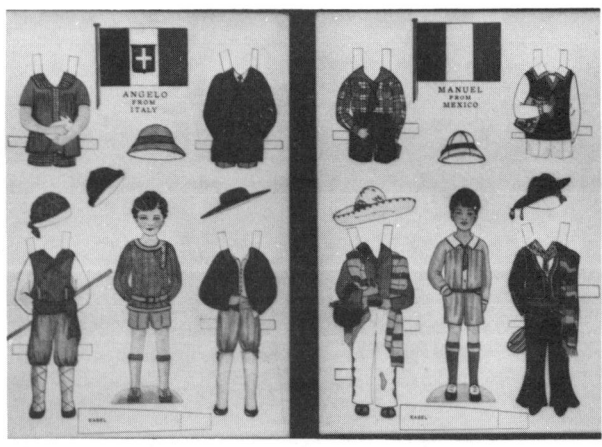

250 *LITTLE AUDREY.*
$15.00
©Harvey Famous Cartoons
no date

D172 Angelo from Italy on left
Manuel from Mexico on right

300 *SHIRLEY TEMPLE*, 1958. $18.00

301 *SHIRLEY TEMPLE*, 1961. $20.00

303 *SHIRLEY TEMPLE*, no date. $25.00

876 *DAINTY DOLLIES*, 1919. $30.00
The dolls are left to right: Alice, Helen, (her hair is trimmed), Dorothy and Elsie.

Courtesy of Jane Sugg

Courtesy of Patti Fertel

867 *MY DOLLY'S CRAYON BOOK*
Inside pages of dolls.

867 *MY DOLLY'S CRAYON BOOK*. $18.00

Courtesy of Joyce McClelland

877 *MY BOOK OF DARLING DOLLIES*, 1920. $30.00

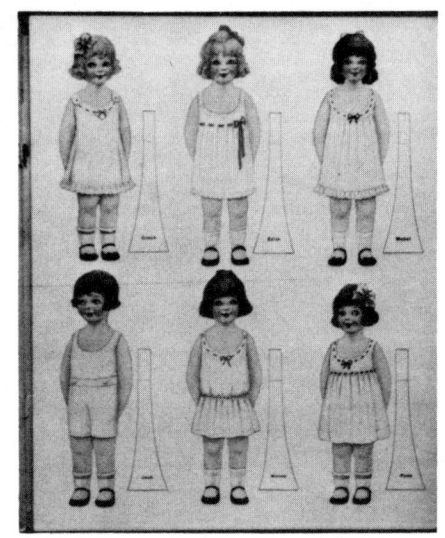

877 Inside page of dolls

886 *SMART FASHIONS*. $22.50
No date, but listed in 1933 catalog

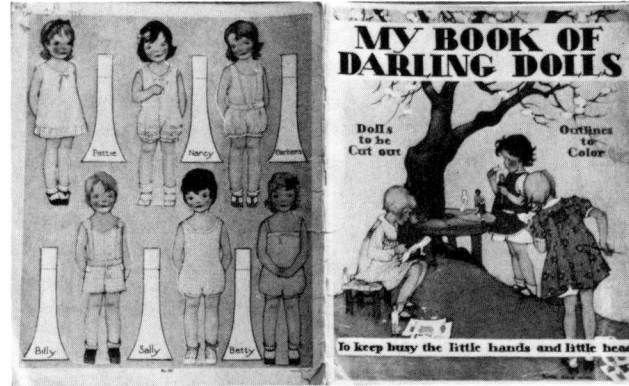

Courtesy of Audrey Sepponen

887 *MY BOOK OF DARLING DOLLS*. $22.50
No date, but listed in 1933 catalog

894 *TOWN AND COUNTRY*. $35.00

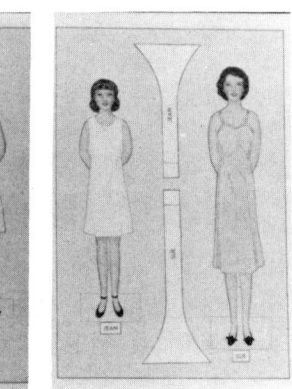

Courtesy of Rosalie Eppert

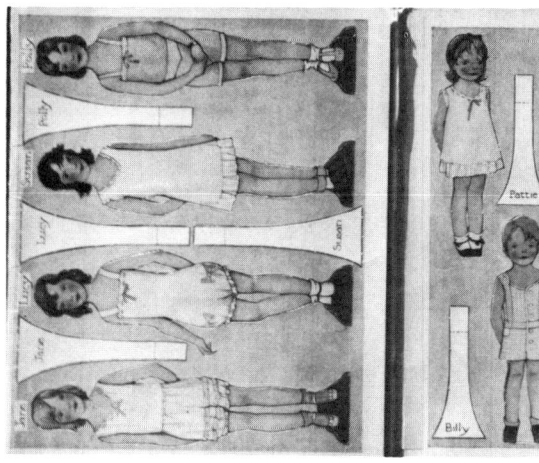

Courtesy of Grayce Piemontesi

895 *MODERN DOLLS A PLENTY.* $30.00
No date but was listed in 1933 catalog

Courtesy of Bonnie Fuson

896 *DOLLIES A'LA MODE.* $30.00

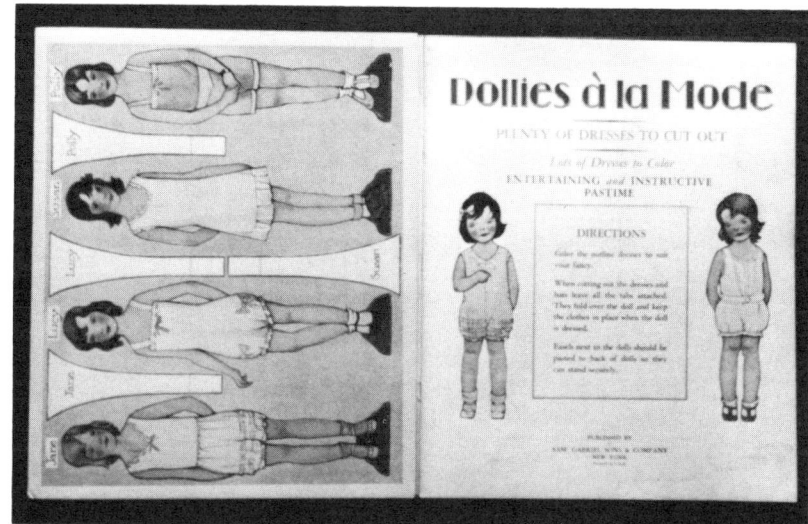

896 Inside front cover and title page

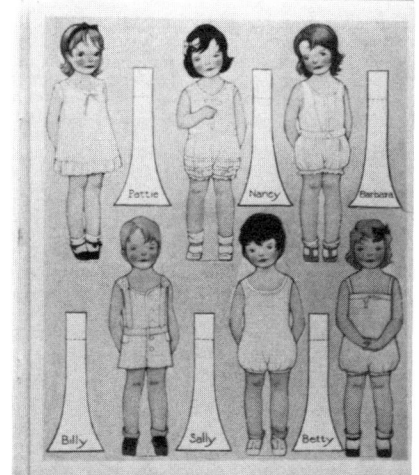

896 Inside back cover

963 *DRESS ME BOOK.* $30.00

Courtesy of Betsy Addison. Photo by Robert Addison

Courtesy of Grayce Piemontesi
896 *FANCY DRESS DOLLS*. $30.00

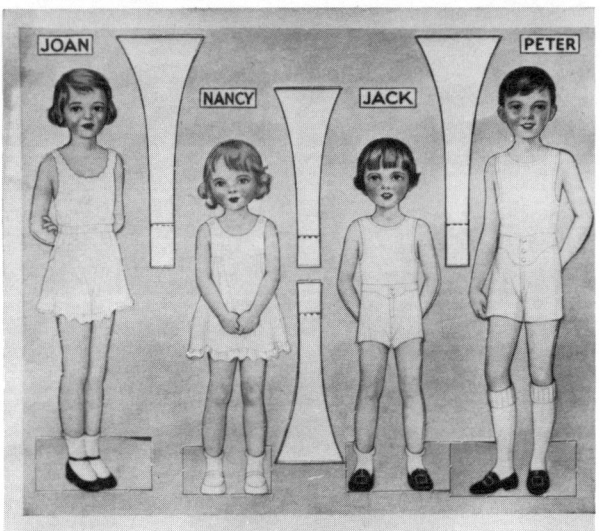
896 Inside front cover

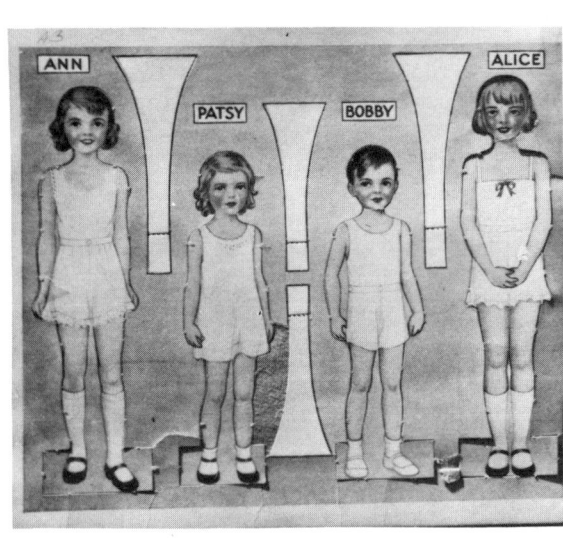
896 Back cover

Courtesy of Grayce Piemontesi
DOLLY SHEETS-JACK, 1922; RUTH, 1922. $10.00 a sheet

Courtesy of Rosalie Eppert
DOLLY DELIGHT-RUTH, 1920. $12.00

Courtesy of Grayce Piemontesi
SUSAN. $22.50
The dolls eyes move when the bow in her hair is moved sideways.

MABEL
This little doll is 5¾" tall. On her back is stamped "Mabel", Sam'l Gabriel Sons & Co. New York-Made in Germany. She resembles the doll on the cover of set D117 *DOLLIES AND THEIR WARDROBES*. She may be from that set which is pictured in the 1926 catalog.

C.R. Gibson Company

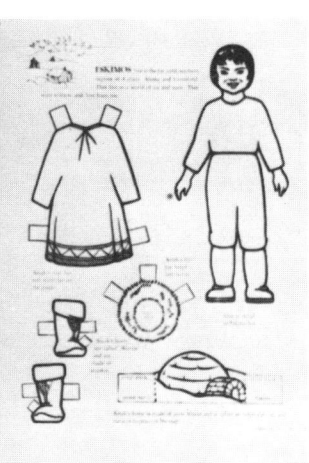

Courtesy of Pam Hunter
4634 *LET'S TELL OTHERS ABOUT JESUS*. $3.00

4936 *BIBLE THINK AND DO*. $3.00
Book 1

4635 *LET'S TELL ABOUT JESUS* - in Latin America, 12 sheets of paper dolls (not pictured)
4939 *BIBLE THINK AND DO BOOK 2*, stand-ups, no paper dolls (not pictured)

Goldsmith Publishing Company

Courtesy of Marilyn Johnson

Courtesy of Jane Sugg

516 *DAISY DOLLY*, 1922. $17.00

516 *JOHNNY JONES*, 1922. $17.00

Courtesy of Jane Sugg

516 *PANSY PRATTLE*, 1922. $17.00

Courtesy of Joyce McClelland

2005 *DAISY DOLLY*, 1930. $16.00

2005 *JOHNNY JONES*, 1930. $16.00

Courtesy of Audrey Sepponen

Charles E. Graham and Company

02 *TEENY WEENY PRETTY DOLLIES* (two dolls from #0225 Snuggly and one doll from #0225 Cuddly)
0212 *DEARIE DOLLS* (four dolls from #0225 Snuggly)
0212 *LOVEY DOLLS* (not pictured; one doll from #0225 Snuggly, three dolls from #0225 Cuddly)
0214 *TINY DOLLS* (dolls on cover from #0225 Cuddly, inside pages are similar to paper dolls in LIttle Folks Magazine in the 1920's)
0214 *DIMPLE DOLLS* (not pictured)
0219 *KIDDIE-KOLORED KUT-OUTS* box set with stand up dolls, doll house and farm

0220 *CUTTING THINGS OUT* (not pictured; box set with paper dolls)
0221 *TINY TWINKLE*
0221 *TUBBY TWINKLE*
0225 *CUDDLY DOLLS WITH DRESSES*
0225 *SNUGGLY DOLLS WITH DRESSES*
0228 *TIPPY TOES* (not pictured)
0229 *CURLY LOCKS*
0237 *LULA-BYE-BYE DOLLS TO DRESS*
0239 *BEAUTY DOLLS TO DRESS*
THE PITTY PATS (not pictured; number not available, dolls same as #0221)

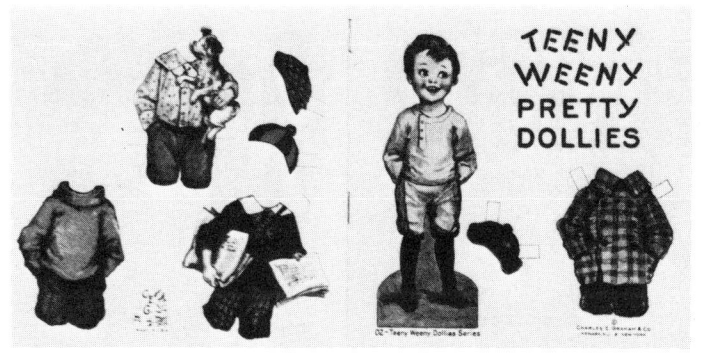

Courtesy of Jane Sugg
02 *TEENY WEENY PRETTY DOLLIES.* $15.00
Front and back cover

02 *TEENY WEENY PRETTY DOLLIES*
Inside pages of dolls and clothes

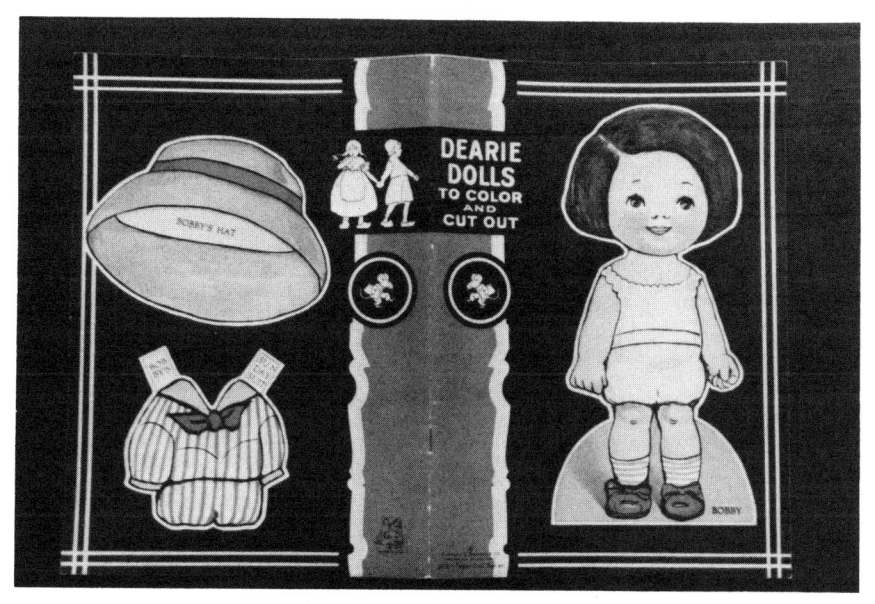

0212 *DEARIE DOLLS.* $15.00
Front and back cover.

0212 *DEARIE DOLLS*
Inside page of Amanda

0212 *DEARIE DOLLS*
Inside page of Dorothy

0212 *DEARIE DOLLS*
Inside page of Kate

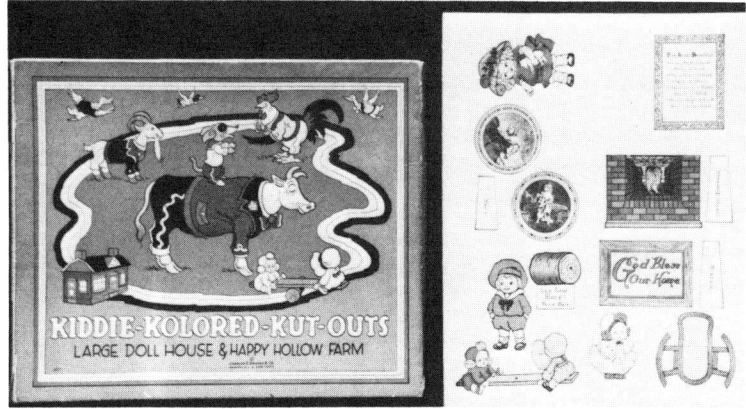

0219 *KIDDIE-KOLORED-KUT-OUTS.* $15.00

87

Courtesy of Rosalie Eppert
0214 *TINY DOLLS*. $15.00

0214 *TINY DOLLS*

0214 *TINY DOLLS*

0221 *TINY TWINKLE*. $18.00

0221 *TUBBY TWINKLE*. $18.00

Courtesy of Jane Sugg
0225 *CUDDLY DOLLS*. $25.00

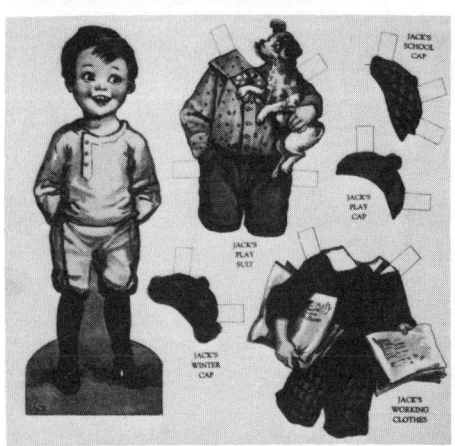
0225 *CUDDLY DOLLS-JACK*

0225 *CUDDLY DOLLS*
Mary Jane and Ida May

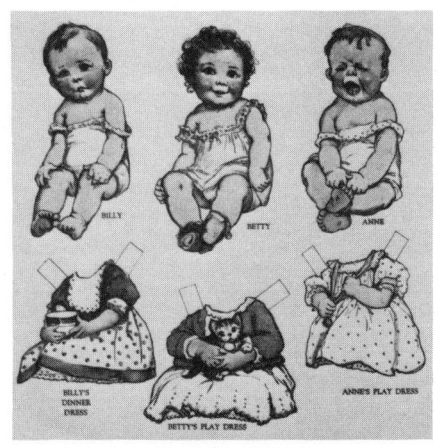
0225 *CUDDLY DOLLS*
Billy, Betty and Anne

88

Courtesy of Norene Allen

0225 *SNUGGLY DOLLS*. $25.00
Dolls are Peggy, Kate, Bobby, Dorothy and Amanda

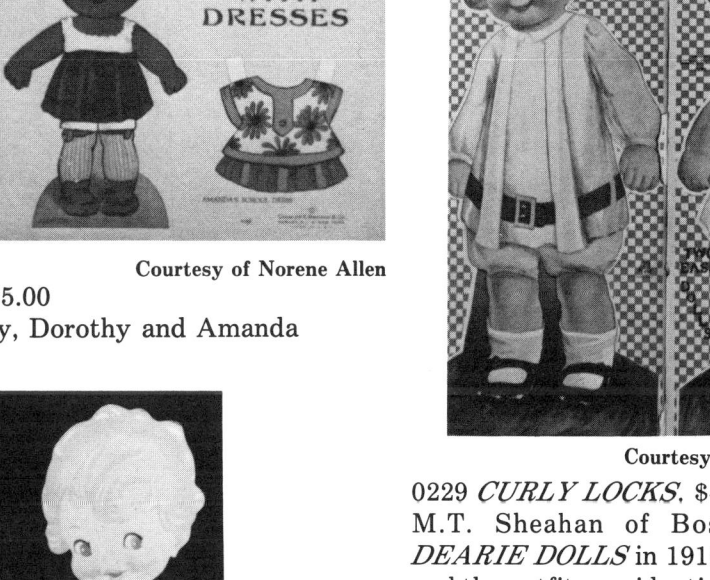

Courtesy of Virginia Crossley

0229 *CURLY LOCKS*. $45.00
M.T. Sheahan of Boston published *DEARIE DOLLS* in 1915. The paper doll and the outfits are identical to the girl doll and her outfits in *CURLY LOCKS*

Courtesy of Virginia Crossley

0237 *LULA-BYE-BYE*. $25.00

0239 *BEAUTY DOLLS TO DRESS*. $25.00

Courtesy of Betsy Slap

Grinnell Lithographic Co., Inc.

C1001 *LIL' PEARL*, 1940. $25.00

Courtesy of Betsy Slap

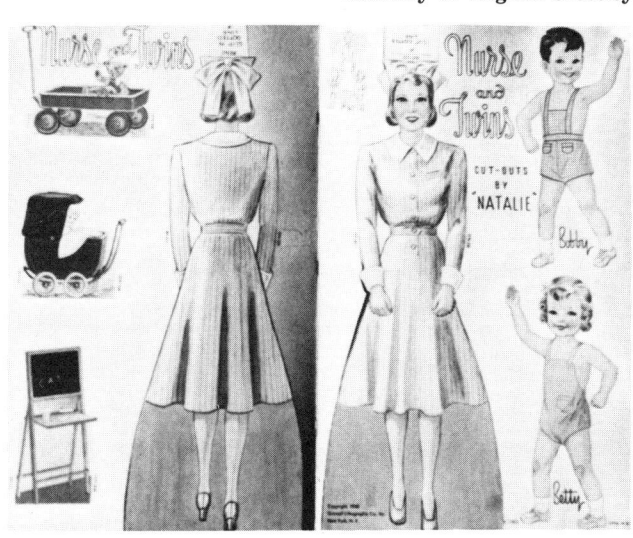

C1003 *NURSE AND TWINS*, 1940. $25.00

Courtesy of Virginia Crossley

C1002 *AMERICAN FAMILY*, 1940. $25.00

Courtesy of Betsy Slap

C1004 *SIX PLAYTIME DOLLS*, 1940. $25.00

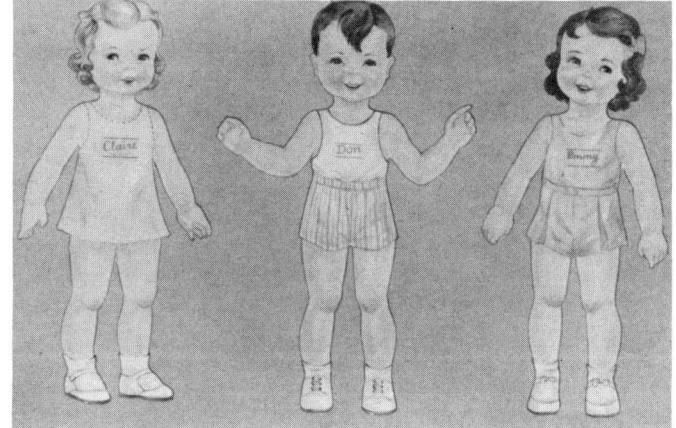

Courtesy of Richard Rusnock

C1010 *FIVE FLYING AMERICANS*, 1940. $25.00

C1010 *FIVE FLYING AMERICANS*
Inside front cover

Courtesy of Betsy Slap

C1005 *MOTHER AND DAUGHTER*, 1940. $25.00

C1011 *SHIPMATES*. 1940. $25.00

C1011 *SHIPMATES*
Inside front cover

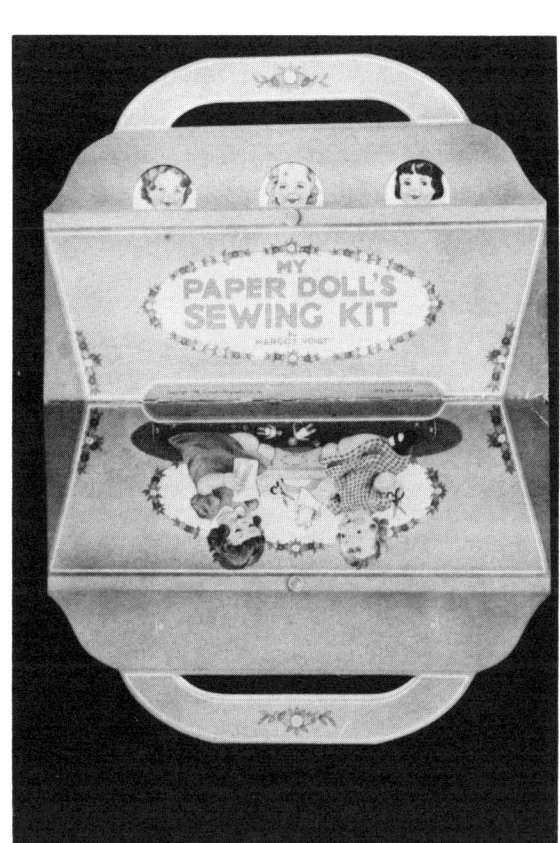
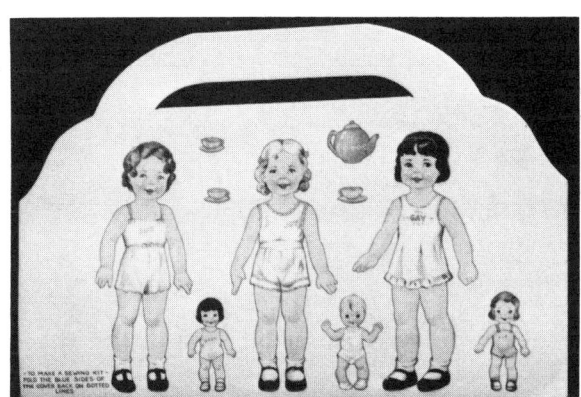

Courtesy of Betsy Slap

C1018 *MY PAPER DOLL'S SEWING KIT*, 1940. $25.00

Courtesy of Betsy Slap

C1015 *SUPER MARKET*, 1940. $25.00

N2009 *SUZIE SWEET*, 1940. $25.00

Courtesy of Betsy Slap

Hamming Publishing Company

Courtesy of Yesteryears Doll Museum, Sandwich, Mass.
THE DOLLS THAT YOU LOVE, 1910. $25.00
(original copyright by L.W. Walter Co. in 1910)

THE DOLLS THAT YOU LOVE
A cut set of the six dolls in the book

Hart Publishing Company

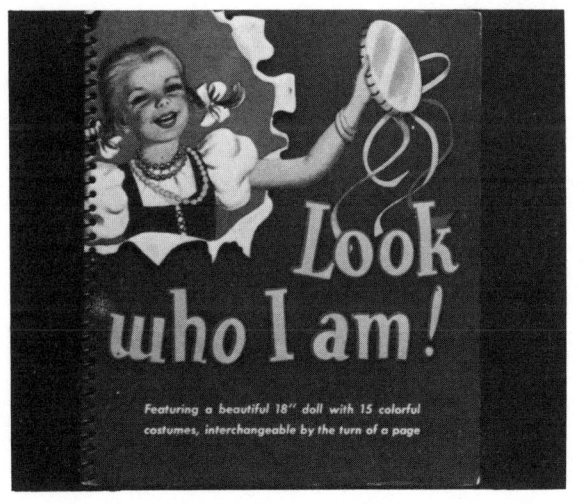 

LOOK WHO I AM!, 1952. $10.00
18″ doll, spiral bound book, costumes change as pages in book are turned.

LOOK WHO I AM!

Harter Publishing Company

H-100 *RAG DOLL SUE*, 1931. $30.00

H-164 *MOTHER GOOSE VILLAGE*, 1935. $12.00

Hobby House Press

Hobby House Press observed its 40th anniversary in 1982. The company was founded by Paul A. Ruddell. He operated the business out of his home by selling books through the mail. He first pioneered in books on antiques and soon after, branched out into books on dolls and the circus. At that time the mail order business was known as Paul A. Ruddell Books. Gradually, books on dolls became their chief product. In the 1950's, the company had begun to reprint out-of-print books on dolls and their other two specialty fields. In the early 1960's, Paul Ruddell formed Hobby House Press and their first original book *Delightful Dolls* by Thelma Bateman, was published.

Son, Gary Ruddell, and a partner established Manor House Press, Inc. in 1969. A year later, Gary took complete control of the company and merged it with the family business. In 1972, Paul A. Ruddell Books, Hobby House Press and Manor House Press moved to space in Riverdale, Maryland. It was in this same year that the first issue of *Doll Reader* was published. It was produced as a tabloid and issued quarterly at first and then became a bi-monthly. In December 1978 the *Doll Reader* changed to a magazine format. Paul Ruddell retired from Hobby House Press in 1972 and Gary is now running the business.

Pictured are four paper doll books published by Hobby House Press. In addition to these paper dolls Hobby House Press also features an original paper doll in each issue of *Doll Reader*. They also published two paper doll booklets: In 1978, *Queen Elizabeth II: Silver Jubilee Paper Doll 1952-1977* and *Princess Caroline of Monaco* in 1979. A reference book *Paper Dolls of Famous Faces, Vol. II*, by Jean Woodcock, was published by Hobby House Press in 1980.

Reference: June/July 1982 *Doll Reader*

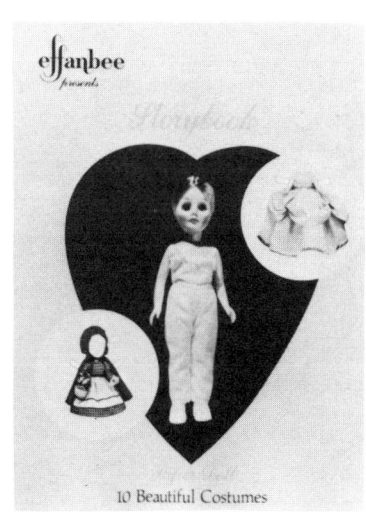

EFFANBEE PRESENTS STORYBOOK © 1979 Hobby House Press. Currently available

EFFANBEE PRESENTS CURRIER AND IVES © 1979 Hobby House Press. Currently available

Courtesy of Virginia Crossley

EFFANBEE PRESENTS THROUGH THE YEARS WITH GIGI 1830-1900 © 1979 Hobby House Press. Currently available

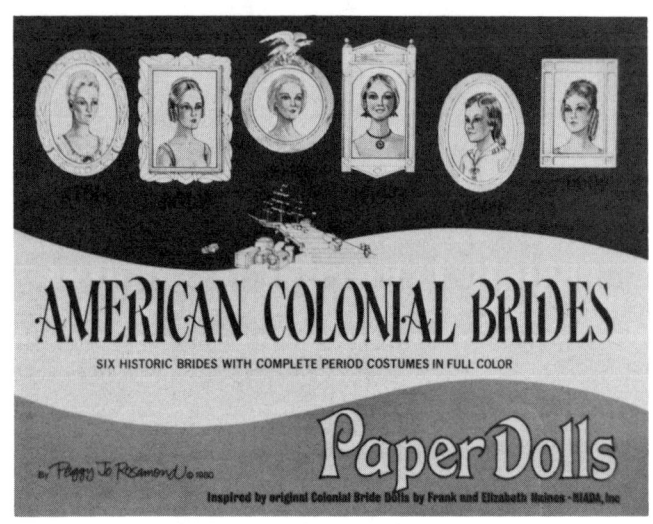

AMERICAN COLONIAL BRIDES © 1980 Peggy Jo Rosamond. Currently available

E.H. Horsman Company

NEW PUSS IN BOOTS PAPER DOLL. $75.00

Courtesy of Rosalie Eppert

House of Dolls

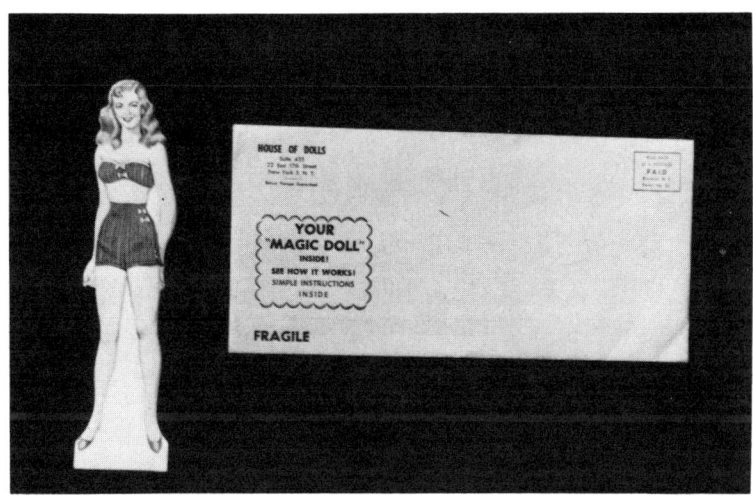

MAGIC DOLL. $12.00

Courtesy of Virginia Crossley

Howell, Soskin Publishers, Inc.

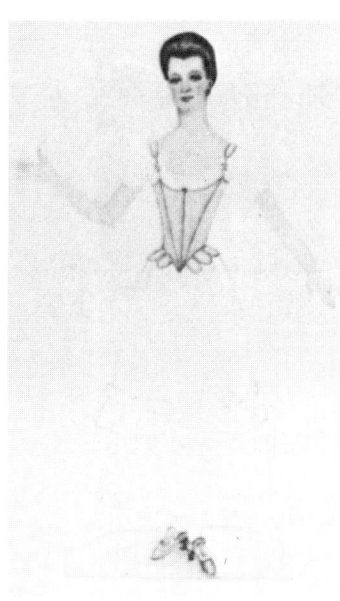
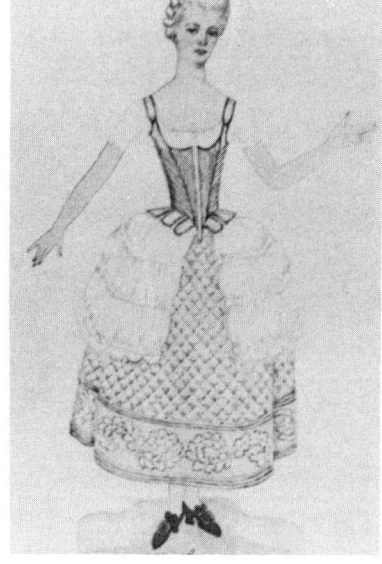

THE MARTHA WASHINGTON DOLL BOOK, 1945. $30.00

NANCY AND JANE, 1945. $15.00

Courtesy of Grayce Piemontesi

Hubbell-Leavens Co., Inc.

TOMMY TOM. $35.00

Photo courtesy of *Midwest Paper Dolls and Toys Quarterly*

DOLLY DIMPLE (not pictured; see Stecher Lithographic Co.)
POLLY DOLLY (not pictured; see E.M. Leavens Co.)

International Paper Goods

60 *FUN FARM FROLICS*, 1932. $35.00

Courtesy of Betsy Slap

60 *FUN FARM FROLICS*
Inside page of paper dolls

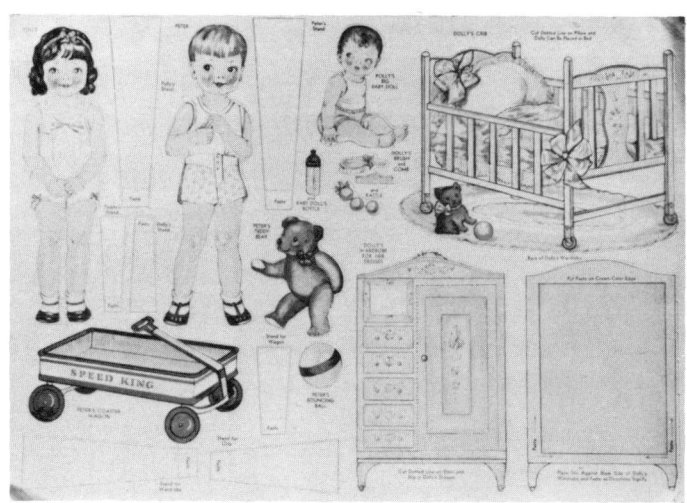

George W. Jacobs and Company

DOROTHY DIMPLE AND HER FRIENDS-PAPER DOLLS OF MANY NATIONS, 1909 © by the Bodley Press Associates, Springfield, Massachusetts. Six sheets in envelope.

PAPER DOLLS OF THE WORLD 1909 © By the Bodley Press Associates, Springfield, Massaschusetts. Six sheets in envelope

POLLY PITCHER AND HER PLAYMATES Series One, 1917

POLLY PITCHER AND HER PLAYMATES Series Two, 1918

THE LETTIE LANE PAPER FAMILY, 1909 (originally published in *Ladies Home Journal*)

First Series-six sheets in a doll house folder

Second Series-six sheets in a doll house folder

Third Series-six sheets in a doll house folder

BETTY BONNET AND HER FRIENDS (not pictured; originally in *Ladies Home Journal)*

First Series-six sheets in folder

Second Series-six sheets in folder

Third Series-six sheets in folder

KITTY CLOVER (originally published in *Ladies Home Journal* as Betty Bonnet series, not pictured)

First Series-six sheets in folder

Second Series-six sheets in folder

CINDERELLA, 1918

POLLY ANN-six sheets in envelope

FAIRY FOLK-six sheets in envelope (not pictured)

BOBBY BEAR-six sheets in envelope (not pictured)

JACK-O'-LANTERN-six sheets in envelope

DOROTHY DIMPLE AND HER FRIENDS, 1909. $8.00 a sheet
Dorthy Dimple (cut set)

DOROTHY DIMPLE AND HER FRIENDS. $8.00 a sheet
Dorothy's Grown-up Sister Sarah

DOROTHY DIMPLE AND HER FRIENDS. $8.00 a sheet
Dorothy's Japanese Doll (cut set)

DOROTHY DIMPLE AND HER FRIENDS. $8.00 a sheet
Clown Friend Toby (cut set)

DOROTHY DIMPLE AND HER FRIENDS. $8.00 a sheet
Sister Susan, (cut set)

DOROTHY DIMPLE AND HER FRIENDS. $8.00 a sheet
Cut set, title not available

Courtesy of Rosalie Eppert
PAPER DOLLS OF THE WORLD, 1909. $8.00 a sheet
Abdul, the Turk, and Pedro, the Spaniard

Courtesy of Rosalie Eppert
PAPER DOLLS OF THE WORLD. $8.00 a sheet
Selim, the Egyptian Camel Boy

Courtesy of Rosalie Eppert
PAPER DOLLS OF THE WORLD. $8.00 a sheet
Dughha-Das, the Hindoo, and His Elephant

Courtesy of Rosalie Eppert
PAPER DOLLS OF THE WORLD. $8.00 a sheet
Black Cloud, the Indian Chief, His Wigwam

PAPER DOLLS OF THE WORLD. $8.00 a sheet
Katrinka, the Little Dutch Girl

PAPER DOLLS OF THE WORLD. $8.00 a sheet
Aileen, the Irish Lass, and MacGregor, the Scotch Lad (cut set)

THE LETTIE LANE PAPER FAMILY

Courtesy of Rosalie Eppert
THE LETTIE LANE PAPER FAMILY 1909. $50.00 for complete set.
The doll house folder shown contained six *LETTIE LANE* sheets. Two of the sheets are pictured.

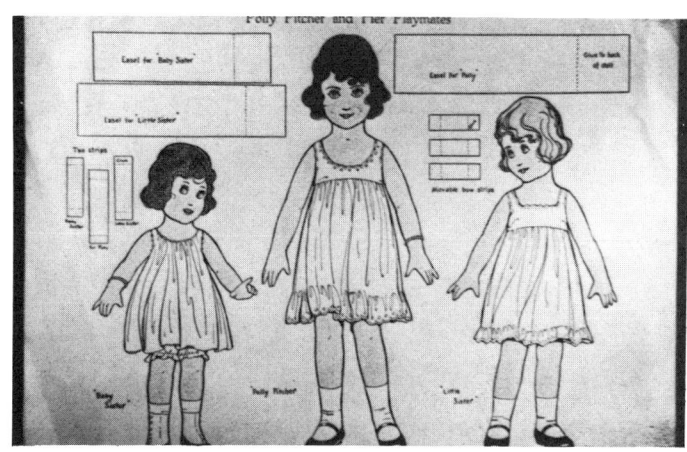

POLLY PITCHER AND HER PLAYMATES SERIES ONE, 1917. $40.00
The folder design is the same as shown for series two.

Courtesy of Jane Sugg
POLLY PITCHER AND HER PLAYMATES SERIES TWO, 1918. $45.00

CINDERELLA, 1918 (cut set). $50.00 for complete uncut set

Courtesy of Rosalie Eppert

POLLY ANN CUT-OUT PAPER DOLLS. $50.00 for complete set

Courtesy of Rosalie Eppert

JACK-O'-LANTERN CUT-OUT PAPER DOLLS. $50.00 for complete set

JAK PAK

301 *WENDY'S WARDROBE.* $2.00 (also #JP 0134)

100

JANEX CORPORATION

The paper dolls in these sets are cardboard with vinyl heads. The clothes are fabric and peel on and off.

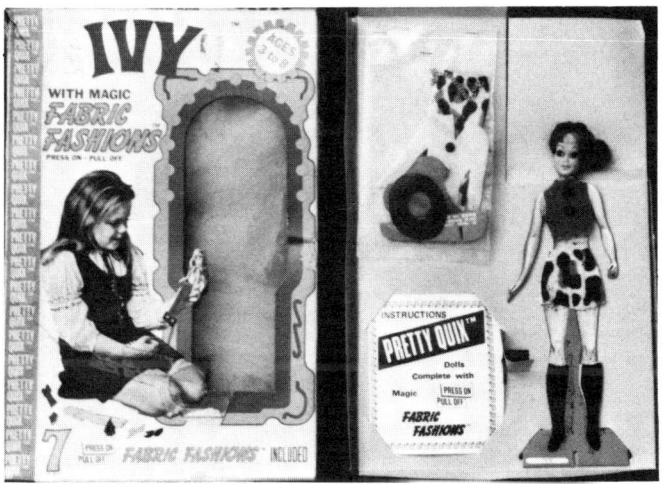

Courtesy of Virginia Crossley
2001 *IVY*, 1971. $5.00

2002 *GLENN*, 1971. $5.00

2000 *HOLLY,* 1971 (not pictured)

4000 *MARC AND JERIE'S WEDDING PARTY* (not pictured)

4001 *ROD AND LIZA JET AWAY* (not pictured)

4002 *GREG AND NOELLE ON CAMPUS* (not pictured)

JAYMAR SPECIALTY CO.-GREAT LAKES PRESS

The Jaymar Specialty Co. was started in 1925 by Jay Jaymar. He began by manufacturing doll clothes that were sold in the five and ten cent stores.

The Great Lakes Press was established in 1936 and began their long association with Jaymar at the time Jaymar was producing doll clothes. Great Lakes Press made the cardboard hangers for Jaymar to hang the doll clothes on. When Jaymar dropped the doll clothes phase of their business, they went into the manufacturing of toy pianos.

Jaymar has been the national distributor for Great Lakes Press since 1939. At that time Great Lakes formed a division of children's games and jigsaw puzzles which later included paper doll box sets.

The following is a list of the known paper doll sets by Jaymar:

905 *FOUR SNAP-IN-PLACE STAND-UP DOLLS*
907 *MOTHER AND DAUGHTER* (not pictured)
909 *WEDDING PARTY*
913 *JET AIRLINE STEWARDESS* (not pictured see #970)
915 *DEBBY DOLLS AND DOLLIES* (not pictured see #992)
970 *JET AIRLINE STEWARDESS*
974 *MOTHER AND DAUGHTER* (not pictured)
975 *BEAUTIFUL BRIDE*
978 *HONEYBUN, BIG DOLL FOR LITTLE GIRLS*
980 *DEBBY DOLLS*

986 *TWO DEBBY DOLLS COMPLETE WITH "MINK FUR"*
988 *FOUR BRIDAL PARTY STAND-UP DOLLS* (not pictured; dolls same as #909)
992 *DEBBY DOLLS AND DOLLIES*
994 *WINKY WINNIE*
996 *BETSEY BATES DEBBY DOLLS* (not pictured)
1976 *TWEEDIE GOES TO THE BEAUTY PARLOR* (not pictured)
1986 *FOUR DEBBY DOLLS, COMPLETE WITH "MINK FUR" MATERIAL*

Courtesy of Virginia Crossley
905 FOUR *SNAP-IN-PLACE STAND-UP DOLLS.* $12.00

970 *JET AIRLINE STEWARDESS PAPER DOLLS.* $12.00

Courtesy of Audrey Sepponen

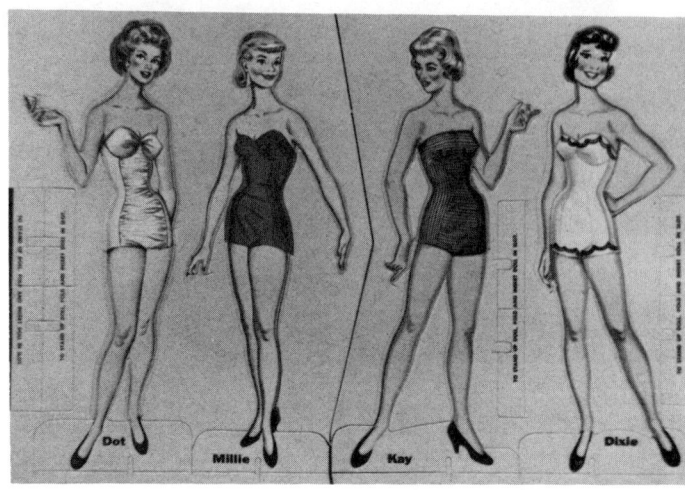

970 *JET AIRLINE STEWARDESS*

975 *BEAUTIFUL BRIDE.* $12.00

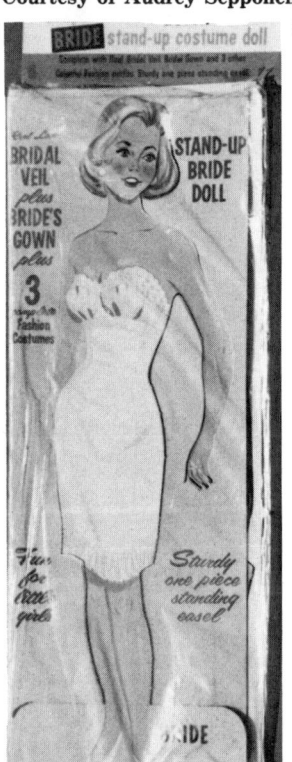

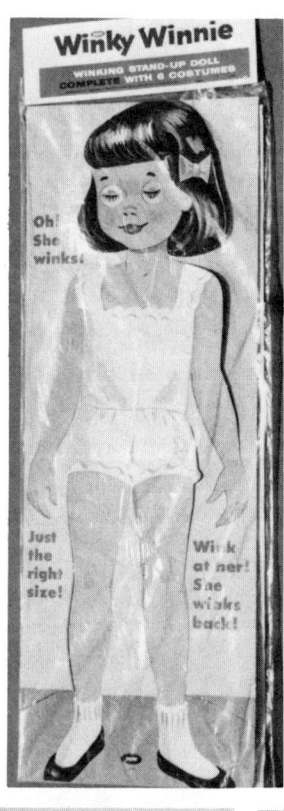

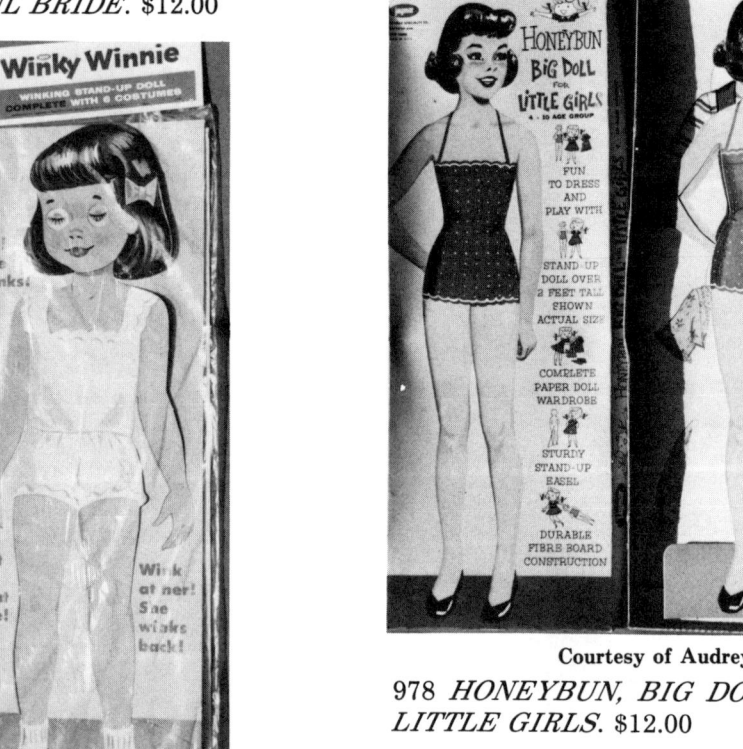

Courtesy of Audrey Sepponen

Courtesy of Audrey Sepponen

978 *HONEYBUN, BIG DOLL FOR LITTLE GIRLS.* $12.00

994 *WINKY WINNIE.* $12.00

Courtesy of Great Lakes Press

986 TWO *DEBBY DOLLS, COMPLETE WITH "MINK FUR".* $12.00

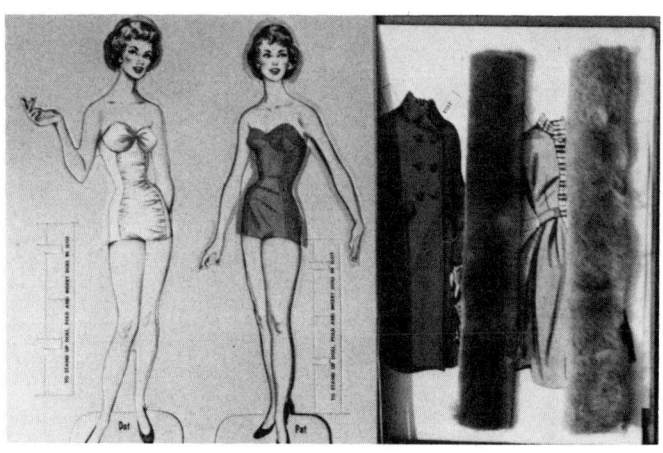

986 TWO *DEBBY DOLLS*
Inside box contents

102

Courtesy of Virginia Crossley

980 *DEBBY DOLLS*. $12.00

Courtesy of Virginia Crossley

992 *DEBBY DOLLS AND DOLLIES*. $12.00

Courtesy of Virginia Crossley

909 *WEDDING PARTY*. $12.00

1986 FOUR *DEBBY DOLLS COMPLETE WITH "MINK FUR"*. $12.00

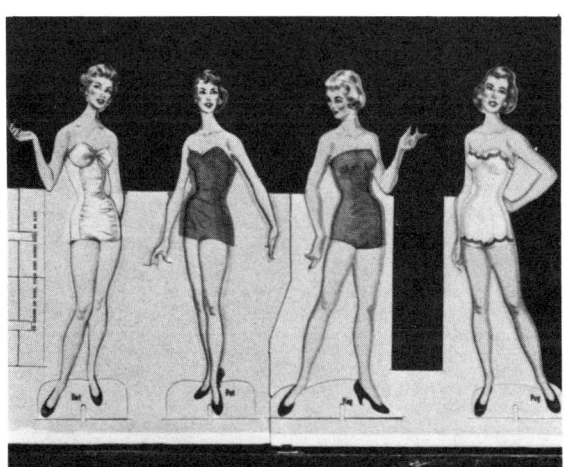

Courtesy of Virginia Crossley

103

Kaufmann and Strauss Company

Courtesy of Maurine Popp

Courtesy of Maurine Popp

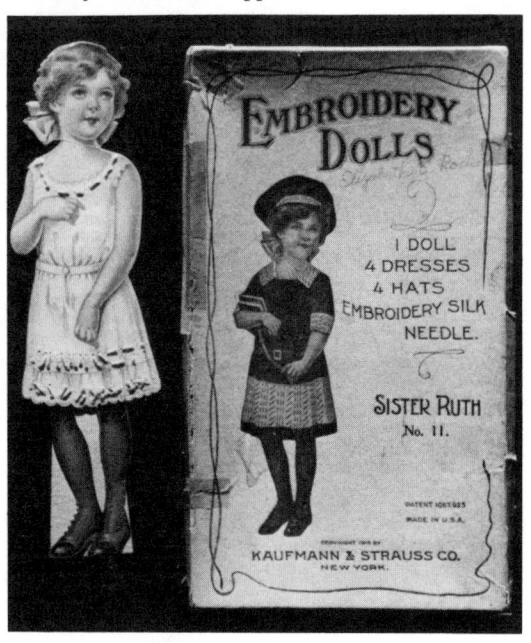

No. 11 *SISTER RUTH*, 1915. $40.00

No. 12 *SISTER HELEN*, 1915. $40.00

Embroidery Dolls
SISTER MARY (not pictured)
BROTHER JACK (not pictured)

Kingston Products Corporation

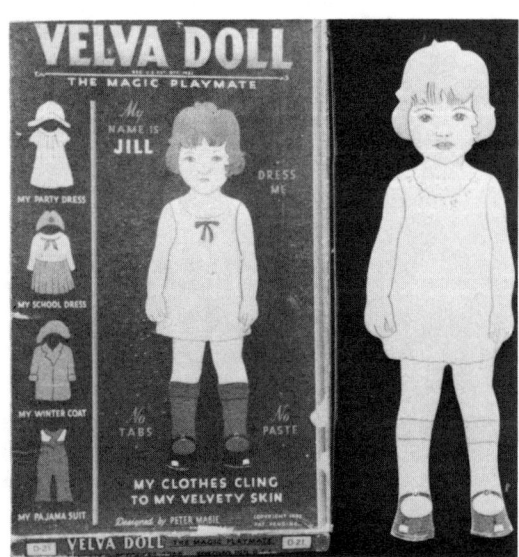
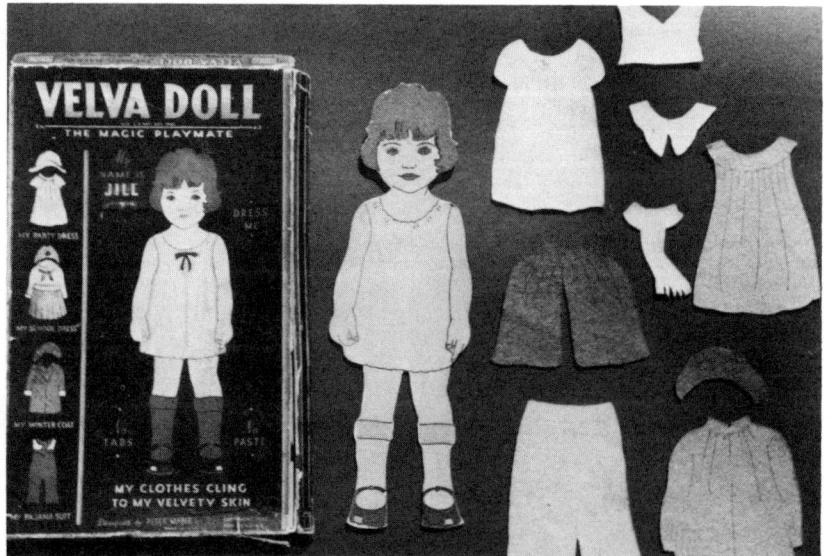

Courtesy of Audrey Sepponen

Courtesy of Betsy Slap

D21 *VELVA DOLL, MY NAME IS JILL (BIG JILL)*, 1932. $17.00
Large 17″ doll known as "Big Jill".

D20 *VELVA DOLL, MY NAME IS JILL*, 1932. $15.00

D23 *VELVA DOLL, BABY*, 1932 (not pictured)
D25 *VELVA DOLLS*, large combination box of Big Jill and Baby (not pictured)
VD202 *VELVA DOLL, VELVA CRAFT* (not pictured)

Kits, Incorporated

1050 *LACEY DAISY*, 1949. $7.00
(clothes lace on the doll)

The Lamp Studio

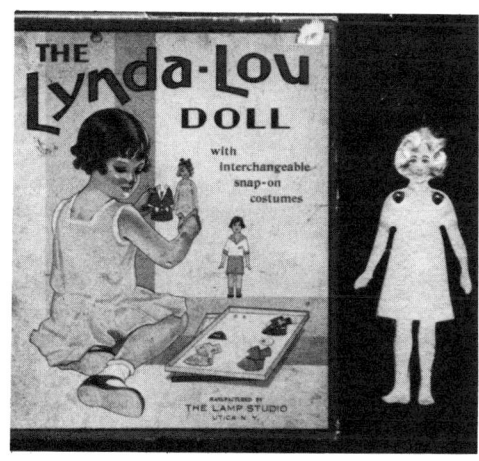

THE LYNDA-LOU DOLL. $15.00
THE LYNDA-LOU DOLL costumes snap on and are of fabric.

Landoll Publishing Company

2129 *DOLLHOUSE CUT OUTS* (not pictured; see Stephens Pub.Co.)

2229 *PAJAMA PARTY* (not pictured; see Stephens Pub. Co.)

E.M. Leavens Company, Inc.

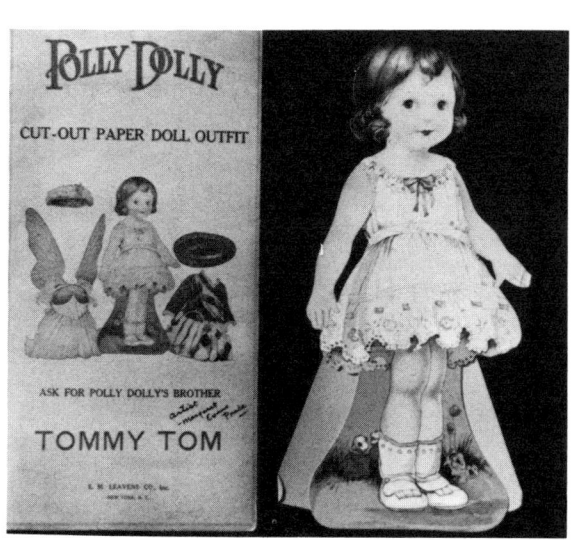

DOLLY DIMPLE (not pictured; see Stecher Lithographic Co.)
TOMMY TOM (not pictured; see Hubbell-Leavens Co.)

POLLY DOLLY. $35.00
Large 16½" doll, came with the outfits pictured on the folder. A smaller 12½" doll has one more outfit than larger doll.

Courtesy of Edith Linn

M.H. LEAVIS

JACK AND JANET PAPER DOLLS
The twins travel around the world and buy costumes in Egypt, Burma, Korea, India, China and Japan. Fourteen costumes in color.

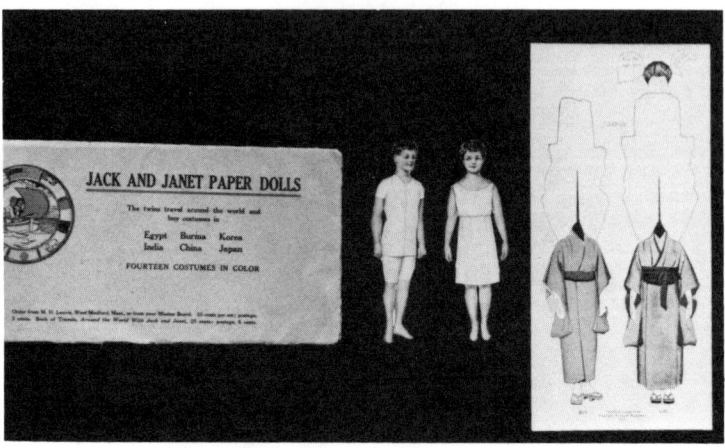

JACK AND JANET PAPER DOLLS. $12.00

Courtesy of Rosalie Eppert

Reuben H. Lilja and Company, Inc.

Mr. Reuben H. Lilja founded his company in 1940. Prior to this time he worked for Rand McNally and Co. in their Children's Books Trade Department.

900 *MISS AMERICA* 1941
901 *AMERICAN BEAUTIES* 1942
902 *MISS HOLLYWOOD* 1942
903 *JAUNTY JUNIORS* 1946
904 *MISS SILVER SCREEN* 1946
905 *DRESS-UP* 1947 (reprint of #901, dolls are redrawn)
906 *MOVIELAND* 1947 (the four dolls are taken from #900, #901, and #902. The dolls are all redrawn)
907 *SAPPHIRE, QUEEN OF THE NIGHT CLUB*
908 *MADAME HATTIE* (reprint of #907, using the two dolls from the back cover)
909 *LITTLE NURSE*
910 *LITTLE DOCTOR*
911 *COSTUME PARTY*
912 *MARY ANN GOES TO MEXICO*
913 *COUNTRY WEEK END WITH KATHY AND JILL* (also published by Childrens Press)
914 *MOTHER AND DAUGHTER* (also published by Childrens Press)
915 *AROUND THE WORLD WITH BOB AND BARBARA* (also published by Childrens Press)
916 *PATSY* (also published by Childrens Press)
917 *AMERICAN BEAUTIES* (reprint of #901, using the two dolls from the back cover)
918 *PAPER DOLLS* (reprint of #901, using the two dolls from the front cover)
919 *MERRY MERMAIDS* (reprint of #903 dolls #2 and #4; redrawn)
920 *PRETTY PENNY AND HER PAL* (reprint of #903 dolls #1 and #3; redrawn)
921 *BIG SISTER* (not pictured; reprint of #914)
922 *WE THREE* (the inside pages of this book are from #916)
923 *TV GLAMOUR GIRLS* (not pictured; reprint of #904)
924 *OUTDOOR FUN* (reprint of #913, redrawn dolls from front cover)
925 *TEEN-AGE TRAVEL FUN* (reprint of #915, redrawn dolls from front cover)
937 *COSTUME PARTY* (not pictured; see #911)
519 *MERRY MERMAIDS* (not pictured; see #919)
520 *PRETTY PENNY AND HER PAL* (not pictured; see #920)
620 *PRETTY PENNY AND HER PAL* (not pictured; see #920)
820 *PRETTY PENNY AND HER PAL* (not pictured; see #920)

Courtesy of Virginia Crossley

900 *MISS AMERICA*, 1941. $25.00

Courtesy of Judy Curtis

901 *AMERICAN BEAUTIES*, 1942. $17.00

902 *MISS HOLLYWOOD*, 1942. $25.00

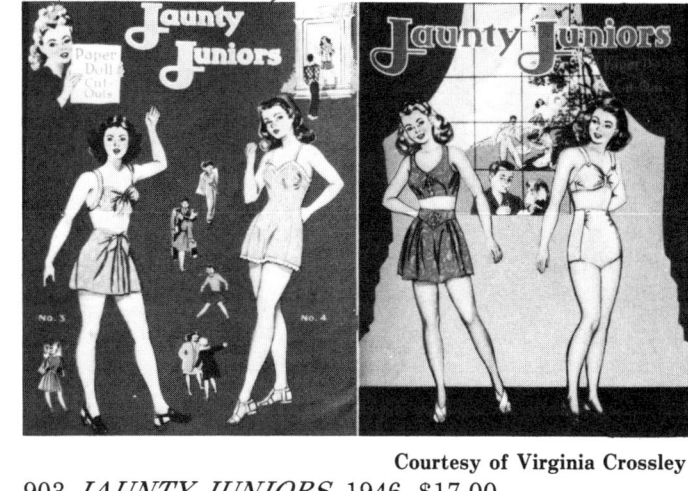

Courtesy of Virginia Crossley

903 *JAUNTY JUNIORS*, 1946. $17.00
There are two editions of the #903 Jaunty Juniors book. One has six pages of outfits, the other only four. Both have identical covers.

904 *MISS SILVER SCREEN* 1946. $20.00
There are two editions of the #904 *Miss Silver Screen* book. One has six pages of outfits, the other only four. Both have identical covers.

Courtesy of Virginia Crossley

905 *DRESS-UP*, 1947. $10.00

906 *MOVIELAND*, 1947. $12.00

Courtesy of Ted Menten

907 *SAPPHIRE, QUEEN OF THE NIGHT CLUB*. $30.00

Courtesy of Rosalie Eppert
908 *MADAME HATTIE.* $20.00

909 *LITTLE NURSE.* $12.00

Courtesy of Judy Curtis
910 *LITTLE DOCTOR.* $12.00

Courtesy of Judy Curtis
911 *COSTUME PARTY.* $12.00

Courtesy of Judy Curtis
912 *MARY ANN GOES TO MEXICO.* $12.00

Courtesy of Judy Curtis
913 *COUNTRY WEEK END WITH KATHY AND JILL.* $12.00

914 *MOTHER AND DAUGHTER.* $12.00

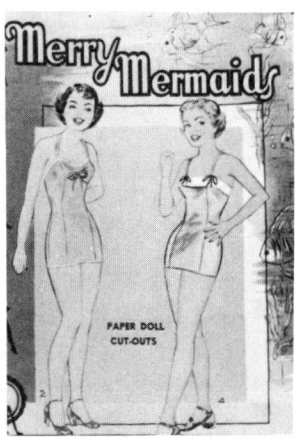
919 *MERRY MERMAIDS.* $7.00

917 *AMERICAN BEAUTIES.* $10.00 (Front and back covers are alike)

915 *AROUND THE WORLD WITH BOB AND BARBARA.* $12.00

916 *PATSY.* $12.00

Courtesy of Virginia Crossley
918 *PAPER DOLLS.* $10.00 (Front and back covers are alike)

Courtesy of Judy Curtis   Courtesy of Virginia Crossley   Courtesy of Virginia Crossley

920 *PRETTY PENNY AND HER PAL.* $7.00

922 *WE THREE.* $7.00

925 *TEEN-AGE TRAVEL FUN.* $5.00

924 *OUTDOOR FUN.* $5.00

Londy Card Corporation

The paper doll series published by the Londy Card Corporation consisted of "Betty Marie" and other members of her family. Every week a new paper doll was presented. The cardboard sheet of "Betty Marie" measures 7¼" x 14½" and is die-cut at her feet and also the slits in the hats have been die-cut. The sheets came in color and were nicely drawn.

These paper doll sheets may have been given away at stores or may have been used as shirt cardboard from cleaning establishments. Unfortunately only four of the sheets have come to light thus far; two are pictured.

5F *BETTY MARIE*, 1932. $5.00

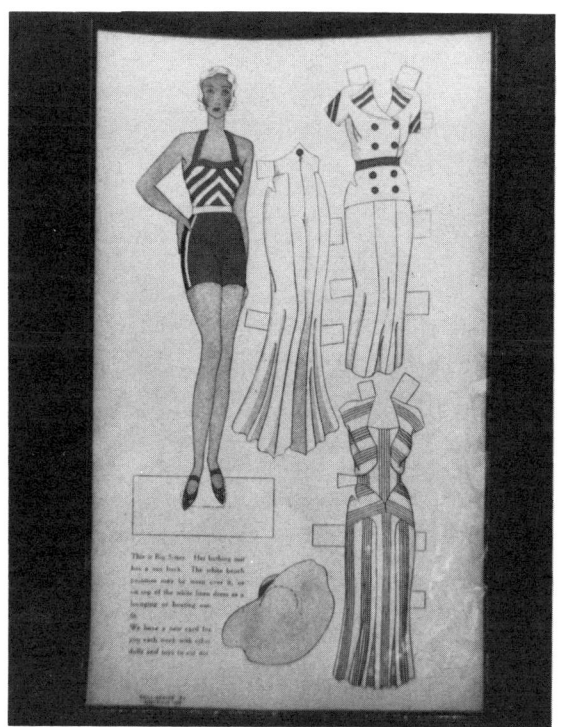

Courtesy of Betsy Addison

5J *BIG SISTER*, 1932. $5.00

5G *BETTY MARIE'S LITTLE SISTER*, 1932 (not pictured)

5L *MOTHER*, 1932 (not pictured)

M.S. Publishing Co.

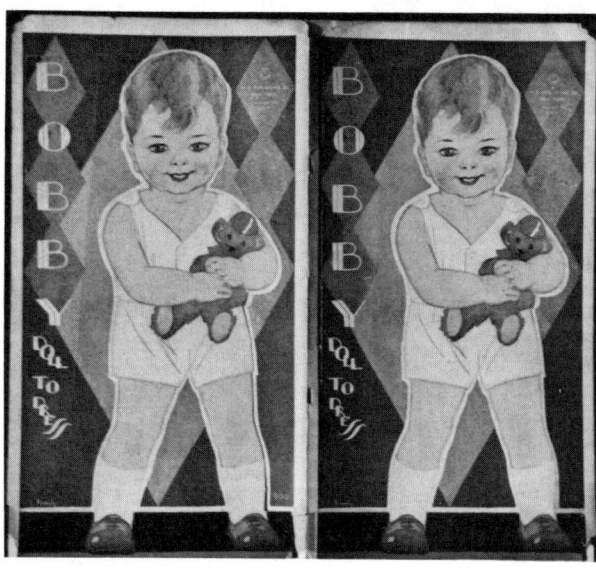

900 *BOBBY, DOLL TO DRESS.* $20.00

Courtesy of Jane Sugg

Magic Wand Corporation

Established 1960
The name "CRAFTMASTER" appears on some sets.

100 *INTRODUCING WENDY AND HER MOMMY*
101 *MY NAME IS CINDY* (not pictured)
104 *JUDY*
105 *BUTCH* (not pictured)
106 *BRIDE AND GROOM*
107 *JACKIE AND CAROLINE*
108 *SWEET SUE*
109 *CAROLINE*
110 *WENDY AND MOMMY* (not pictured; may be same as #100)
111 *TRESSY,* 1964
112 *TINY TEARS WITH ROCK-A-BYE CRADLE*
114 *BEWITCHED,* 1965
115 *TABATHA* (not pictured)
116 *DOLLS OF THE FOUR SEASONS,* 1967 (not pictured)
117 *GRANNY,* 1967

118 *SUPER TWINS,* 1967 (not pictured)
119 *MIMI-MODS,* 1968
120 *TEENY MIMIS,* 1968 (not pictured)
121 *BLACK IS BEAUTIFUL,* 1969
201 *3 HIGH FASHION MODELS*
204 *THE FIRST LADY,* 1963
1010 *MAGIC PRINCESS,* 1964
1011 *PAINT ME PRETTY,* 1969
17401 *PAPER DOLLS,* 1970 (not pictured)
17402 *PAPER DOLLS,* 1970 (not pictured)
17403 *PAPER DOLLS,* 1970 (not pictured)
90010 *BRIDE AND GROOM,* 1970
DRESS DAWN AND HER FRIENDS (stock number and picture not available)
FIREBALL XL5, Steve and Venus (stock number and picture not available)

104 *JUDY.* $6.00

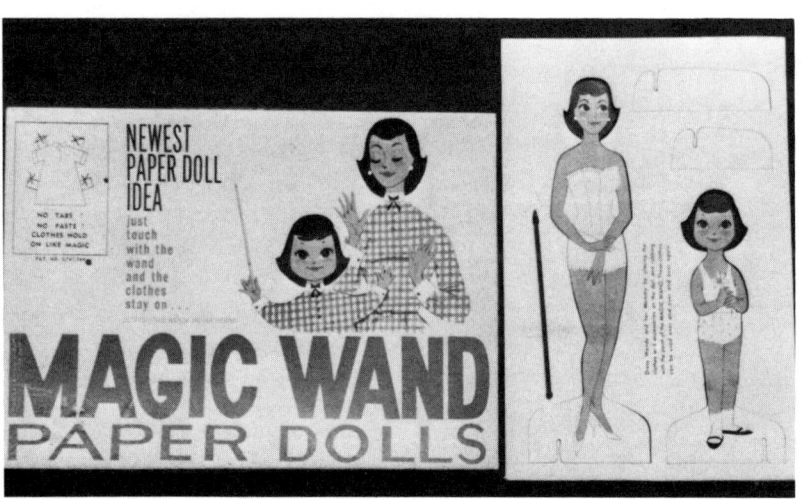

Courtesy of Virginia Crossley

100 *MAGIC WAND PAPER DOLLS, WENDY AND HER MOMMY.* $5.00

Courtesy of Virginia Crossley

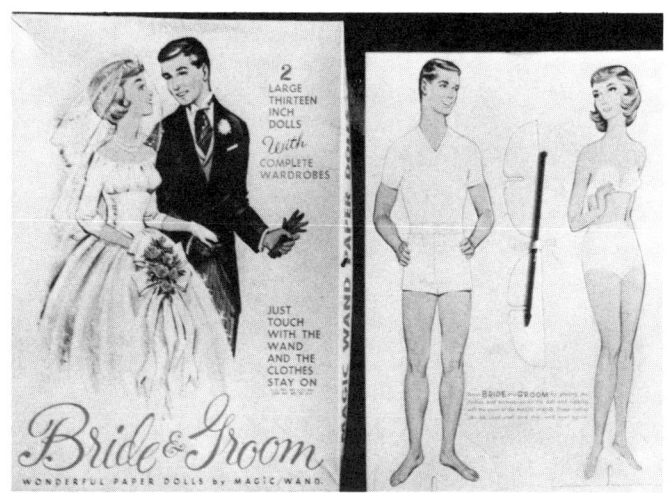

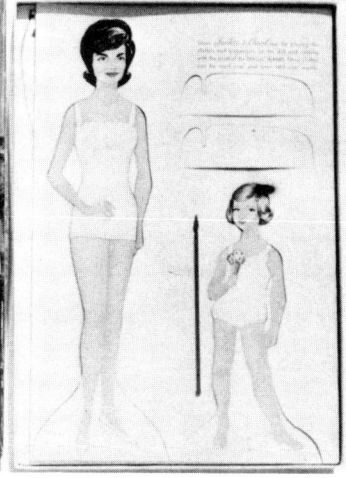

106 *BRIDE AND GROOM*. $6.00

107 *JACKIE AND CAROLINE*. $20.00

108 *SWEET SUE*. $5.00

109 *CAROLINE*. $18.00

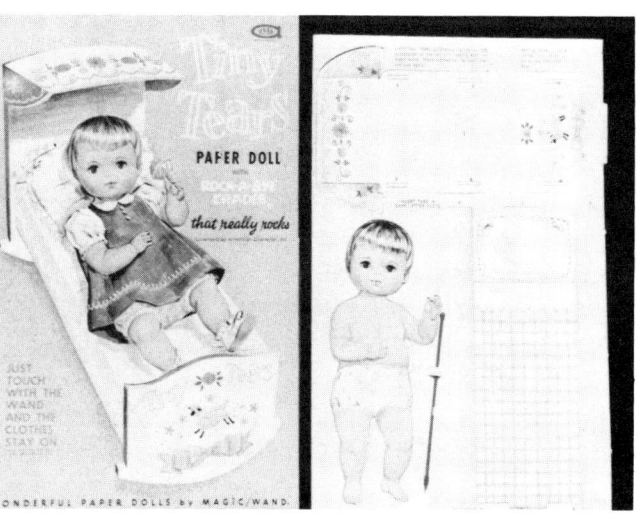

111 *TRESSY*, 1964. $6.00

112 *TINY TEARS*. $6.00

117 *GRANNY*, 1967. $5.00

Courtesy of Virginia Crossley
121 *BLACK IS BEAUTIFUL*, 1969
$3.00

204 *THE FIRST LADY*, 1963. $25.00

119 *MINI-MODS*, 1968. $3.00

114 *BEWITCHED* © 1965 Screen Gems. $20.00

1010 *MAGIC PRINCESS*, 1964. $8.00

90010 *BRIDE AND GROOM*, 1970. $5.00

201 Three *HIGH FASHION MODELS*. $5.00

1011 *PAINT ME PRETTY*, 1969. $5.00

McLoughlin Brothers

John McLoughlin established his first print shop in 1828 and began publishing children's books shortly afterward. When his two sons, John and Edmund, took over the firm in the late 1840's, the company became known as McLoughlin Bros. The company developed into the foremost producer of children's books in the country. The firm continued to publish until 1920 when it was sold to The Milton Bradley Company. It continued as a division of Milton Bradley until 1944.

McLoughlin Bros. produced paper dolls in abundance, starting in the late 1850's. Their paper dolls produced from the turn of the century to 1944 are covered here.

236 *THE NEW MODEL BOOK OF DOLLS*, 1904
239 *OUR DOLLIES MODEL BOOK*, 1909
244 *THE DOLLS' HOUSE MODEL BOOK* (stand-ups; not pictured)
509 *THE PLAYHOUSE CUT OUT STORY BOOK*, 1932 (cut/paste book; not pictured)
515 *PLAY TIME CIRCUS*, 1932 stand-ups (not pictured)
517 *THE THREE BEARS HOME*, 1933 stand-ups
521 *FUN WITH SCISSORS, CRAYON, BRUSH AND PENCIL* (not pictured; no paper dolls)
538 *WIDE WORLD COSTUME DOLLS* (not pictured; reprint of #236)
540 *FASHION BOOK OF ROUND ABOUT DOLLS*, 1936 (reprint of #545 & #555 Ten Round-About)
541 *STAND-UP HAPPY ANIMAL PAPER DOLLS*, 1934 (not pictured)
542 *MULTI-HEAD PAPER DOLLS*, 1933
544 *NURSERY RHYME PARTY DOLLS IN COSTUME*
545 *DIANE AND DAPHNE ROUND ABOUT DOLLS*, 1933
545 *THE NEW PRETTY VILLAGE* (stand-ups; not pictured)
547 *MARCELLA'S RAGGEDY ANN DOLL BOOK*, 1940
548 *DEBBIE DOLLS*, 1937
549 *THE LITTLE RED SCHOOL HOUSE KINDERGARTEN*, 1940
550 *MARY AND MADGE THE ROUND ABOUT DOLLS*
551 *LET'S PLAY PAPER DOLLS*, 1938 (reprint of The Sewing Book of the Round About Dolls)
552 *THE PARTY OF THE PAPER DOLLS*, 1938
553 *FUNNY BUNNIES*, 1938
555 *TEN ROUND ABOUT DOLLS*, 1936
555 *WINNIE'S NEW WARDROBE*, 1939 (some editions called "Winnie and her Wardrobe")
556 *REAL SLEEPING DOLL* 1939
557 *BIG GIRL*, 1939
558 *FINGER FUN DOLLS*, 1939 (not pictured; not paper dolls with outfits)
559 *THE NEW ROUND ABOUT DOLL BOOK*, 1939
560 *RADIO CUT-OUTS*, 1935 (stand-ups; not pictured)
561 *18 LITTLE MOVIE STARS*, 1939
700 *THE ROUND ABOUT DOLLS*, 1933 (not pictured; reprint of #545 Diane and Daphne)
704 *DEBBIE DOLLS* (not pictured; reprint of #548)
707 *BIG GIRL* (not pictured; reprint of #557)
707 *BIG SISTER*, 1940 (reprint of #557)
2014 and 2026 *SOMETHING TO DO FOR EVERY DAY* (not pictured; no paper dolls)
2028 *THE DRESS PARADE OF THE ROUND ABOUT DOLLS* (not pictured)
2710 *DEBBIE DOLLS*, 1937 (reprint of #548, except these dolls are heavy statuette type dolls and come in a folder)
2950 *THE FASHION BOOK OF ROUND ABOUT DOLLS*, 1936 (three part folder, includes two dolls from #545 Diane and Daphne, and four dolls from #555 Ten Round About Dolls. The dolls are heavy statuette type of dolls)
2952 *ROUND ABOUT DOLLS ON PARADE*, 1941 (three part folder; reprint of The Sewing Book of the Round About Dolls listed further on)
2953 *THE DRESS PARADE OF THE ROUND ABOUT DOLLS* not dated, circa 1937. (three part folder with patterns and cloth material to make outfits for the dolls. The paper patterns can be colored and used as dresses also.)

The following have no stock number:
THE FASHION BOOK OF THE ROUND ABOUT DOLLS, 1936 (not pictured; same as #2950 except this is a four part folder and has three dolls from #545 (two alike) and five dolls from #555)
THE SEWING BOOK OF THE ROUND ABOUT DOLLS, 1937 (four part folder, includes four dolls (two each of two dolls) scissors, crayons, embroidery floss etc.)
DOLLS TO CUT OUT AND DRESS, 1929
OUR DOLLIES, 1905 (not pictured; the contents of this box set are the same as book #239)

McLoughlin Bros. numbered sheets:
0100 Young school age girl and five outfits and hats
0100 School age girl of about 10 years, five outfits and hats
0100 Lady with five outfits and hats
0100 Small girl, four outfits and hats (not pictured)
0101 *DOLLS OF ALL NATIONS* (4 different sheets, for pictures see #236)

0102 Bride with four outfits and hats
0104-D Young lady with five sport outfits and hats
0105-A Gentleman with four outfits and hats
0105-B Bride with four outfits and hats (not pictured)
0105-C Young Lady and four outfits and hats
0106 *CINDERELLA* (not pictured)
0109-D Little Girl and outfits
0110-B Two ladies, six outfits and hats
4009-A Baby, seven outfits, carriage, bathtub (not pictured)
4010-A Two girls with six outfits and hats (not pictured)
4010-B Two ladies with six outfits and hats
4011-B Two Ladies with six outfits and hats
4011-C Two ladies with six outfits and hats
4011-D Two ladies with six outfits and hats

McLoughlin Bros. Sheets without numbers:
CELIE, 1900 This doll is used again four years later in 1904, in book #236. Her name is changed to Edna and the outfits are different
ETHEL, 1900 (not pictured; this doll was used again in book #236)
KATIE (circa 1900)
LIZZIE (circa 1900)
MAMIE (circa 1900)
NELLIE (circa 1900)

The following is a list of McLoughlin Bros. "Model" books published before 1910. They are stand-up toys, not paper dolls.

DOLLS' HOUSE MODEL BOOK, 1905 #244
MODEL BOOK OF ANIMALS
MODEL BOOK OF FURNITURE, 1904
MODEL BOOK OF LITTLE FOLKS' ARMY
MODEL BOOK OF OBJECTS
MODEL BOOK OF SOLDIERS
MODEL BOOK OF TRAINS

Courtesy of Betsy Addison

236 *THE NEW MODEL BOOK OF DOLLS*, 1904. $45.00

THE NEW MODEL BOOK OF DOLLS

517 *THE THREE BEARS' HOME*, 1933. $25.00
There are no outfits for the dolls

Courtesy of Betsy Slap

The twelve dolls pictured from "Our Dollies Model Book" are made up of different parts; feet, skirt, waist, head and hat. Different combinations can be made to create many different dolls. This set was also produced as a box set a few years earlier in 1905.

Courtesy of the Detroit Public Schools Children's Museum

239 *OUR DOLLIES MODEL BOOK*

239 *OUR DOLLIES MODEL BOOK,* 1909. $45.00

239 *OUR DOLLIES MODEL BOOK*

239 *OUR DOLLIES MODEL BOOK*

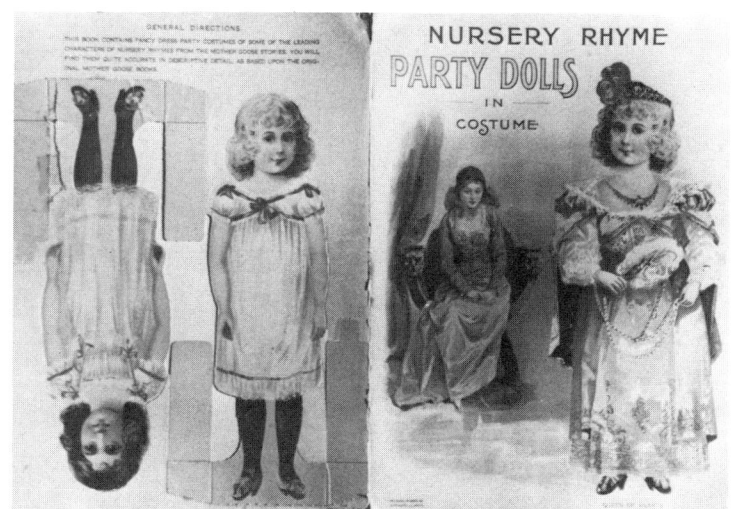

544 *NURSERY RHYME PARTY DOLLS IN COSTUME.* $30.00

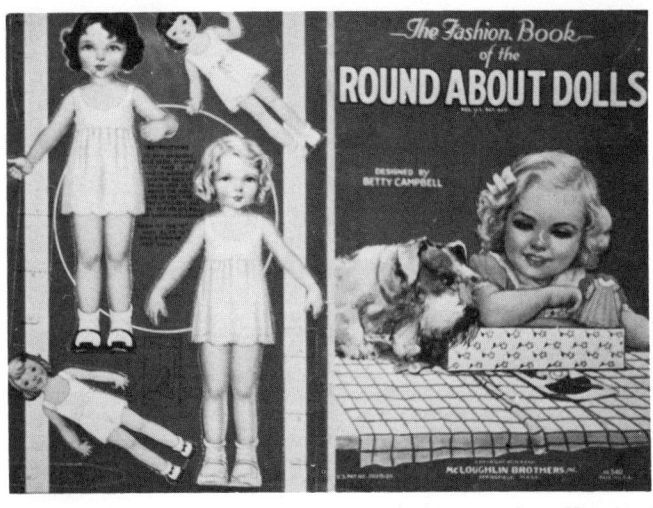

Courtesy of Jean Woodcock

540 *THE FASHION BOOK OF THE ROUND ABOUT DOLLS*, 1936. $20.00

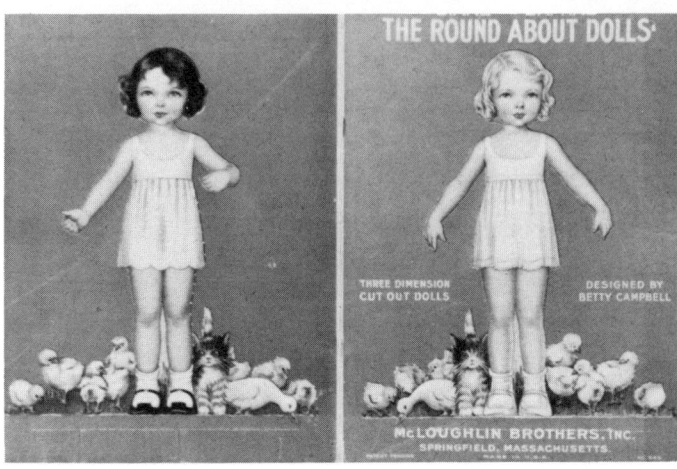

Courtesy of Shirley Hedge

545 *DIANE AND DAPHNE THE ROUND ABOUT DOLLS*, 1933. $25.00

547 *MARCELLA'S RAGGEDY ANN DOLL BOOK* ©1940 Johnny Gruelle Co. $27.00

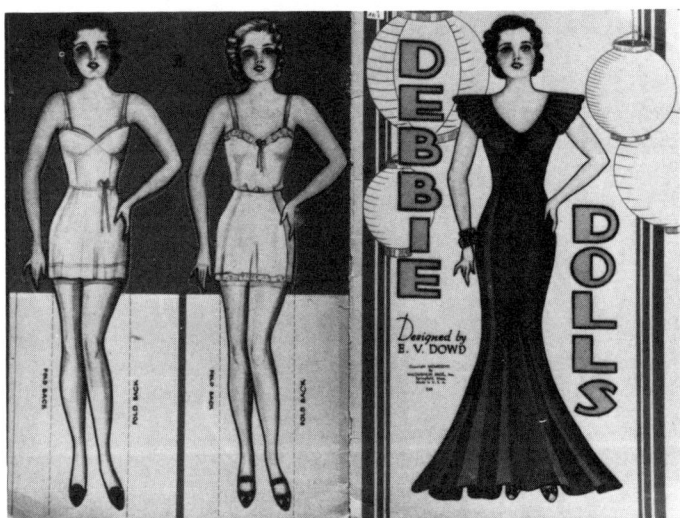

Courtesy of Carol Carey

548 *DEBBIE DOLLS*, 1937. $25.00

542 *MULTI-HEAD PAPER DOLLS*, 1933. $35.00

Courtesy of Jane Sugg

116

Courtesy of Betsy Slap

549 *THE LITTLE RED SCHOOL HOUSE KINDERGARTEN*, 1940. $25.00

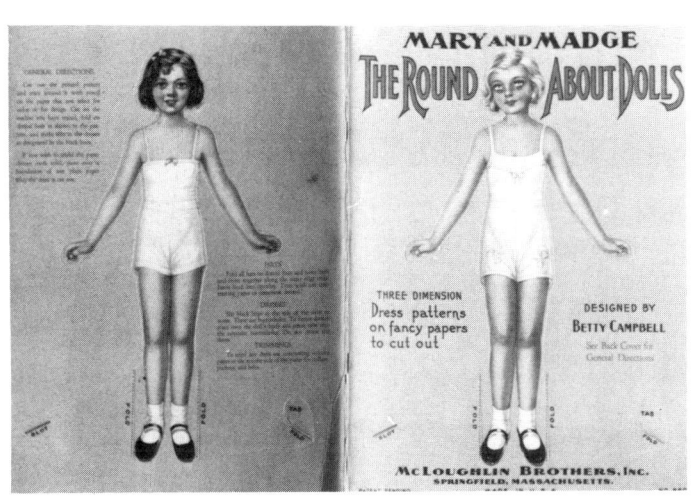

Courtesy of Betsy Slap

550 *MARY AND MADGE THE ROUND ABOUT DOLLS*. $25.00

551 *LET'S PLAY PAPER DOLLS*, 1938. $20.00

Courtesy of Jean Woodcock

553 *FUNNY BUNNIES*, 1938. $35.00

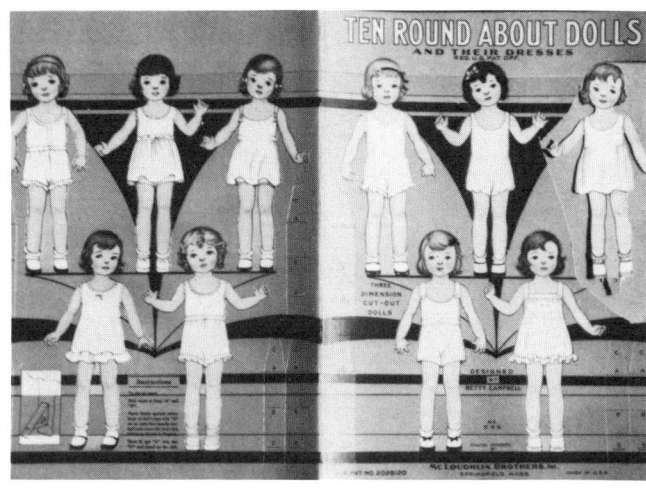

555 *TEN ROUND ABOUT DOLLS*, 1936. $25.00

Courtesy of Shirley Hedge

552 *THE PARTY OF THE PAPER DOLLS*, 1938. $20.00

552 *THE PARTY OF THE PAPER DOLLS*

2710 *DEBBIE DOLLS*, 1937. $25.00
same dolls as #548 but statuette and in folder

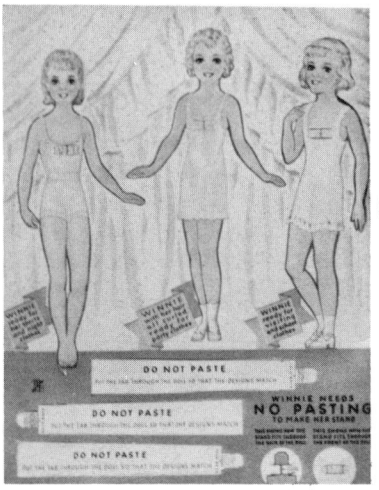

555 *WINNIE AND HER WARDROBE*, 1939. $25.00

Courtesy of Jane Sugg

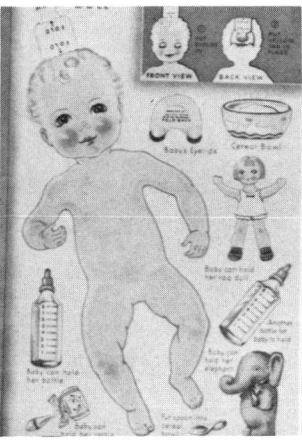

Courtesy of Betsy Slap

556 *REAL SLEEPING DOLL*, 1939. $22.50

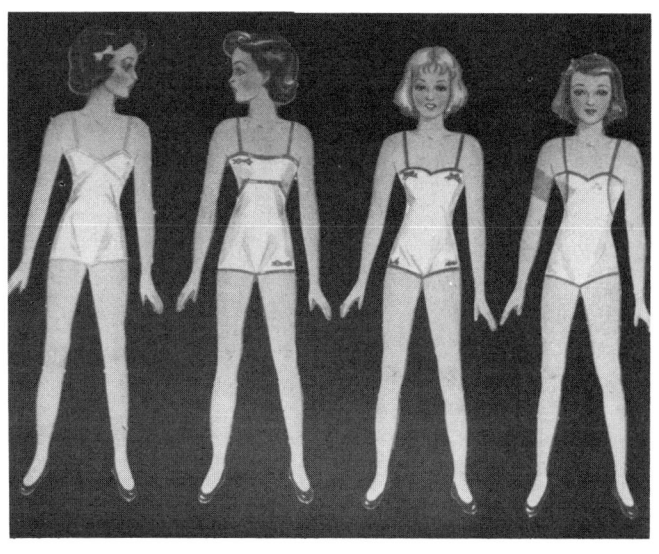

557 *BIG GIRL*, 1939. $15.00
(Cut set)

Courtesy of Emma Terry

559 *THE NEW ROUND ABOUT DOLL BOOK*, 1939. $20.00

Courtesy of Virginia Crossley

707 *BIG SISTER*, 1940. $9.00
Reprint of #557, using two of the four dolls twice.

Courtesy of Shirley Hedge

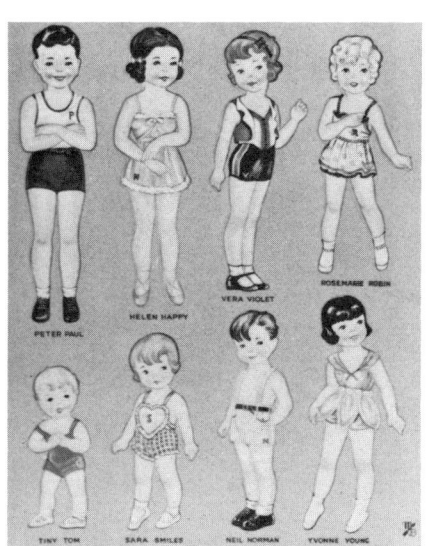

561 *EIGHTEEN LITTLE MOVIE STAR PAPER DOLLS*, 1939. $35.00

2950 *THE FASHION BOOK OF ROUND ABOUT DOLLS,* 1936. $30.00

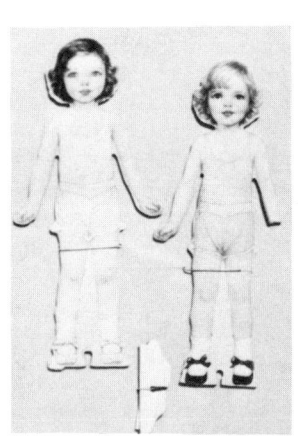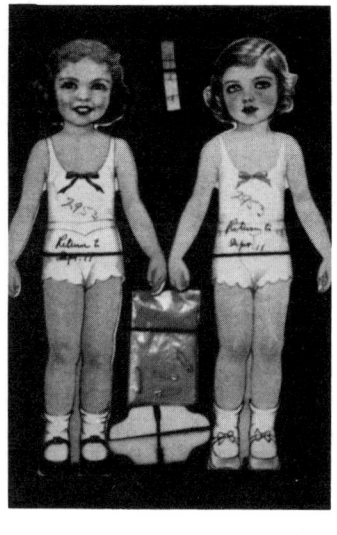

Courtesy of Shirley Hedge

2952 *ROUND ABOUT DOLLS ON PARADE,* 1941. $30.00

2953 *THE DRESS PARADE OF THE ROUND ABOUT DOLLS.* $40.00

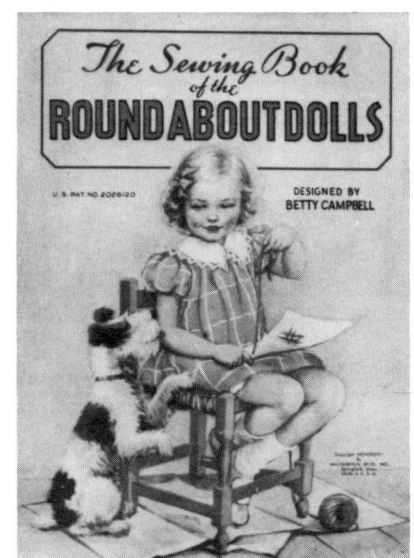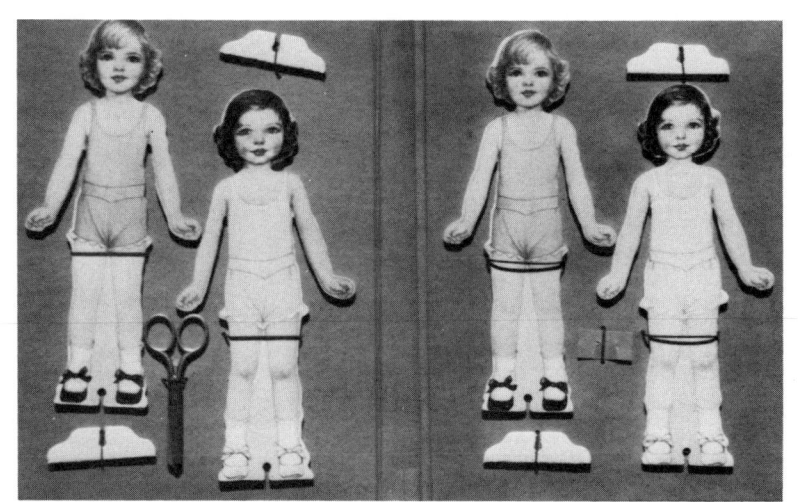

THE SEWING BOOK OF THE ROUND ABOUT DOLLS, 1937. $35.00

Courtesy of Jane Sugg

DOLLS TO CUT-OUT AND DRESS, 1929. $17.00

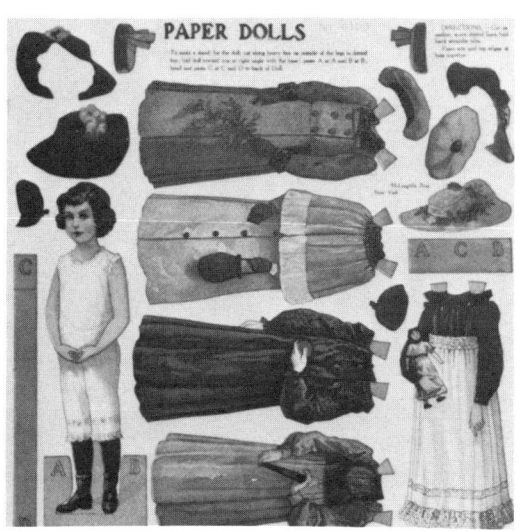

Courtesy of Pam Hunter

Numbered Sheet 0100. $15.00-18.00.

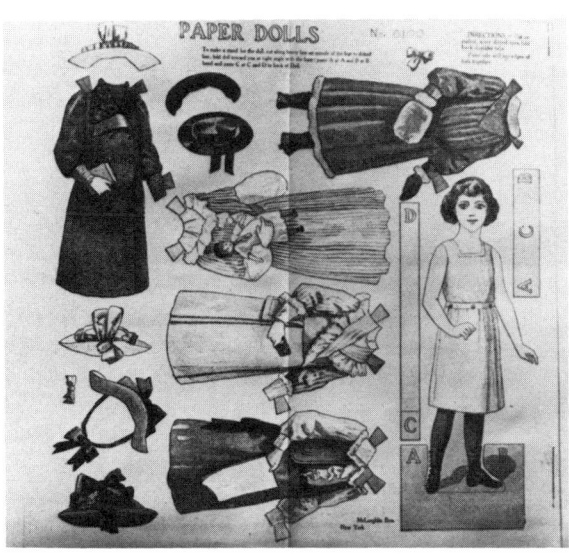

Courtesy of Suzanne Tessey

Numbered Sheet 0100. $15.00-18.00

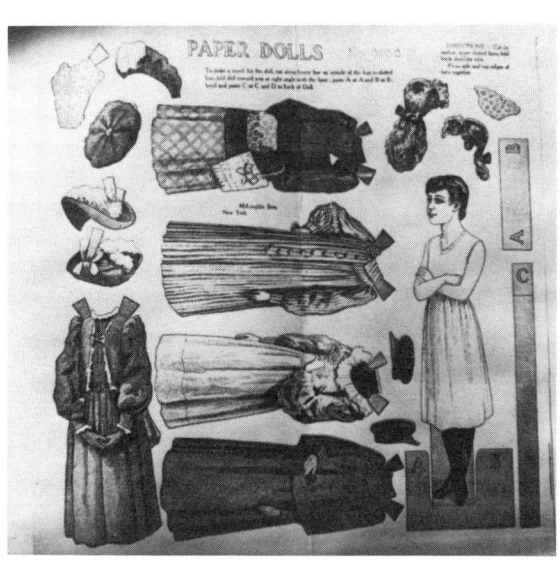

Courtesy of Suzanne Tessey

Numbered Sheet 0100 $15.00-18.00

Courtesy of Detroit Public Schools Children's Museum

0102 *BRIDE*
Hat on far left does not belong to set

Courtesy of Pam Hunter

Numbered Sheet 0104 Set-D. $15.00-18.00

Courtesy of Suzanne Tessey

0105 SET-A. $15.00-18.00
(not all outfits are shown)

Courtesy of Pam Hunter

0105 SET-C. $15.00-18.00

Courtesy of Betsy Addison. Photo by Robert Addison

0110 SET-B. $15.00-18.00

Courtesy of Suzanne Tessey

Unidentified cut set from a McLoughlin sheet. $15.00-18.00

Courtesy of Pam Hunter

4010 SET-B is a reprint of sheet #0110 Set-B. The address given on this reprint is Springfield, Mass., so the date is after 1920. The original #0110 was done while the company was still in New York. The reprint is on a poor quality pulp paper. $15.00-18.00

Courtesy of Audrey Sepponen

4011 SET-B. $15.00-18.00

Courtesy of Audrey Sepponen

4011 SET-C. $15.00-18.00

Courtesy of Suzanne Tessey

4011 SET-D. $15.00-18.00

CELIE
Date 1900 Reprinted in book #236 with new outfits. $12.00-15.00

NELLIE   Courtesy of Dot Trippel
Hat in lower right of picture belongs to Mamie. $12.00-15.00

Courtesy of Suzanne Tessey

KATIE. $12.00-15.00
(not all outfits are shown)

Courtesy of Suzanne Tessey

MAMIE. $12.00-15.00
(not all outfits are shown)

Courtesy of Suzanne Tessey
LIZZIE. $12.00-15.00
(not all outfits are shown)

Courtesy of Detroit Public Schools Children's Museum

The little boy and two girls pictured here are not identified. They were found at the Detroit Public Schools Children's Museum with the paper doll of the Bride #0102 which is pictured with the numbered sheets. These three dolls are of the same fine quality as the Bride and it seems probable that these dolls are also from McLoughlin sheets.

Merrimack Publishing Corporation

A subsidiary of B. Shackman Co., Inc.

B. Shackman and Co. was founded in 1898 by Bertha Shackman in Wilkes Barre, Pa. The business was later moved to New York City, and the four Shackman sons eventually took over the firm. The business is still owned and run by descendants of the original family.

The Merrimack Publishing Corporation is the publishing subsidiary of B. Shackman. Over the years they have created over 1,000 nostalgic paper items produced from antique originals.

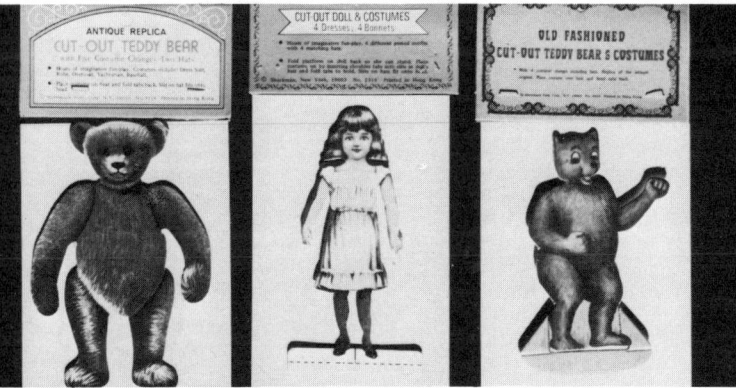

#9116, #2318, #4955
Currently available

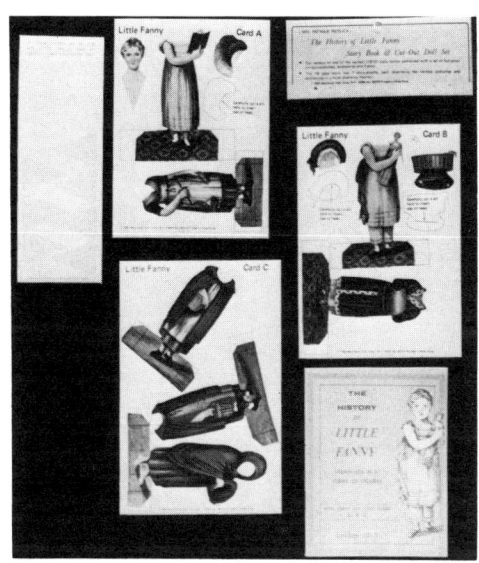

90374 *THE HISTORY OF LITTLE FANNY*
Currently available

Top-#3684
Bottom-#3237S
Currently available

1810 *PETER RABBIT & FRIENDS*
Currently available

The following additional paper dolls are just a sample of the many paper dolls produced by the company:
A-1714 *ALICE IN WONDERLAND*
1977-S *ANTIQUE PAPER CUT OUT DOLL AND CLOTHES*
A-2043 *SET OF SIX POST CARDS OF PAPER DOLLS*
2308 *COLLECTOR'S MINIATURE CUT-OUT PAPER DOLLS & COSTUMES*
2372 *SUNBONNET BABIES*
3052 *KATE GREENAWAY*

Merry Manufacturing Company

In 1962 the Merry Manufacturing Co. bought out the DeJournette Co. and began to produce their own paper dolls. In addition to paper dolls the company produced Miss Merry Play Sets such as pretend nail polish and cosmetics sets and nurse kits. For the boys there were Mr. Merry Play Sets, One was the popular "Really Neat" set which had play shaving cream, band-aids, a toy razor and toy blades. By the late 1960's these sets and the paper dolls came to an end, as the company was sold.

4360 *BRENDA LEE*. $12.00
©1964 by Brenda Lee & Weston Mfg. Corp and Merry Mfg. Co.

Courtesy of Shirley Hedge

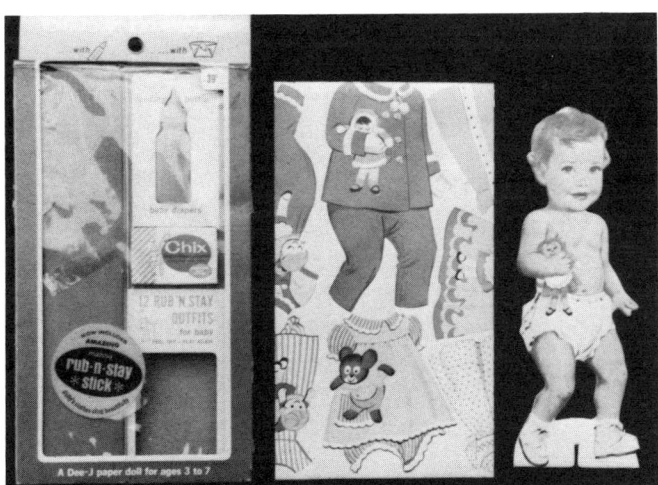

Courtesy of Audrey Sepponen

4350 *BABY MERRY*, 1964. $8.00
(has bottle and diaper)

Courtesy of Audrey Sepponen

6402 *BRIDE OF FRANKENSTEIN.* $12.00
© 1964 Merry Mfg. Co. and Universal Pictures Co. Inc.

Courtesy of Audrey Sepponen

4362 *JODI.* $6.00

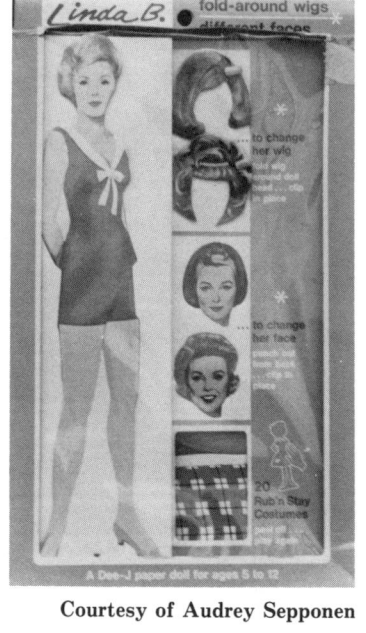

Courtesy of Audrey Sepponen

4361 *LINDA B.* 1964. $6.00

6504 *WENDY WALKS*, 1965. $10.00

Courtesy of Audrey Sepponen

6403 *DONNA REED.* $12.00
© 1964 Merry Mfg. Co. and Todon of California

Courtesy of Audrey Sepponen

6501 *TONI.* $6.00

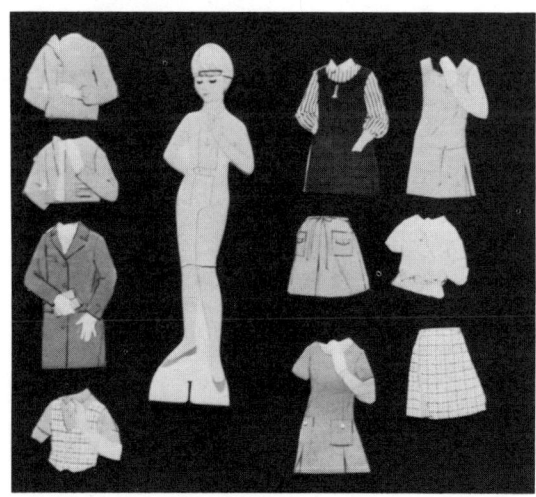

8½" doll by Merry Mfg. Co. dated 1964. Name of set not available

6502 JO (not pictured)
MINDY (number and picture not available)
MISS MERRY (number and picture not available)

Milton Bradley Company

The Milton Bradley Co. was founded in 1860 in Springfield, Mass., by Milton Bradley. In that year, while working at the Wason Locomotive Car Works, he became interested in lithography and purchased a lithographic press. Since it was the only press in Massachusetts outside of Boston he began receiving orders in great quantity and was able to start his own business. When business slowed down that first year, Mr. Bradley developed a game called "The Checkered Game of Life". He ran it off on his press and with the help of only one man, assembled and boxed the game. Mr. Bradley took several hundred of the games to New York and sold them to sales managers and news vendors until, by the end of the second day, all were sold. That winter Mr. Bradley produced and sold 40,000 copies of the game. When the Civil War broke out the following spring Milton Bradley stopped the game production to work as a draftsman on plans for the new percussion-lock Springfield rifle.

In the fall of 1861 Bradley went back to game-making as he noticed the soldiers needed something to take their minds off the war and their living conditions. He invented a kit called "Games for Soldiers". It was a small flat kit and contained nine games: backgammon, Checkered Game of Life, chess, checkers and five variations of dominoes. From this time foreward, Milton Bradley would remain firmly planted in the game-making industry and in a few short years would become the leading manufacturer of games in the country.

In the summer of 1869 Mr. Bradley heard a lecture given by Elizabeth Peabody, founder of the kindergarten movement in the U.S.A. He was so impressed with the kindergarten theory that he agreed to publish a book on kindergarten education based on a method devised by a Mr. Froebel in Germany. The method used supplementary educational material and Milton Bradley agreed to manufacture these products. For years these materials were a non-profitable part of the business but were something in which Mr. Bradley believed totally; so he continued to manufacture them. The original materials have since been up-dated many times but are still being sold as learning aids in elementary schools.

Games, of course, still accounted for the biggest share of production and continued to do so up to present times. For their 100th anniversary, a modern version of the first Milton Bradley game "Checkered Game of Life" was produced. The new "Game of Life" reflected the modern times with personal achievement and monetary success while the original game of 100 years prior dealt with high ideals of morality and happy old age.

One very popular game of 1966 was the game of "Twister". The company had doubts of its success when it was presented to them. It was not your usual board game. In this game the participants became the playing pieces and moved from one colored circle to another on a vinyl sheet. To become a successful game it had to be demonstrated, and when the Milton Bradley Co. persuaded Johnny Carson to play the game with Zsa Zsa Gabor on the "Tonight Show", the game became an instant hit.

Sometimes a game, thought to be too involved or difficult, was passed over. Such an incident occurred in the 1930's when the executives turned down the game of Monopoly. The inventor took his game over to Parker Bros. in Salem, Mass., where the game was accepted and went on to become the largest selling game in the world.

Milton Bradley died in 1911, but the company ran smoothly along until 1932. Then, because of the great Depression, operations had to be curtailed. By the end of 1941, the company was on the brink of bankruptcy, and to protect their interests, the holders of preferred stock insisted on a reorganization. They knew they had to find a man for president who had the vision of Milton Bradley. Such a man was James Shea, Sr., who left his position in another firm to become the new president of Milton Bradley just one week before the country entered World War II. War rationing of raw materials, including paper, made it next to impossible for Milton Bradley to continue manufacturing their products. So the company turned over a good portion of their facilities to war products. They manufactured gun stocks in their wood working department, and the company was given a contract with the Coca-Cola Co. to supply game kits for the Armed Forces. This started to put the company back on its feet, and each year since, there has been a steady growth.

In 1914 the first sets of "Bradley's Tru-Life Paper Dolls" were published. In the 1914 catalog three sets are listed and each is listed as "new". According to the catalog the paper dolls were "painted by an American artist from life models". These paper dolls sold in a variety of sets.

In 1920 Milton Bradley acquired a controlling interest in McLoughlin Bros. of New York. The McLoughlin operation was moved to Springfield, Mass., and became a separate division of the company until 1944. During this time McLoughlin Bros. published many paper dolls. Some of them were reprinted under the Milton Bradley name.

The "Magic Mary" paper dolls were first published by the company in 1946 and are still being produced almost 40 years later! "Magic Mary" was invented by an engineer in Ohio for his two daughters who loved paper dolls. He devised a way of hiding a magnet inside the doll and attaching small pieces of metal to the dresses so that they would cling to the doll. After obtaining a patent on his idea in 1943, he tried to interest manufacturers with the doll but wound up selling the patent to a Mrs. Wright of Cleveland. She took the idea to Milton Bradley but the executive with whom she spoke rejected it. She then inquired her way to the president's office and was able to stop him as he came out of his office. Mr. Shea immediately saw the possibilities of the magnet paper doll and Mrs. Wright had a signed contract before she left. The first "Magic Mary" was introduced in their 1946 catalog. The set, #4132, was drawn by Emma McKean. In 1948, a new "Magic Mary" doll was drawn by Betty Campbell in such a way as to accept the original dresses by Emma McKean plus a few new outfits by Betty Campbell. The number on the new set was #4132-B. It was in 1950 when this same "Magic Mary" paper doll was used again, but this time all the clothes were drawn by Betty Campbell. The stock number was changed to #4010-1 (still used today) and three other paper dolls were added to the line: "Magic Mary Ann" #4010-2, "Magic Mary Jane" #4010-3 and "Magic Mary Lou" #4010-4. These three dolls were originally in set #4489A by Betty Campbell. The dolls in the series would change every three or four years, but the names remained the same. The last sets were copyrighted in the 1970's but are still being produced and sold in the stores today.

Bibliography: *It's All in the Game* by James J. Shea
The Milton Bradley Story by James J. Shea, Jr.

All the known Milton Bradley paper dolls are listed here.

4010-1 *MAGIC MARY* new in 1950, (doll from #4132-B, clothes new)
4010-1 *MAGIC MARY*, 1955
4010-1 *MAGNETIC MAGIC MARY*, 1958
4010-1 *MAGIC MARY*, 1962 (same doll as year 1958, few new clothes added)
4010-1 *MAGIC MARY*, 1966
4010-1 *MAGIC MARY*, 1972
4010-1 *MAGIC MARY*, 1972 (same set as above 1972 set only box is smaller and box covered changed slightly)
4010-2 *MAGIC MARY ANN* new in 1950, (from #4489A)
4010-2 *MAGIC MARY JANE*, 1955
4010-2 *MAGIC MARY ANN*, 1958 (not pictured)
4010-2 *MAGIC MARY ANN*, 1962 (not pictured)
4010-2 *MAGIC MARY ANN*, 1966
4010-2 *MAGIC MARY ANN*, 1972
4010-3 *MAGIC MARY JANE* new in 1950, (from #4489A)
4010-3 *MAGIC MARY LOU*, 1955
4010-3 *MAGIC MARY JANE*, 1958
4010-3 *MAGIC MARY JANE*, 1962 (not pictured)
4010-3 *MAGIC MARY JANE* 1966
4010-3 *MAGIC MARY JANE*, 1972
4010-3 *MAGIC MARY JANE*, 1975 (new doll, clothes the same as year 1972)
4010-4 *MAGIC MARY LOU* new in 1950, (from #4489A)
4010-4 *MAGIC MARY ANN*, 1955
4010-4 *MAGIC MARY LOU*, 1958
4010-4 *MAGIC MARY LOU*, 1962 (doll in same pose as 1958, but re-drawn)
4010-4 *MAGIC MARY LOU*, 1966
4010-4 *MAGIC MARY LOU*, 1972
4030 *THE ANIMATED CINDERELLA DOLL*
4042 *TWO-GUN PETE* new in 1950, (magnetic paper doll)
4043 *BRONCO BESS* new in 1950, (magnetic paper doll)
4053 *CUTIE PAPER DOLLS* (two dolls from McLoughlin #552)
4101 *THE ANIMATED GOLDILOCKS DOLL WITH THE THREE BEARS*
4106 *RAGGEDY ANN CUT OUT DOLLS*, 1941 (dolls from McLoughlin #547, new clothes)
4110 *SIX ANIMATED NURSERY RHYME DOLLS*
4112-1 *JEANS 'N THINGS*-Bells and Beads, 1971
4112-2 *JEANS 'N THINGS*-Rags and Jeans, 1971
4132 *MAGIC MARY* (drawn by Emma McKean, new in 1946 catalog)
4132-B *MAGIC MARY* (doll drawn by Betty Campbell, clothes from #4132)
4236 *SUNNY THE WONDER DOLL*
4319 *BRADLEY'S TRU-LIFE PAPER DOLLS* (new in 1914 catalog, contains 3 dolls)
4319 *BRADLEY'S TRU-LIFE PAPER DOLLS* patented March 21, 1916 (box cover is same as above 1914 set but dolls are new)
4320 *BRADLEY'S TRU-LIFE PAPER DOLLS* (new in 1914 catalog, contains 6 dolls)
4321 *BRADLEY'S TRU-LIFE PAPER DOLLS* (new in 1914 catalog, contains 12 dolls)
4374 *PEGGY AND POLLY*, 1934 (issued under two different box covers. Reprint of Diane and Daphne McLoughlin #545)
4382 *BETTY AND BARBARA, ROUND ABOUT DOLLS*, 1934 (McLoughlin #545 and #550)
4396 *JEAN AND JOAN AND THEIR FRIENDS*, 1934 (not pictured; from McLoughlin #545 & #550)
4414 *THREE DOLLS WITH ROUND ABOUT DRESSES* (same set as #4489A, new box cover)
4425 *TELEVISION DOLLS*
4441 *PATTY DUKE*, 1963 (not pictured)
4447 *THE TWINS, ROUND ABOUT DOLLS*, 1935 (McLoughlin #555 Ten Round About Dolls)
4489 *WOOD DOLLS WITH ROUND ABOUT DRESSES* (dolls originally from McLoughlin #545)
4489A *WOOD DOLLS WITH ROUND ABOUT DRESSES* (new in 1949 catalog)
4552 *FIVE ROUND ABOUT WOOD DOLLS* (McLoughlin #555 Ten Round about Dolls)
4716 *CUTIE DOLLS* (one doll)
4717 *CUTIE DOLLS* (two dolls)
4727 *DOLLIES DRESSES TO COLOR AND CUT OUT*
4727 *LITTLE FOLKS DOLL'S SET* (three dolls same as the 1914 set of #4319, only this set contains six crayons and all outfits are to be colored)
4727 *THE MODS*, 1967 (not pictured)
4746 *NURSERY RHYME DOLLS*, 1957 (four dolls, not pictured; see #4110)
4785 *SLEEPY TIME GIRL* (doll has eyes that move and is from McLoughlin #545)
4790 *CUTIE PAPER DOLLS* (four dolls from McLoughlin #549)
4792 *TWINKLEY EYES*, The Baby Doll Who Looks Around (eyes move)
4815 *MAGNETIC SUE*, 1947
4833 *WINNIE*, The Great Big Baby Doll (not pictured; doll same #4792 but eyes do not move)
4847 *MERRIE WITH THE GO-ROUND DRESSES* (McLoughlin #545)
4900 *DELUXE MAGIC MARY DRESS DESIGNERS KIT*, 1959 (doll same as #4010-1, year 1955)
4944 *NEW FOLDING DOLL HOUSE* listed in 1922 catalog, no paper dolls
7007 *I WISH I WERE*, 1964 game with paper dolls and outfits

The following is a list of Bradley's picture cut-outs.

8206 *NURSERY RHYMES* (jointed dolls)
8207 *BILLY BOBTAIL AND HIS FRIENDS* (jointed dolls)
8208 *PICTURE BUILDING WITH CUT-OUTS* Folio One
8209 *PICTURE BUILDING WITH CUT-OUTS* Folio two
8210 *POSTER PATTERNS*
8211 *CUT-OUT DOLLS AND ANIMALS THAT WILL STAND*
8212 *FAIRY TALES* (jointed dolls)
8213 *THE FAMILY* (jointed dolls)
8214 *ALICE IN WONDERLAND* (jointed dolls)
8215 *MOTHER GOOSE* (jointed dolls)
8216 *TOYLAND* (jointed dolls)
8219 *THE HAPPY HOUR PORTFOLIO* (some cut-outs are included)
8243 *DESIGNS FOR BEGINNERS IN WOODWORK*
8244 *POSTER DESIGNS*
8249 *BRADLEY'S FURNITURE CUT-OUTS*
8256 *BRADLEY'S WINDOW DECORATIONS*
8297 *BRADLEY'S CHARACTER DOLLS*
8298 *THE HAPPY FAMILY*, 1923 (five paper dolls to color, including outfits)
8299 *OTHER GIRLS AND BOYS* (patterns of dolls in other lands)

The following 8300 numbers are all stand-ups

8301 *DUTCH VILLAGE*
8302 *JAPANESE VILLAGE*
8303 *ESKIMO VILLAGE*
8304 *ARABIAN VILLAGE*
8305 *AFRICAN VILLAGE*
8306 *PILGRIM VILLAGE*
8307 *INDIAN VILLAGE*
8308 *FILIPINO VILLAGE*
8309 *ABRAHAM LINCOLN* (His home in Indiana)
8360 *HINDU VILLAGE*
8361 *GEORGE WASHINGTON* (Mt. Vernon Home)
8362 *THE LANDING OF COLUMBUS*
8363 *SANTA CLAUS* (village church, children, toys, houses etc.)
8364 *CHINESE VILLAGE*
8365 *MEXICAN VILLAGE*
8366 *OLDE JAMES TOWNE*
8450 *CHILDREN'S PARTY* (novelty cut-outs for parties)
8451 *CHILDREN'S GIFT SHOP* (designs for gifts children can make)
8452 *LITTLE NEIGHBORS OF MANY LANDS*, 1926 (stand-ups)
8462 *THE ORANGE INDUSTRY* (stand-ups)
8463 *THE DATE INDUSTRY* (stand-ups)
8468 *HAPPY FAMILY DOLLS*
9251 *WALTON'S PLAYSET*, 1974 (stand-ups)

The following have no stock number

KOMICAL KUT-OUTS WITH CRAYONS (jointed dolls)
BRADLEY'S TRU-LIFE PAPER DOLLS, 1914 Some sets had no stock number on the box cover

4132 *MAGIC MARY*, 1946. $10.00
The first *Magic Mary*

The Milton Bradley Paper Dolls are reproduced by permission of the Milton Bradley Company.

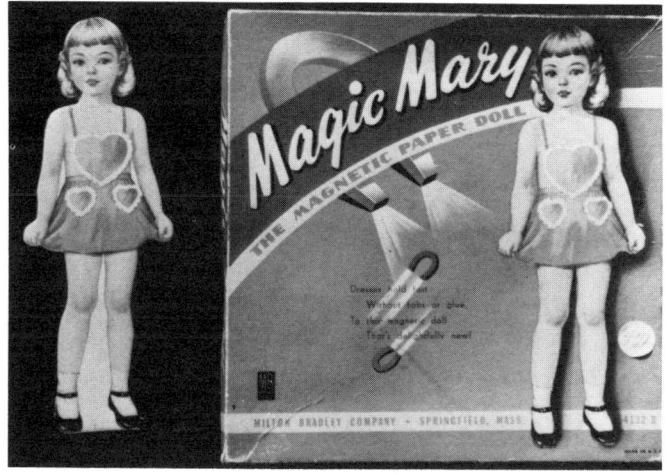

Courtesy of Rosalie Eppert

4132-B *MAGIC MARY*, new in 1948. $8.00
The second *Magic Mary*

Courtesy of Emma Terry

4010-1 *MAGIC MARY*, new in 1950. $7.00

4010-2 *MAGIC MARY ANN*, new in 1950. $7.00

4010-3 *MAGIC MARY JANE*, new in 1950. $7.00

Courtesy of Emma Terry

4010-4 *MAGIC MARY LOU*, new in 1950. $7.00

4010 *MAGIC MARY*, 1955. $7.00

Courtesy of Virginia Crossley

4010-2 *MAGIC MARY JANE*, 1955. $7.00

4010-3 *MAGIC MARY LOU*, 1955. $7.00

4010-4 *MAGIC MARY ANN*, 1955. $7.00

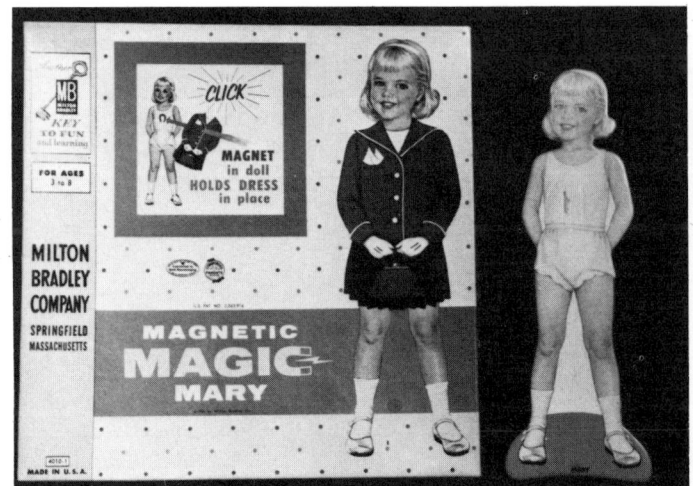

Courtesy of Virginia Crossley

4010-1 *MAGNETIC MAGIC MARY*, 1958. $7.00

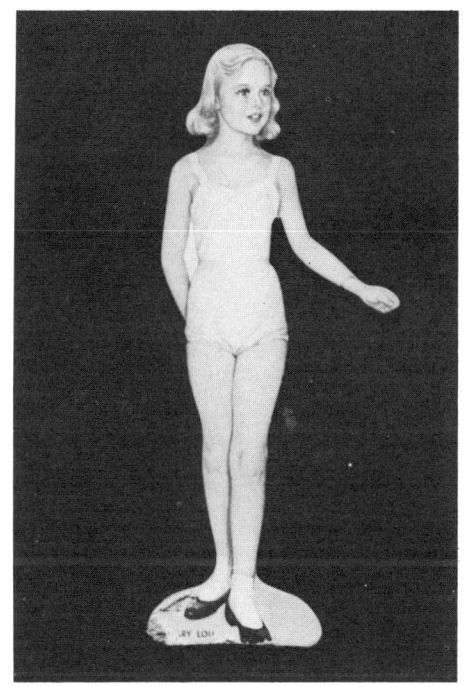

MAGIC MARY LOU, 1958. $7.00
Box not available

Courtesy of Virginia Crossley

MAGIC MARY JANE, 1958. $7.00
Box not available

Courtesy of Milton Bradley Co.
4010-1 *MAGIC MARY*, 1962. $6.00

4010-4 *MAGIC MARY LOU*, 1962. $6.00

4010-1 *MAGIC MARY*, 1966. $5.00

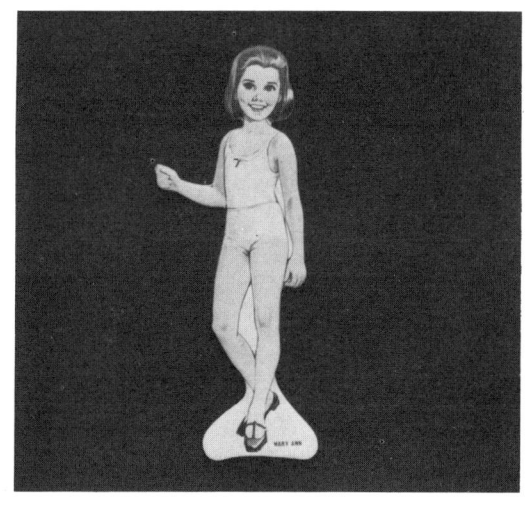

4010-2 *MAGIC MARY ANN*, 1966. $5.00

4010-3 *MAGIC MARY JANE*, 1966. $5.00

4010-4 *MAGIC MARY LOU*, 1966. $5.00

Courtesy of Virginia Crossley

4010-1 *MAGIC MARY*, 1972. $3.00

Courtesy of Virginia Crossley

4010-2 *MAGIC MARY ANN*, 1972. $3.00

Courtesy of Virginia Crossley

4010-3 *MAGIC MARY JANE*, 1972. $3.00

Courtesy of Virginia Crossley

4010-4 *MAGIC MARY LOU*, 1972. $3.00

4010-3 *MAGIC MARY JANE*, 1975. $2.00

Courtesy of Milton Bradley Co.

4900 *DELUXE MAGIC MARY*, 1959. $8.00
Dress Designers Kit

Courtesy of Virginia Crossley

4900 *DELUXE MAGIC MARY*, 1959
Doll and instructions

Courtesy of Audrey Sepponen

4030 *THE ANIMATED CINDERELLA DOLL*. $8.00

Courtesy of Audrey Sepponen

4042 *TWO-GUN PETE*, New in 1950. $8.00

4043 *BRONCO BESS*, new in 1950. $8.00

133

Courtesy of Milton Bradley Co.
4053 *CUTIE PAPER DOLLS.* $15.00

4053 *CUTIE PAPER DOLLS*
Box contents

Courtesy of Milton Bradley Co.
4110 6 *ANIMATED NURSERY RHYME DOLLS.* $8.00
Includes six dolls and six scenes

Courtesy of Betsy Slap
4101 *THE ANIMATED GOLDILOCKS DOLL.* $15.00

4106 *RAGGEDY ANN CUTOUT DOLLS* © 1941
Johnny Gruelle Co. $35.00

4106 *RAGGEDY ANN*
Dolls of Marcella, Raggedy Ann, Jane and Betty

 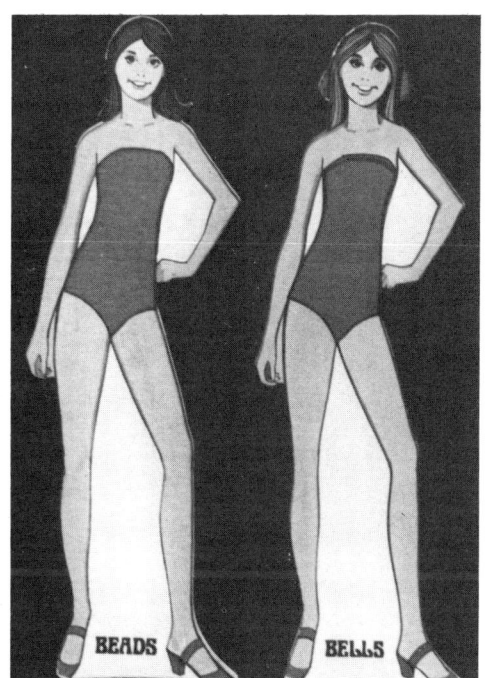 

4112-1 *JEANS'N THINGS, BELLS & BEADS*, 1971. $4.00

Courtesy of Milton Bradley Co.

4236 *SUNNY THE WONDER DOLL*. $8.00

4236 *SUNNY THE WONDER DOLL*
The outfits have tabs that slide under the belt at the doll's waist

4112-2 *JEANS'N THINGS, RAGS & JEANS*. $4.00

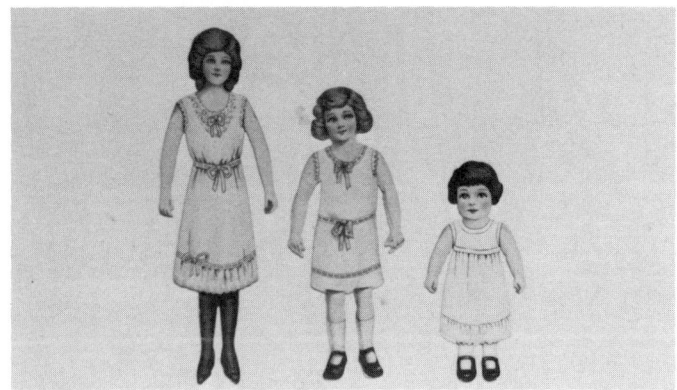
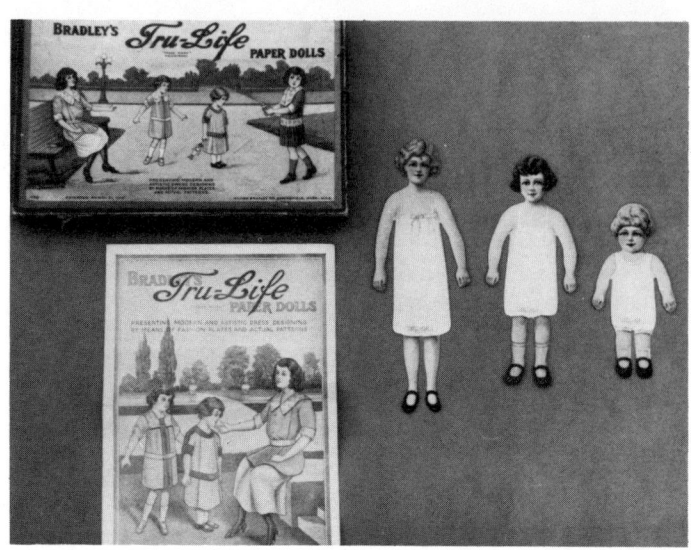

4319 *BRADLEY'S TRU-LIFE PAPER DOLLS*, 1914
These three dolls were also in Bradley's Tru-Life set #4320 in duplicate for a total of six dolls. The two dolls in each size are identical except one has blonde hair, the other brunette. Set #4321 contained four dolls of each size for a total of twelve dolls. The box cover and pamphlet are the same as the 1916 set pictured. Some early boxes of these sets did not have the stock number printed on the box.

Courtesy of Audrey Sepponen
4319 *BRADLEY'S TRU-LIFE PAPER DOLLS.* $35.00
Patented March 21, 1916

Courtesy of the Atlanta Toy Museum

Courtesy of Emma Terry
4374 *PEGGY AND POLLY*, 1934. $18.00

Courtesy of Milton Bradley Co.
4374 *PEGGY AND POLLY*, 1934. $18.00
Same as set on left, different cover

4382 *BETTY AND BARBARA*, 1934. $18.00

Courtesy of Milton Bradley Co.
4425 *TELEVISION DOLLS.* $12.00

4414 Three *DOLLS WITH ROUND ABOUT DRESSES*. $18.00

Courtesy of Audrey Sepponen

4447 *THE TWINS, ROUND ABOUT DOLLS*, 1935. $10.00

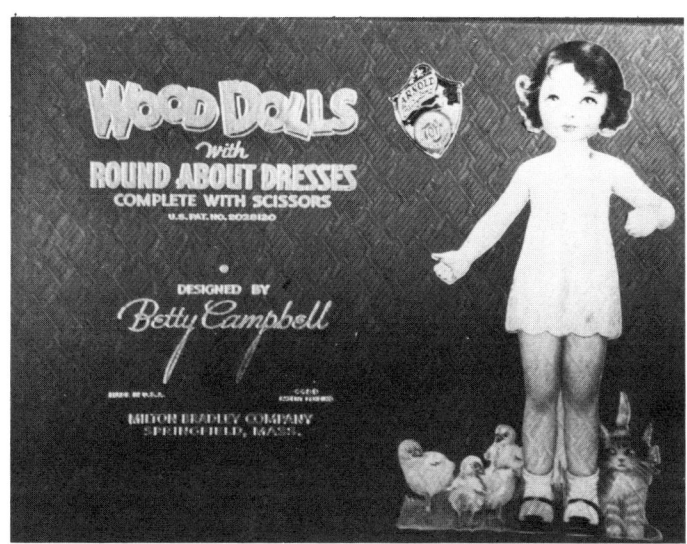

4489 *WOOD DOLLS WITH ROUND ABOUT DRESSES*. $20.00

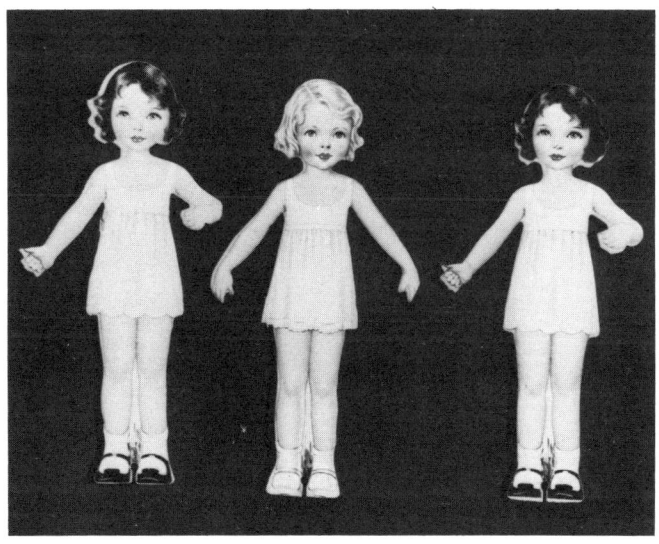

4489 There are three dolls in the set. Some sets have two of the blonde dolls and one brunette.

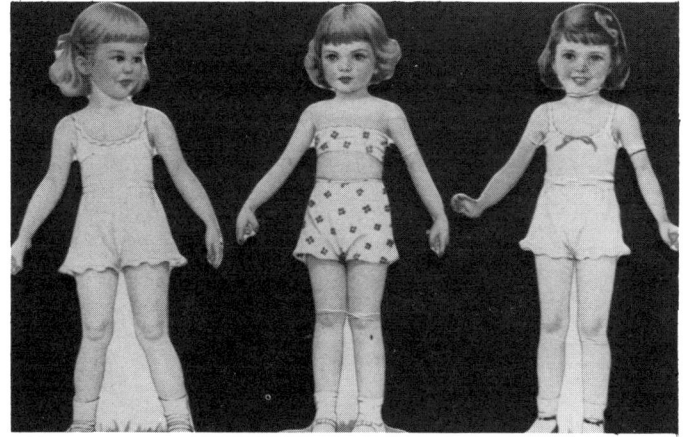

4489A *WOOD DOLLS WITH ROUND ABOUT DRESSES*, new in 1949. $20.00

4552 *FIVE ROUND ABOUT WOOD DOLLS.* $20.00

4552 The five dolls and one page of outfits

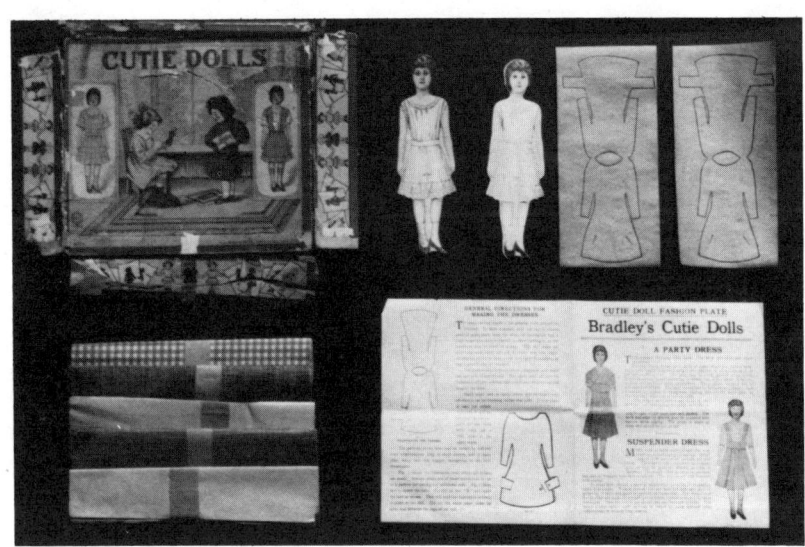
Courtesy of Emma Terry
4717 *CUTIE DOLLS* (2 doll set). $30.00

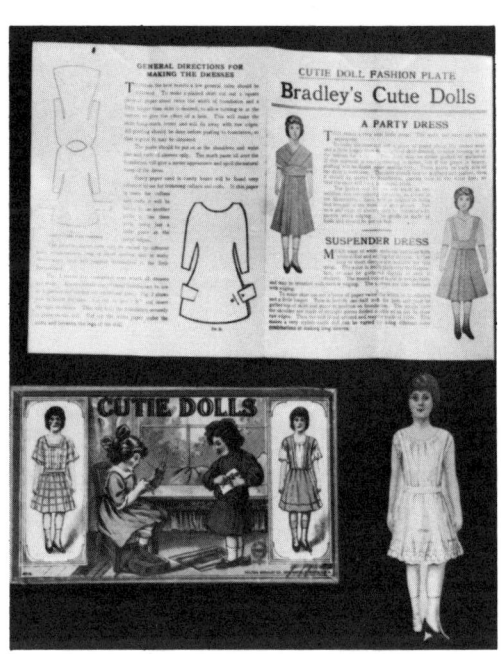
Courtesy of Virginia Crossley
4716 *CUTIE DOLLS* (1 doll set). $25.00

Courtesy of Zelda Cushner
4727 *DOLLIES DRESSES.* $35.00

4727 *DOLLIES DRESSES*
Doll and one sheet of clothes (to be colored)

4727 *LITTLE FOLKS DOLL'S SET.* $25.00

4727 *LITTLE FOLKS DOLL'S SET*
The dolls, one sheet of clothes and crayons.

Courtesy of Grace Battjes

4785 *SLEEPY TIME GIRL.* $12.00

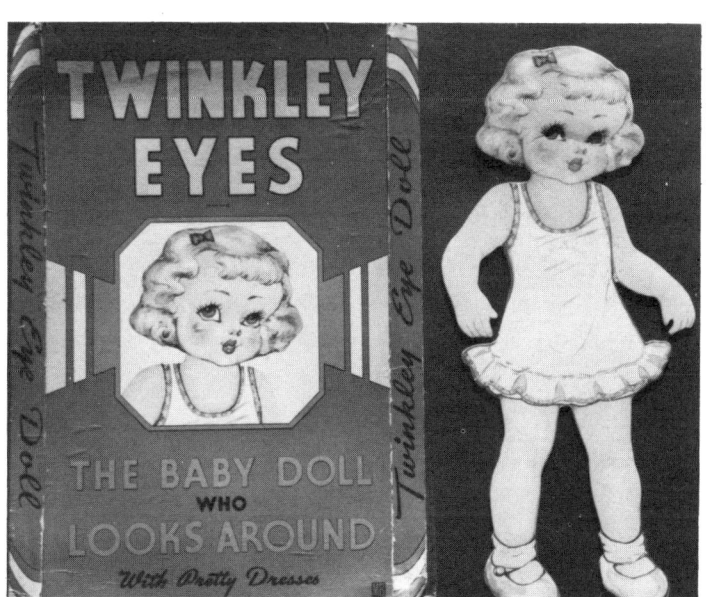

4792 *TWINKLEY EYES.* $12.00
(The set of Winnie #4833 is identical to this set except the eyes on the doll are not movable)

Courtesy of Milton Bradley Co.

4790 *CUTIE PAPER DOLLS.* $15.00

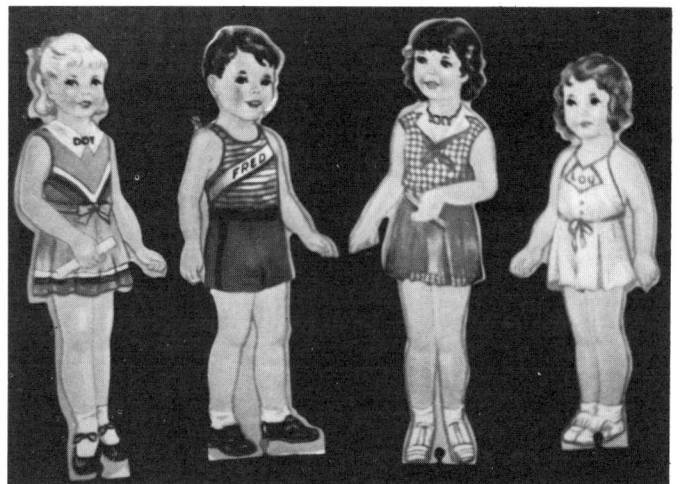

4790 *CUTIE PAPER DOLLS*
The four dolls in the set

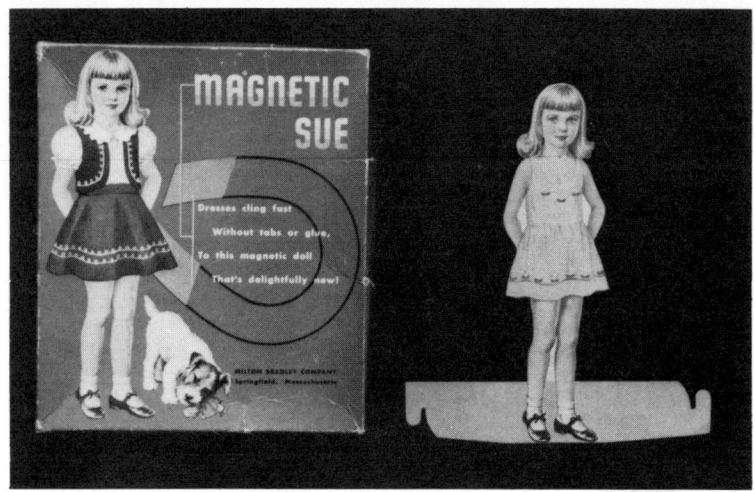

4815 *MAGNETIC SUE*, 1947. $10.00

Courtesy of Emma Terry

Courtesy of Milton Bradley Co.

4847 *MERRIE WITH THE GO-ROUND DRESSES*. $10.00

7007 *I WISH I WERE*, 1964. $6.00

Mold Trim Products

THE DOLLY BALLET, 1955 (not pictured; contains ten plastic dolls and sixty costumes)

My Ladye Faire Doll Company

Courtesy of Rosalie Eppert

MY LADYE FAIRE DOLL, EVENING GOWN SERIES #1. $35.00

National Art Company

Courtesy of Audrey Sepponen

MOTHER GOOSE CUT OUT PICTURE BOOK. $20.00

National Paper Box Company, Inc.

N12-29 *CIRCUS TWINS.* $5.00

N11-29 *WILD WEST TWINS.* $5.00

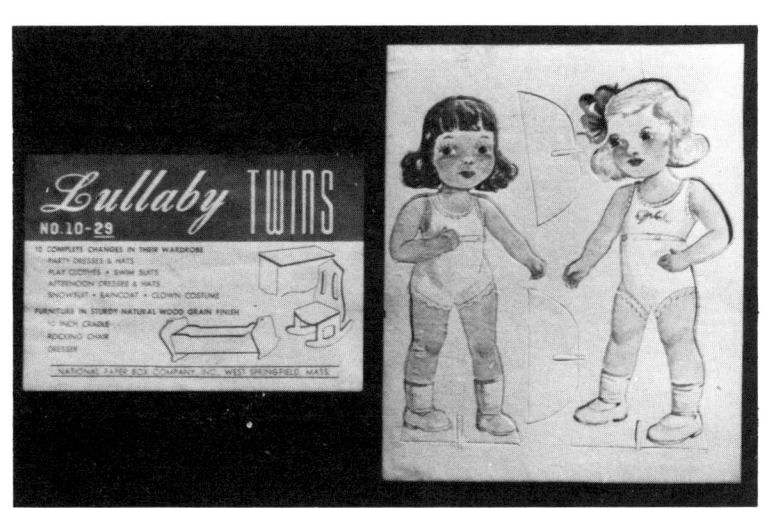

N10-29 *LULLABY TWINS.* $5.00

National Syndicate Displays, Inc.

Courtesy of Audrey Sepponen
77 *"STAND-UP" DOLLS*, 1942. $10.00

77-1 *SCHOOL DAYS*, 1943. $10.00

Courtesy of Audrey Sepponen
77-2 *BIRTHDAY PARTY*, 1944. $8.00

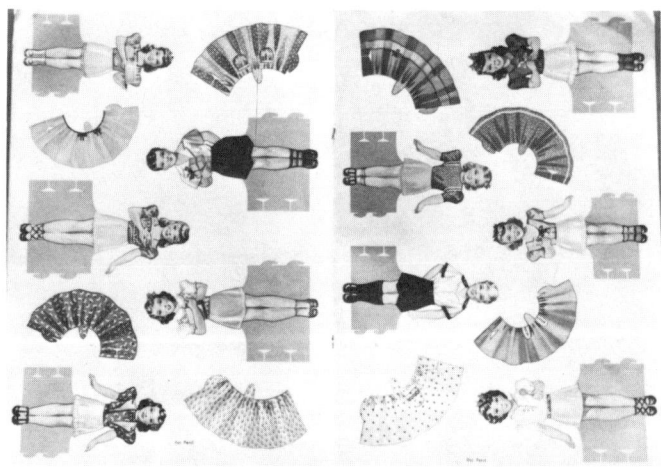

77-2 *BIRTHDAY PARTY*
Inside pages

Courtesy of Audrey Sepponen
777 *"STAND-UP" CUT OUT DOLLS WEDDING BOOK*. $10.00

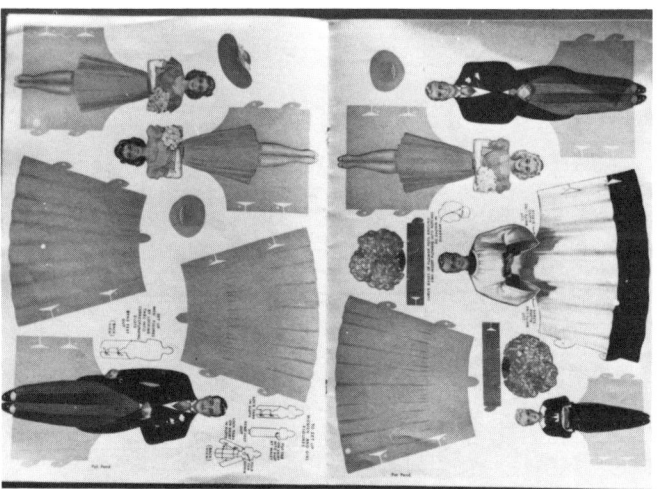

#777 Inside pages

Near East Foundation

BIBLE LAND CHILDREN, 1934. $8.00

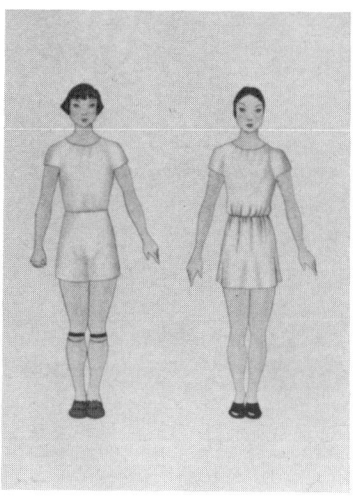

Inside page of dolls

O.W. Nelson

Each of the O.W. Nelson paper dolls came with three outfits and three hats. The outfits are marked "c 1914, O.W. Nelson". The dolls also say "c 1914 O.W. Nelson" plus "American Lithographic Co., N.Y." These dolls were also used for advertising Minard's Liniment. On the advertising version, the words, "I Talk For Minard's Liniment", were added at the bottom of the doll's stand, and the present that the doll is holding becomes a box containing the liniment. You will note the doll from the Atlanta Toy Museum is wearing an outfit that hides her pink dress that can be seen on the advertising doll.

Courtesy of Jane Sugg
20½" *MINARD'S LINIMENT DOLL*. $50.00

Courtesy of Jane Sugg
20½" *MINARD'S LINIMENT DOLL*. $50.00

20½" O.W. NELSON DOLL, 1914. $50.00

Courtesy of Virginia Crossley

20½" O.W. NELSON DOLL, 1914. $50.00
Pictured are two of the doll's outfits. The third outfit is shown with the doll's advertising counterpart.

Courtesy of the Atlanta Toy Museum

New York Book Company

Courtesy of Rosemary McBurnett

DOLLS OF ALL NATIONS 1911. $20.00

Elizabeth (American)

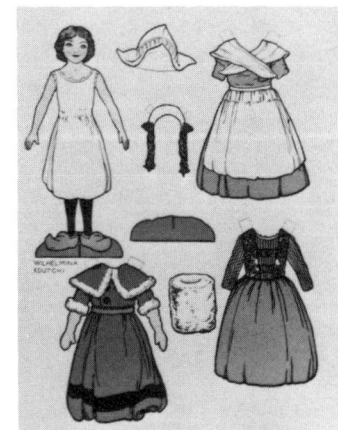

Wilhelmina (Dutch)

Pitti Sing (Japanese)

Minne-ha-ha (Indian)

San Toy (Chinese)

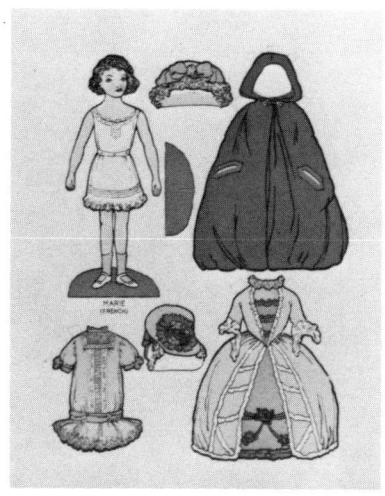
Marie (French)

Carmencita (Spanish)

Romola (Italian)

The Nourse Company

The Nourse Company evolved from the Platt and Nourse Company which originally began as Platt and Peck. When Mr. Platt left the Platt and Nourse Company to form a new book company with Arnold Munk, the Nourse Company operation lasted for a few years before it was bought out by Platt and Munk. Older books originally published by Platt and Peck and Platt and Nourse continued to be sold by the Nourse Co. along with new original books. Many of the earlier Platt and Nourse books were also reprinted by the Platt and Munk Co.

There were at least three paper doll books published originally by the Nourse Company in 1921 after Mr. Platt had departed from the firm. One of the books, "Dolls from Fairyland", by Lois Lenski, was a companion book to "Dolls From The Land Of Mother Goose" that had been published in 1918 by Platt and Nourse. A completely un-cut book has not been found, but the dolls are pictured here. Some of the costumes depict Goldilocks, Snowdrop, Hansel, Gretel and Jack the Giant Killer. Another book is "Nayan Dolls No. 1". (If there is a Nayan Dolls No. 2, a copy has yet to show up.) The third book is the delightful "Teddy Bear and His Friends To Dress".

The following were sold by the Nourse Company:

BEAUTIFUL DOLLS FOR CHILDREN TO DRESS, 1915 (see Platt and Peck for picture)
DOLLIES TO DRESS LIKE FATHER AND MOTHER (see Platt and Munk #225 for picture)
DOLLS FROM FAIRYLAND, 1921 (pictured)
DOLLS FROM THE LAND OF MOTHER GOOSE, 1918 (see Platt and Munk #221 for picture)
MARY AND TEDDY CUT OUT DOLLS (originally published by Platt and Nourse)
NAYAN DOLLS No. 1, 1921 (pictured)
PLAYROOM TOYS TO CUT OUT, 1921 (paper toys)
TEDDY BEAR AND HIS FRIENDS TO DRESS, 1921 (pictured)
TOY ANIMALS I CAN MAKE (paper toys)
TOY ARMY I CAN MAKE (paper toys)

Courtesy of Grayce Piemontesi
NAYAN DOLLS NO. 1. $30.00

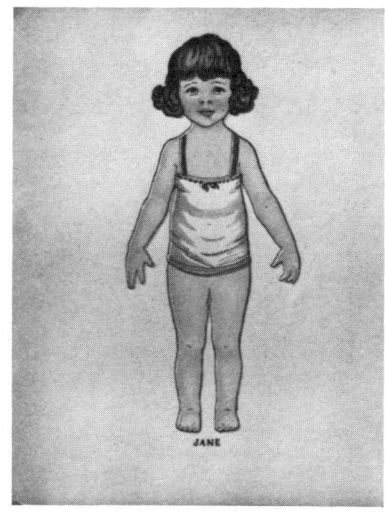
JANE

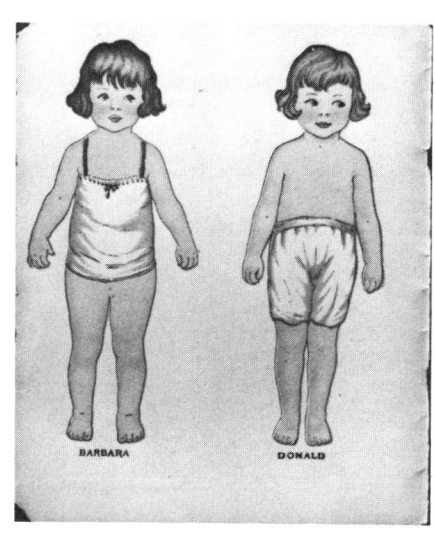
BARBARA   *DONALD*

Courtesy of Jean Woodcock

TEDDY BEAR AND HIS FRIENDS TO DRESS, 1921. $40.00

DOLLS FROM FAIRYLAND, 1921. $25.00

Novel Products Corporation

 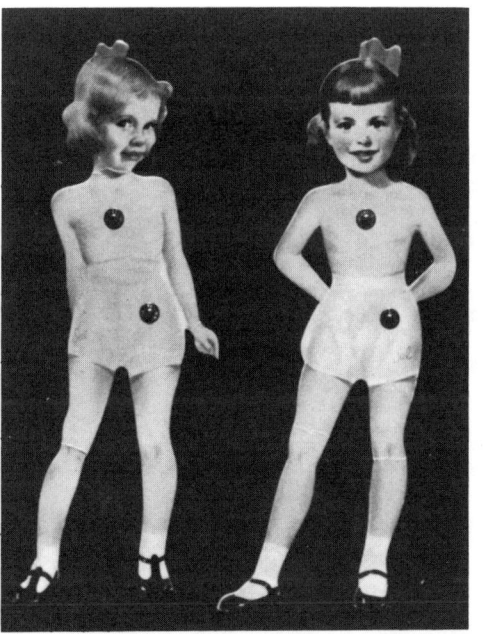

SUE AND SAL, THE SNAP-ON SISTERS. $10.00

Nutmeg Press

 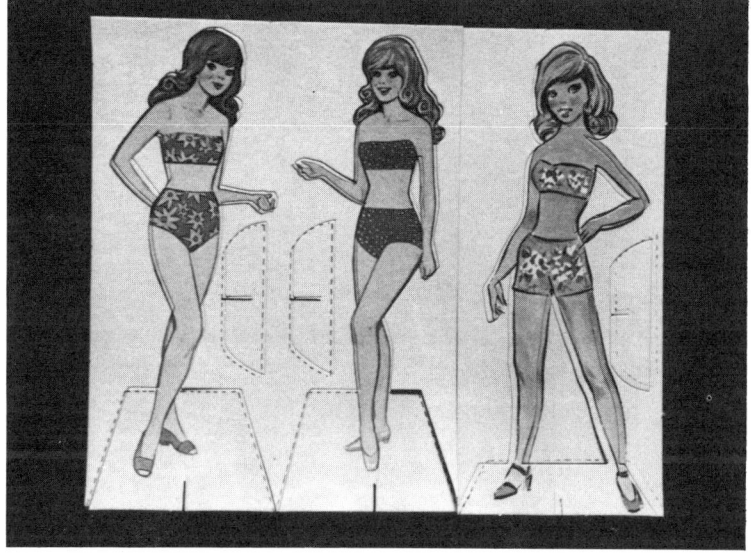

954 *DRESS-UPS*. $4.00   954 *DRESS-UPS*

Olde Deerfield Doll House

This set of paper dolls depicts a true story, the massacre of Deerfield, Massachusetts, in 1704. The paper dolls are of six children. Five of the children represent captives that were carried off to Canada by the Indians. The sixth paper doll is of the Indian, Arosen, who later married one of the captives. Included in the set are six very small books that relate to and illustrate in color the true story of each of the characters portrayed.

Two of the children belonged to the family of John Williams. The Williams house is pictured on the front of the folder and Arosen's wigwam is shown on the back. When cut out and folded, these pieces are able to stand up. They measure 9½" x 21¼" each.

OLDE DEERFIELD DOLLS, 1919. $60.00

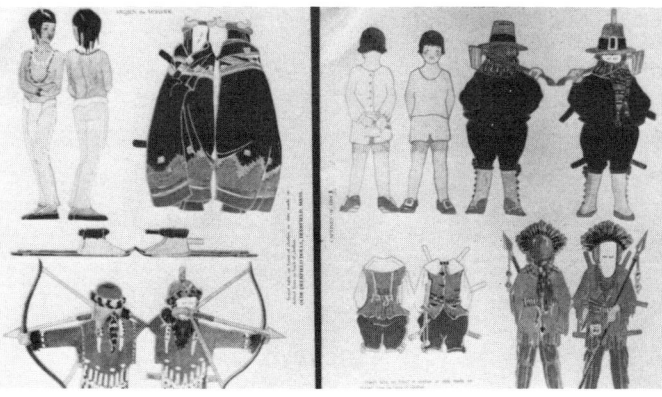 

Ottenheimer Publishers, Inc.

The following paper doll books are not pictured:

2060-5 *MY FAIR LADY*, 1965   2961-0 *MY FAIR LADY*, 1965
2960-2 *MY FAIR LADY*, 1965   5860-2 *MY FAIR LADY*, 1965

J. Ottmann Lithograph Company

The Ottmann Co. also published a book of stand-up toys called "Buster Brown's Parade".

Courtesy of Audrey Sepponen
BUSTER BROWN AND TIGE. $75.00

Courtesy of Jane Sugg
CHANTICLEER PAPER DOLL. $75.00

FLUFFY RUFFLES, 1907. $60.00

Courtesy of Rosalie Eppert
TEDDY BEAR PAPER DOLL. $75.00

L.C. Page and Company

The following paper doll books are not pictured:

THE LITTLE COLONEL DOLL BOOK, 1910
A hardcover book with 48 sheets of paper dolls and outfits. There are ten paper dolls. All dolls were from the *LITTLE COLONEL SERIES* of story books by Annie Fellows Johnston.

THE MARY WARE DOLL BOOK, 1914
A hardback book with 48 sheets of paper dolls and outfits. There are ten paper dolls. This is a companion volume to the *LITTLE COLONEL DOLL BOOK* listed above. All dolls were from the *LITTLE COLONEL SERIES* of story books by Annie Fellows Johnston.

Paper Palace

The Paper Palace was established by Robert Middlestetter in 1981. His first paper doll book is called "Victoria" and contains 14 pages. Besides the paper dolls and outfits there are background scenes which include a millinery shop, a street scene and a parlor set. "Victoria" is currently on the market and a second paper doll book is planned for the near future.

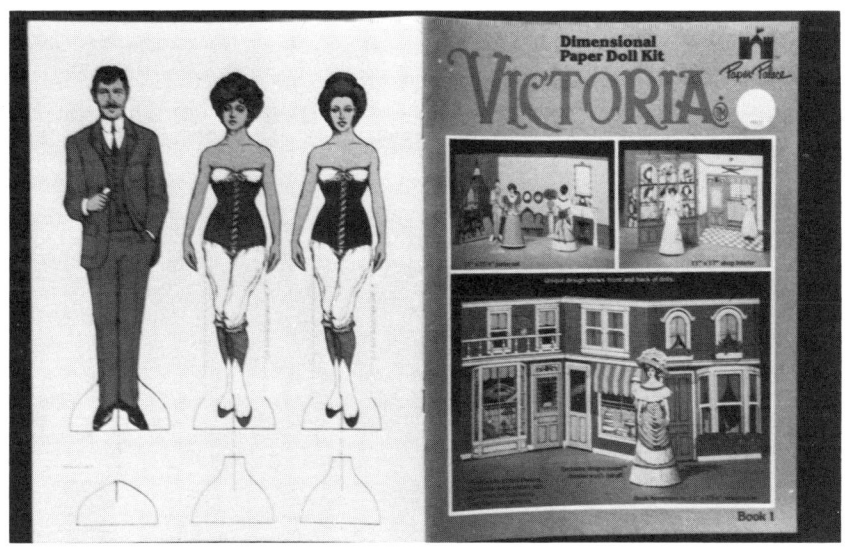

VICTORIA ©1981 Paper Palace, Dimensional Paper Doll Kit, Book I, currently available

Parker Brothers, Inc.

George Parker invented and published his first game in 1883 when he was only 16 years old. The name of his first game was "Banking". While still in high school he published two more games, and by the age of 18, he had introduced five more games to the public. One of these last five games was a new edition of the old game of "Dr. Busby". The game had been invented years before by the Ives Co. of Salem, Massachusetts. George Parker bought the rights to the game, and a few years later he bought out the rights to all the old Ives games. One of these games, "The Mansion of Happiness" was among the first board games made in America, which Mr. Parker reissued.

In just five years since he published his first game, the business had grown so large that Parker needed someone to share the responsibilities. When his older brother Charles joined him, the firm became known as Parker Brothers. Eleven years later in 1898 their oldest brother Edward joined the firm.

George Parker spent hour after hour testing each new game the company produced. He would play the games with friends and employees, always alert to how they reacted and how well they were able to understand and follow the rules. He continued to write the rules for all games produced even after the firm had grown into a large corporation.

In 1893 at the Chicago World's Fair, Parker Brothers won the highest award for their games; and at the St. Louis World's Fair a decade later, the company won the Grand Prize. Parker Brothers has been in the game business for 100 years now. The list of games produced through the years is endless, but any history of Parker wouldn't be complete without mention of their most popular and biggest selling game in the world, "Monopoly® ." The game came on the market in 1935 and was an instant hit with children and adults of all ages. In the newest Parker catalog, there are now four editions of "Monopoly® " ranging from their regular edition to their electronic edition. Other old favorites such as "Risk® ", "Clue® " and "Sorry® " are now in company with such new games as "Annie™" and "Garfield™" In 1968 Parker Brothers was sold and is now a part of General Mills.

Paper dolls by Parker Brothers made their appearance in 1917. Their catalog that year listed five "Improved Paper Doll Outfits" ranging from 50 cents to $1.50. The dolls had jointed arms and legs. The larger sets included a large girl doll, a medium sized girl and a small boy. The smaller sets had only two dolls including the small boy and either one of the girl dolls.

These "Improved Paper Doll Outfits" were sold by Parker Brothers until 1934. Since the crepe paper outfits found in the Parker sets are similar, and in some cases identical, to the Dennison's outfits it may be assumed that Dennison supplied Parker with the printed crepe paper and most likely all the inside paper material in the boxes. Although no Parker sets have been found containing Dennison Dolls, the booklet of instructions shows dolls from Dennison set #33.

In the Parker Brothers 1939 catalog, the Magic Dolls of "Princess Elizabeth" and "Princess Margaret Rose" are featured. These dolls are of heavy cardboard and have a special surface that allows the cloth clothes to cling to the dolls. Two other magic dolls, "Susie" and "Baby Doll" are also in this 1939 catalog. The Magic Dolls of "Princess Elizabeth" and "Princess Margaret Rose" were also sold in England and Canada by the Somerville Paper Boxes Limited. It's very possible that Parker Brothers bought the rights from Somerville. More Magic Dolls, including a large 14½" "Miss America", were introduced in the 1950's, and still others in the 1960's.

As Parker Brothers enters their second century of operation, they are now into additional products such as video cartridges and other electronic games. Also, they have recently entered the field of publishing children's books.

Bibliography: *75 Years of Fun, The Story of Parker Brothers, Inc.*
100 Years of Fun, The Story of Parker Brothers 1883-1983

AMERICAN MISS MAGIC DOLL, 1957
IMPROVED PAPER DOLL OUTFIT, 1917, large size with deep double-deck box (not pictured)
IMPROVED PAPER DOLL OUTFIT, 1917, large 16 x 10½" size
IMPROVED PAPER DOLL OUTFIT, 1917, large 16 x 10" size
IMPROVED PAPER DOLL OUTFIT, 1917, small 14 x 9¼" size (not pictured)
IMPROVED PAPER DOLL OUTFIT, 1917, small 13½" x 9" size
LOVEY AND DOVEY MAGIC DOLLS, 1951
THE MAGIC BABY DOLL (not pictured; listed in 1939 catalog)
THE MAGIC DOLL, SUSIE (not pictured; listed in 1939 catalog)
THE MAGIC DOLL listed in 1947-48 catalog

MAGIC DOLL, large 14" doll listed in 1948-49 catalog
MAGIC DOLL, small 7¼" doll listed in 1948-49 catalog
THE MAGIC DOLL, for the *LITTLE DRESSMAKER* (reprint of the original "Susie" listed above)
MAGIC DOLL, 1961
MAGIC DOLL, 1961 (different from above)
MAGIC DOLL, 1963
MISS AMERICA MAGIC DOLL, listed in 1953 catalog
PAPER DOLL OUTFIT #802, 1917
PRINCESS ELIZABETH MAGIC DOLL, 1939
PRINCESS MARGARET ROSE MAGIC DOLL, 1939

Courtesy of Parker Bros.

AMERICAN MISS MAGIC DOLL, 1957. $15.00

Courtesy of Virginia Crossley

IMPROVED PAPER DOLL OUTFIT. $35.00
Size 16 x 10½"

The three dolls from IMPROVED PAPER DOLL OUTFIT

Courtesy of Parker Bros.

IMPROVED PAPER DOLL OUTFIT, 1917. $32.50
The inside contents of the third largest set. The box cover is the same for all sets of IMPROVED PAPER DOLL OUTFITS

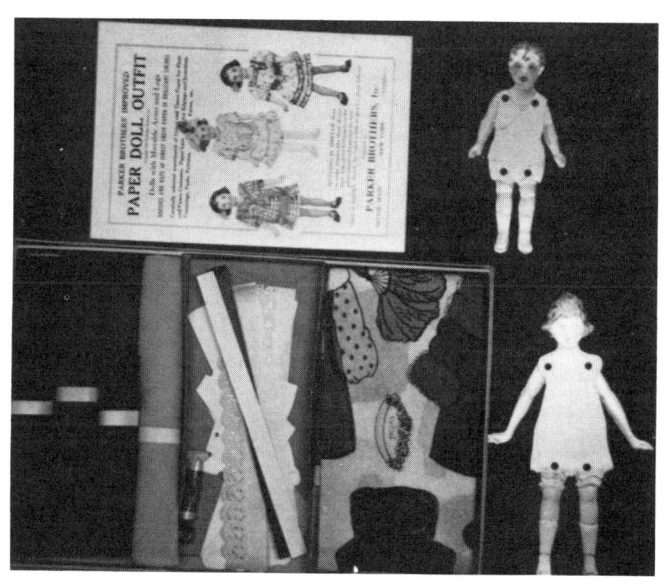

Courtesy of Parker Bros.

IMPROVED PAPER DOLL OUTFIT, 1917. $30.00
The inside contents of the smallest set

IMPROVED PAPER DOLL OUTFIT
Instruction booklet. Notice the dolls pictured are from Dennison set #33.

Courtesy of Audrey Sepponen

LOVEY AND DOVEY MAGIC DOLLS, 1951. $15.00

THE MAGIC DOLL. $15.00
Listed in 1947-48 catalog (reprint of Princess Elizabeth)

Courtesy of Rosalie Eppert
THE MAGIC DOLL. $15.00
Listed in 1948-49 catalog

Courtesy of Rosalie Eppert
THE MAGIC DOLL. $12.00
Listed in 1948-49 catalog

Courtesy of Parker Bros.

THE MAGIC DOLL, for the *LITTLE DRESSMAKER.* $12.00

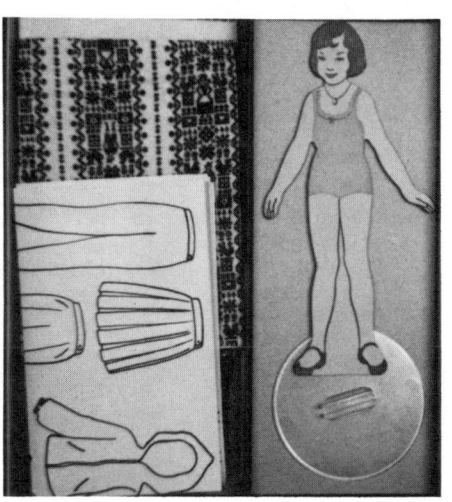

MAGIC DOLL, 1961. $8.00

Courtesy of Parker Bros.

MAGIC DOLL, 1961. $8.00

Courtesy of Parker Bros.
Box contents of *MAGIC DOLL*, 1961

Courtesy of Parker Bros.
MAGIC DOLL, 1963. $8.00

Box contents of *MAGIC DOLL*, 1963

Courtesy of Parker Bros.
MISS AMERICA MAGIC DOLL. $18.00
Listed in 1953 catalog

MISS AMERICA MAGIC DOLL

Courtesy of Parker Bros.
802 *PAPER DOLL OUTFIT*, 1917. $30.00

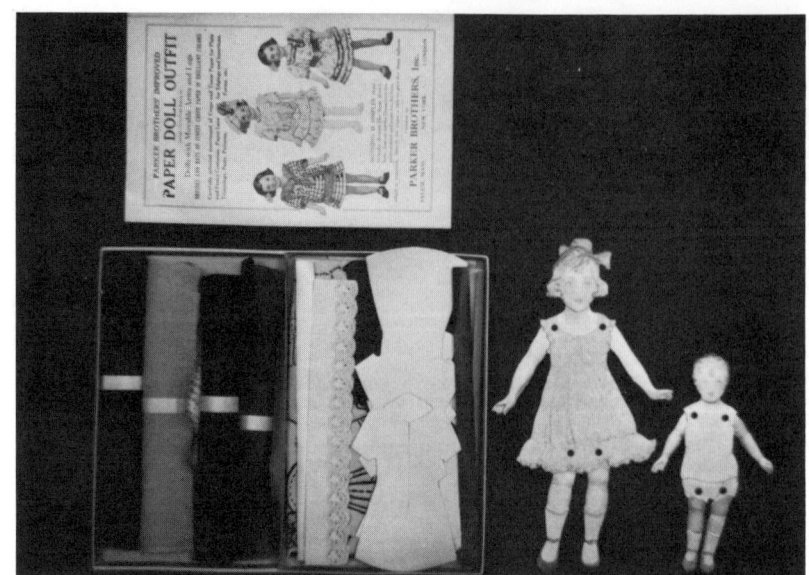

Box contents of *PAPER DOLL OUTFIT* #802

Courtesy of Parker Bros.
PRINCESS ELIZABETH MAGIC DOLL.
$25.00

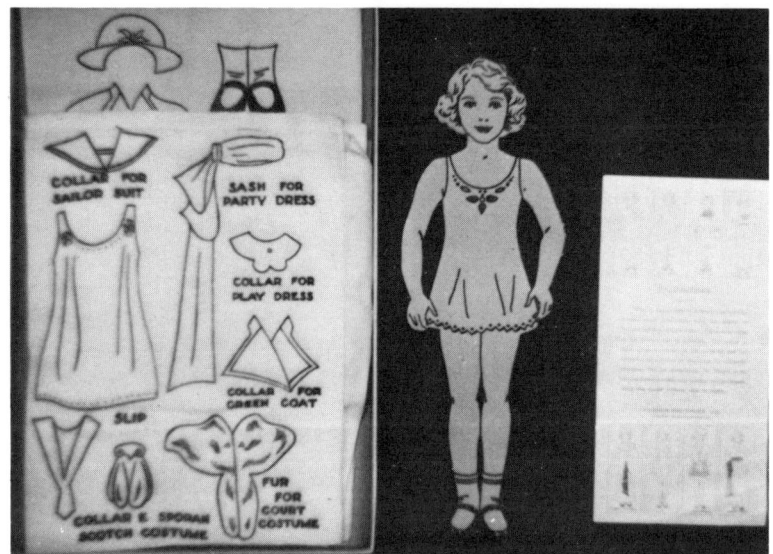

Box contents of *PRINCESS ELIZABETH MAGIC DOLL*

Courtesy of Betsy Slap
PRINCESS MARGARET ROSE MAGIC DOLL. $25.00

Patcher Company

Courtesy of Virginia Crossley

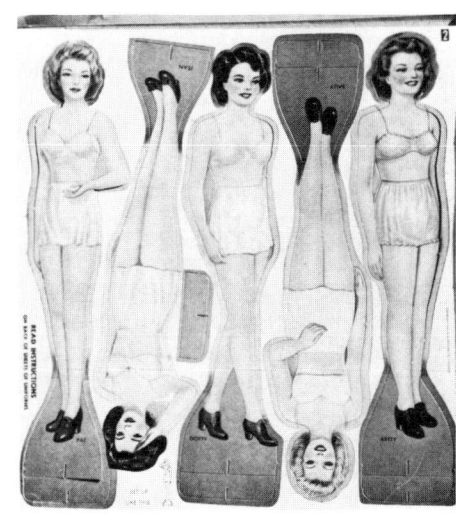

#80 *BILD-A-SET, 10 BEAUTIFUL JUNIOR GIRLS IN UNIFORMS*, 1943 $35.00

Pinkham Press

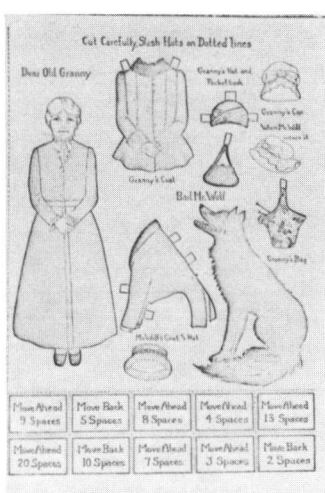

TRIPLE-JOY-BOOK, 1927. $25.00
Story, Paper Dolls and Game

Courtesy of Jean Woodcock

Pla-Mor Toy Company

FOLLIES GIRL, JACKIE. $17.50
Paper doll puzzle

Courtesy of Richard Rusnock

Platt and Munk Company, Inc

The Platt and Munk Company was established in 1920. Mr. Platt had previously been a partner in the Platt and Nourse Co. and, before that, the Platt and Peck Co. which also published books.

The Platt and Munk Co. published some of the most beautiful books for children and, later, activity sets were included in their line of products. Paper dolls were produced right from the start, though some were reprints of paper dolls previously published by the Platt and Nourse Co.

In the late 1960's Platt and Munk became a division of Questor Education Products. Four of the company's most recent paper doll sets were reprinted in 1969 by Platt and Munk as a division of Child Guidance Products, Inc. which was a division of Questor. The four sets are "Early American Dolls", "Betsy Ross", "Dolls of Far-Off Lands" and "Dolls Across the Sea".

190 *TEDDY BEAR AND HIS FRIENDS*-Box set which includes three paper doll books. The paper dolls in these books originated in the Nourse Co. book of *TEDDY BEAR AND HIS FRIENDS*, 1921. The three books are:
    190A *BEAR AND MONKEY*
    190B *KITTY AND DOGGIE*
    190C *PIGGY AND BUNNY*
205 *MODERN DOLLS TO CUT OUT AND DRESS*, box set (dolls same as #210 below)
210 *BETTY ANN AND HER FRIENDS*-Box set which includes three paper doll books:
    210A *BETTY ANN AND AUDREY*
    210B *JEAN AND TOMMY*
    210C *JANET AND DICK*
220 *DOLLS' OPEN HOUSE*, 1963
220 *BEAUTIFUL DOLLS FOR CHILDREN TO DRESS* (not pictured: see Platt & Peck)
221 *DOLLS FROM THE LAND OF MOTHER GOOSE* (reprint of the original Platt & Nourse book)
222 *TEDDY BEAR AND HIS FRIENDS TO DRESS* (not pictured; see Nourse Co.)
224A *EARLY AMERICAN DOLLS*, 1963 (four dolls from #242)
224B *BETSY ROSS*, 1963 (four dolls from #242)
225 *DOLLIES TO DRESS LIKE FATHER AND MOTHER* (reprint of original Platt & Nourse book)
225A *GAY DOLLS*, 1942 (two dolls from #229)
225B *PARTY DOLLS*, 1942 (two dolls from #229)
225B *PRETTY DOLLS TO CUT OUT, COLOR AND DRESS*
225C *PRETTY DOLLS*, 1942 (two dolls from #229)
225D *YOUNG MISS DOLLS*, 1942 (two dolls from #229)
226A *COSTUME DOLLS*, 1962 (four dolls from #243)
226B *HISTORICAL DOLLS*, 1962 (four dolls from #243)
227A *BETTY ANN AND HER FRIENDS* (four dolls from #229)
227B *PLAYTIME DOLLS* (four dolls from #229)
228A *DOLLS ACROSS THE SEA*, 1965 (four dolls from #241)
228B *DOLLS OF FAR-OFF LANDS*, 1965 (four dolls from #241)
229 *JUNIOR MISS DOLLS*, 1942
230B *BETTY AND PEGGY*, 1937 (two dolls from #240, date 1937)
230C *JANET AND JEANNE* 1937 (two dolls from #240, date 1937)
230D *GOING ABROAD DOLLS*, 1937 (two dolls from #240, date 1937)
235A *I'M GROWING UP DOLLS*, 1937 (four dolls from #240, date 1937)
235B *MARY LOU AND HER FRIENDS*, 1937 (four dolls from #240, date 1937)
240 *AT HOME ABROAD DOLLS*, 1937
240 *MODERN DOLLS*, 1957
241 *FOREIGN DOLLS*, 1957
242 *COLONIAL DOLLS*, 1960
243 *CENTURY DOLLS*, 1960
245 *WILLIAMSBURG COLONIAL DOLLS*, 1967
330 *BETTY AND JACK* (for picture see Platt & Nourse, also Platt & Peck "Beautiful Dolls")
331 *PRETTY DOLLS TO DRESS*
335 *DOROTHY AND RUTH* (for picture see Platt & Nourse, also see Platt & Peck book of "Beautiful Dolls")
360 *THE LITTLE CHERUBS*, 1921
370 *THE LITTLE BUNTINGS*, 1921 (two girl dolls)
370 *THE LITTLE BUNTINGS*, 1921 (one girl and one boy doll)
390 *LITTLE BOY BLUE*, 1921
1250 *EARLY AMERICAN DOLLS*, 1969 (reprint, see #224A)
1251 *BETSY ROSS*, 1969 (reprint, see #224B)
1252 *DOLLS OF FAR-OFF LANDS*, 1969 (reprint, see #228B)
1253 *DOLLS ACROSS THE SEA*, 1969 (reprint, see #228A)

Courtesy of Richard Rusnock

Courtesy of Richard Rusnock

190B *KITTY & DOGGIE*
This is one of three books contained in the box pictured on the left. For pictures of the remaining dolls, see *TEDDY BEAR AND HIS FRIENDS TO DRESS* pictured with the Nourse Co. paper dolls.

190 *TEDDY BEAR AND HIS FRIENDS*. $40.00

205 *MODERN DOLLS TO CUT OUT AND DRESS.* $30.00
The paper dolls in this set are the same as pictured for #210

Photo Courtesy of Richard Rusnock

Courtesy of Mary Kelley
210 *BETTY ANN AND HER FRIENDS.* $30.00

Courtesy of Mary Kelley
210A *BETTY ANN AND AUDREY*

Courtesy of Mary Kelley

210B *JEAN AND TOMMY*

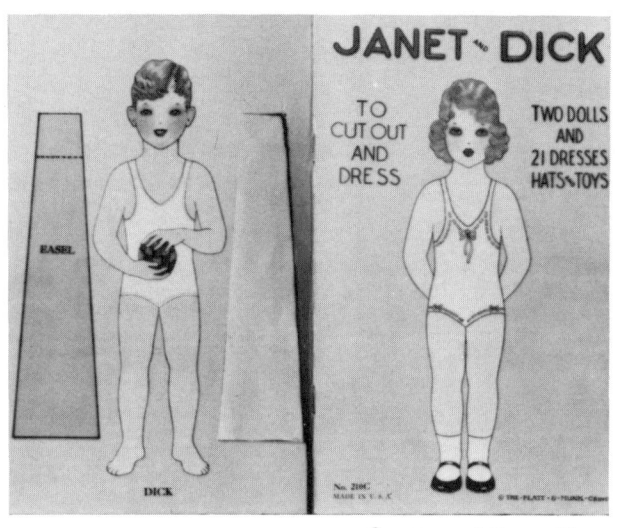

Courtesy of Emma Terry

210C *JANET AND DICK*

220 *DOLLS' OPEN HOUSE*, 1963. $10.00

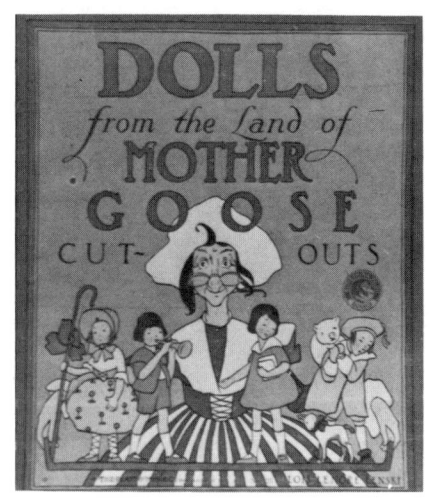

221 *DOLLS FROM THE LAND OF MOTHER GOOSE*. $22.50

224A *EARLY AMERICAN DOLLS*, 1963. $6.00

Photo Courtesy of Elsie Stevens

224B *BETSY ROSS*, 1963. $6.00

Courtesy of Jane Sugg

225 *DOLLIES TO DRESS LIKE FATHER AND MOTHER*. $20.00

Courtesy of Edith Linn

225A *GAY DOLLS*, 1942. $6.00

Courtesy of Audrey Sepponen

225B *PARTY DOLLS*, 1942. $6.00

Courtesy of Jean Woodcock

225B *PRETTY DOLLS TO CUT OUT, COLOR AND DRESS*. $35.00

Courtesy of Virginia Crossley

225D *YOUNG MISS DOLLS*, 1942. $6.00

226A *COSTUME DOLLS*, 1962. $8.00

226B *HISTORICAL DOLLS*, 1962. $8.00

Courtesy of Mary Kelley

227B *PLAYTIME DOLLS*. $12.00
The sets of 227A and 227B each contain four dolls from the eight doll set of *JUNIOR MISS DOLLS* #229. The dolls for 227A are pictured. The four dolls in *PLAYTIME DOLLS* will be found pictured with #229.

Courtesy of Audrey Sepponen

227A *BETTY ANN AND HER FRIENDS*. $12.00

228A *DOLLS ACROSS THE SEA*, 1965. $6.00

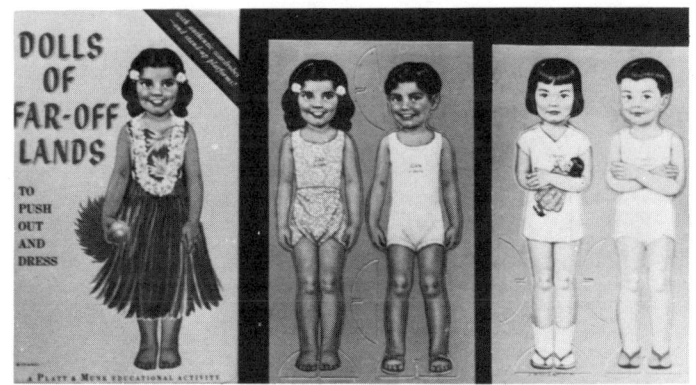
228B *DOLLS OF FAR-OFF LANDS*, 1965. $6.00

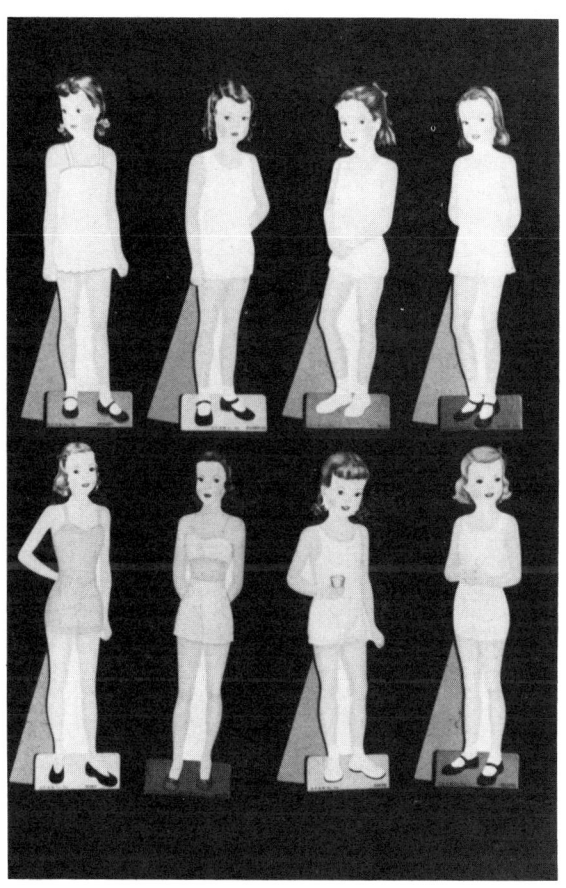

Courtesy of Mary Kelley
229 *JUNIOR MISS DOLLS*, 1942. $20.00

229 *JUNIOR MISS DOLLS*
Top row, left to right: Audrey, Patricia, Joan and Betty Ann. Bottom row, left to right: Mary, Nancy, Edith and Elaine.

230B *BETTY AND PEGGY*, 1937. $8.00

Photo Courtesy of Pam Hunter

230C *JANET AND JEANNE*, 1937. $8.00

230D *GOING ABROAD DOLLS*, 1937. $8.00

Courtesy of Betsy Addison
235A *I'M GROWING UP DOLLS*, 1937. $18.00

Courtesy of Mary Kelley
235B *MARY LOU AND HER FRIENDS*. $18.00

The sets of 235A and 235B each contain four dolls from the eight doll set of *AT HOME ABROAD DOLLS*, #240.

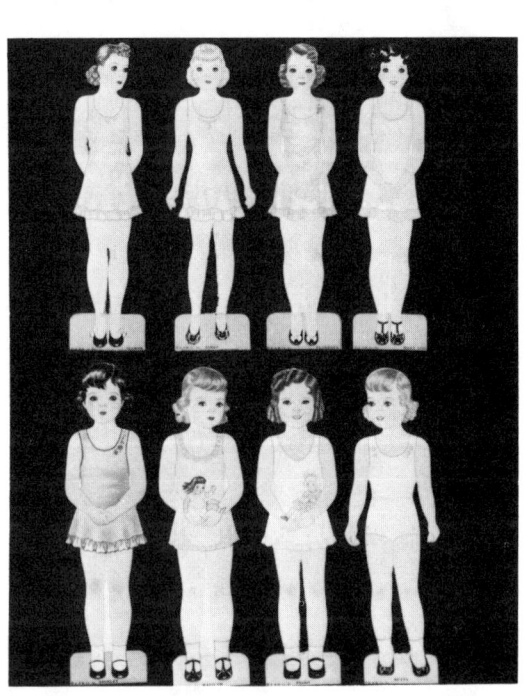

240 *AT HOME-ABROAD DOLLS*, 1937. $30.00   240 *AT HOME-ABROAD DOLLS*

 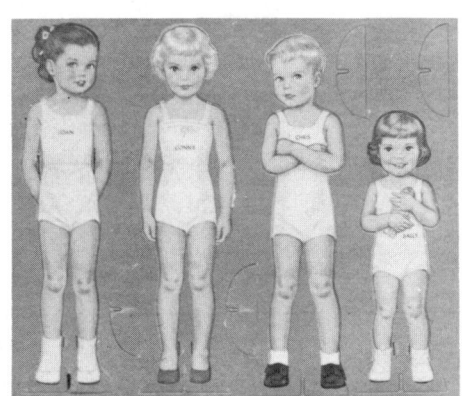 

240 *MODERN DOLLS*, 1957. $20.00

162

241 *FOREIGN DOLLS*, 1957. $20.00

241 *FOREIGN DOLLS*

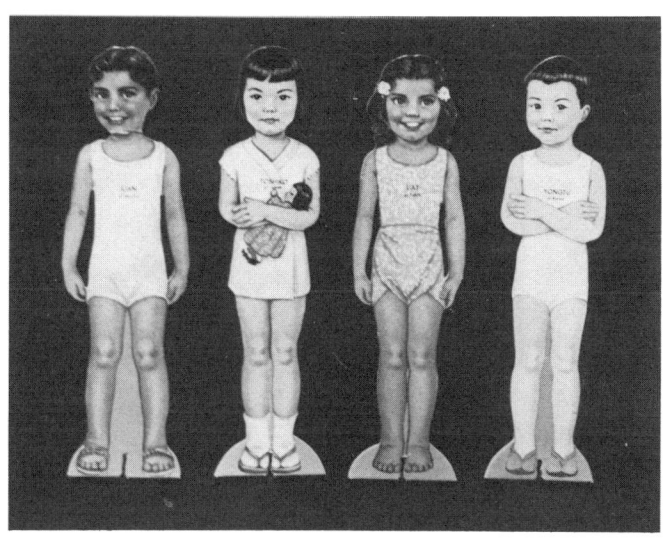

241 *FOREIGN DOLLS*

242 *COLONIAL DOLLS*, 1960. $20.00

242 *COLONIAL DOLLS*

242 *COLONIAL DOLLS*

243 *CENTURY DOLLS*, 1960. $20.00

243 *CENTURY DOLLS*

243 *CENTURY DOLLS*

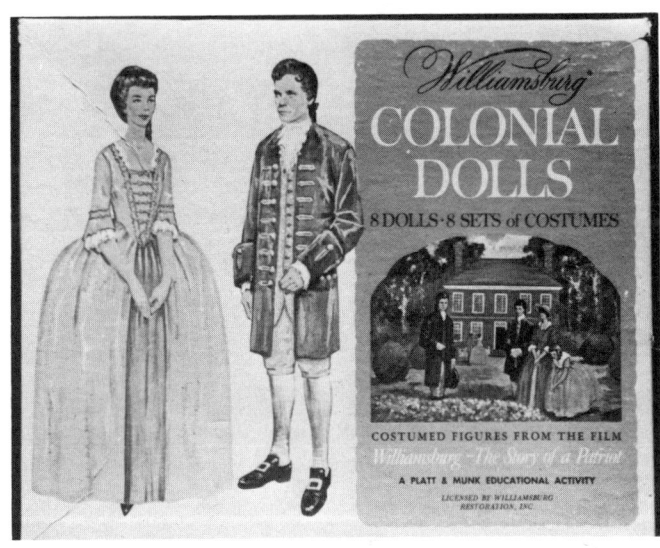
245 *WILLIAMSBURG COLONIAL DOLLS* © 1967 Williamsburg Restoration, Inc. Re-issued by Colonial Williamsburg Foundation and is currently available. Box C, Williamsburg, Va. 23187

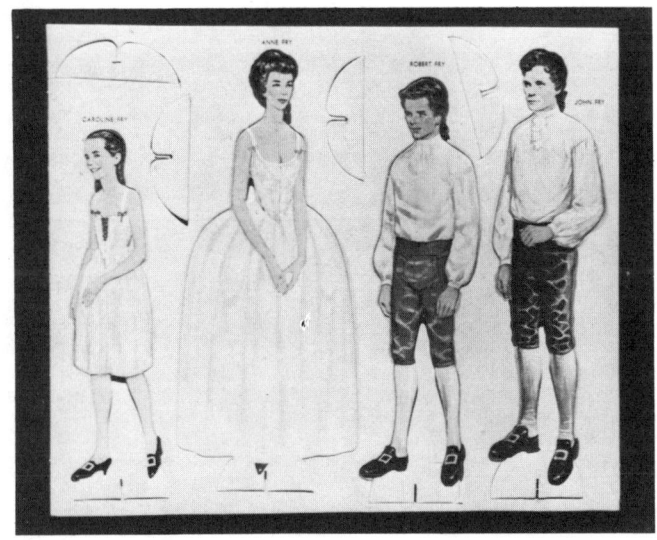
245 *WILLIAMSBURG COLONIAL DOLLS*

245 *WILLIAMSBURG COLONIAL DOLLS*

Courtesy of Betsy Addison

331 *PRETTY DOLLS TO DRESS*. $20.00

Courtesy of Jane Sugg

360 *THE LITTLE CHERUBS*, 1921. $30.00

360 *THE LITTLE CHERUBS*, 1921.
Doll from back cover

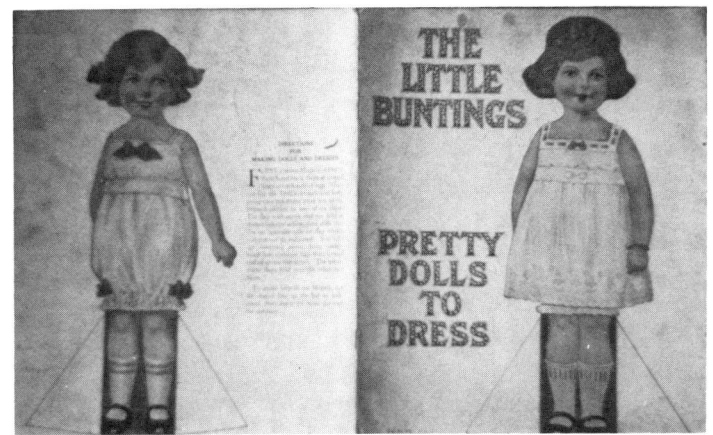

Courtesy of Betsy Addison

370 *THE LITTLE BUNTINGS*, 1921. $30.00

Courtesy of Betsy Slap

370 *THE LITTLE BUNTINGS*, 1921. $30.00
The doll on the back cover is from *Little Boy Blue* #390.

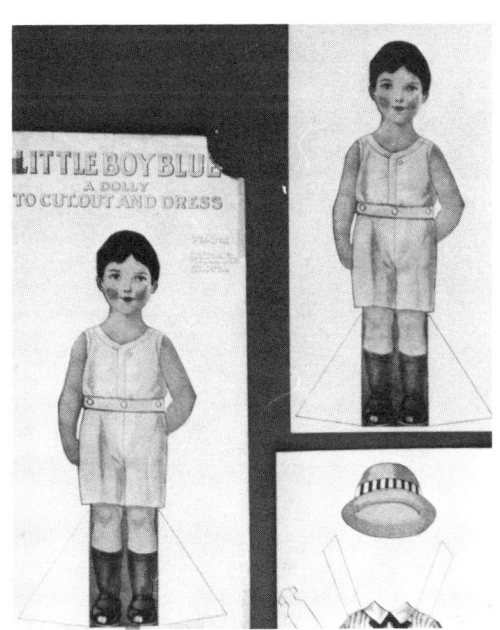

Courtesy of Audrey Sepponen

390 *LITTLE BOY BLUE*, 1921. $30.00

The Platt and Nourse Company

The Platt and Nourse Company emerged from the Platt and Peck Company. Mr. Platt left the company in 1920 and joined up with Arnold Munk to form the Platt and Munk Publishing Company. For a few years the Nourse Company operated alone and then was bought by Platt and Munk.

DOLLS FROM THE LAND OF MOTHER GOOSE, 1918 (see Platt and Munk #221 for picture)
DOROTHY AND RUTH DOLLS TO DRESS (dolls are from *BEAUTIFUL DOLLS* above)
MARY AND TEDDY CUT OUT DOLLS (not pictured)
MY LITTLE DEARS TO DRESS (not pictured)
PRETTY DOLLS TO DRESS (see Platt and Munk #331 for picture)

BEAUTIFUL DOLLS FOR CHILDREN TO DRESS, 1915 (see Platt and Peck for picture)
BETTY AND JACK DOLLS TO DRESS (dolls are from *BEAUTIFUL DOLLS* above)
DOLLIES TO DRESS LIKE MOTHER AND FATHER (see Platt and Munk #225 for picture)

Courtesy of Marilyn Johnson
BETTY AND JACK DOLLS TO DRESS. $20.00

Courtesy of Marilyn Johnson
DOROTHY AND RUTH DOLLS TO DRESS. $20.00

Platt and Peck

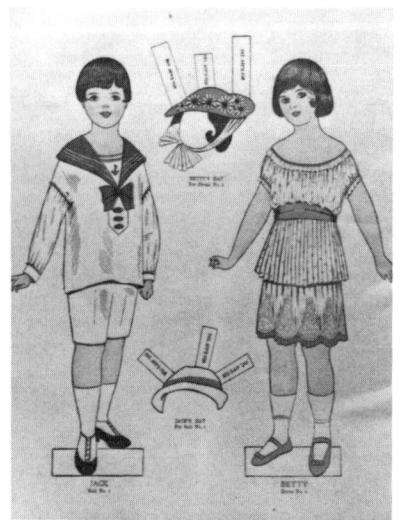
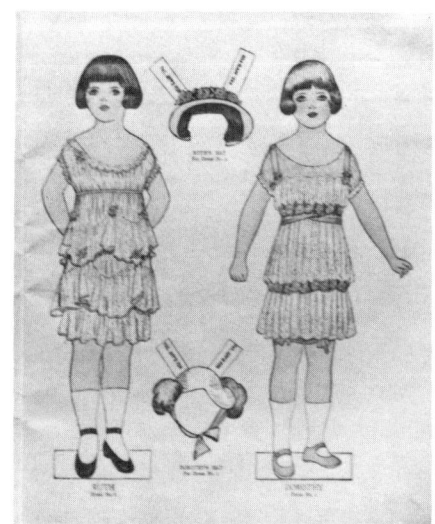

Courtesy of Virginia Crossley
BEAUTIFUL DOLLS FOR CHILDREN TO DRESS, 1915. $30.00

Playtime House

Playtime House produced paper dolls, games, picture puzzles, toys and blocks. Since this company is no longer in business there is no way to obtain dates on the following paper dolls. However, it is known that the company participated in the Toy Fair of 1947 in New York; so this bit of information may be useful in dating the sets.

310 *NANCY*
313 *DOROTHY*
313 *SHIRLEY*
313 *IRENE*
314 *PEGGY*

320 *CONNIE AND HER BIG WOOLLY WARDROBE*
3151 *THREE GLITTER DOLLS AND THEIR WARDROBES* (These three dolls are the same as #313 Shirley and Irene, and #314 Peggy, but with new names.)
3152 *GLITTER DOLLS*

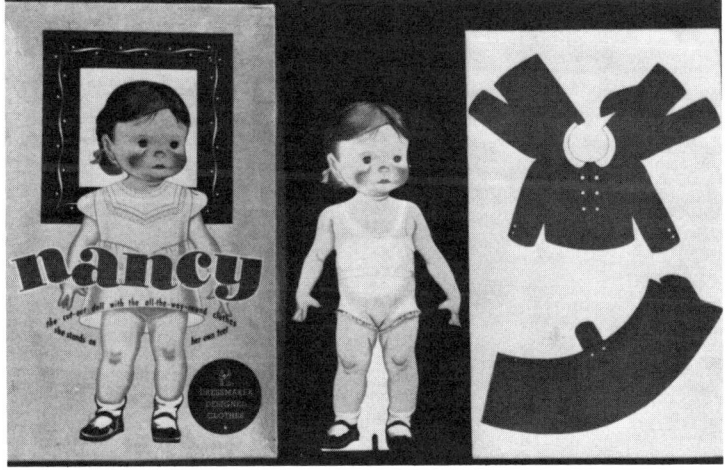

Courtesy of Virginia Crossley

310 *NANCY*. $10.00

313 *DOROTHY*. $5.00

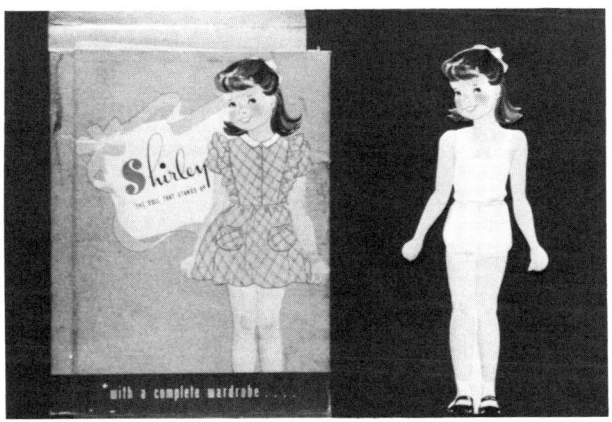

313 *SHIRLEY*. $5.00

313 *IRENE*. $5.00

Courtesy of Virginia Crossley

314 *PEGGY*. $5.00

Courtesy of Rosalie Eppert

320 *CONNIE AND HER BIG WOOLY WARDROBE*. $10.00

167

3151 *THREE GLITTER DOLLS.* $10.00

3151 The three dolls from *THREE GLITTER DOLLS*

3152 *GLITTER DOLLS.* $12.00

Courtesy of Betsy Slap

Pleasure Books, Inc.

FAIRY TALE CUT OUT DOLLS AND FURNITURE, 1936. $15.00

Courtesy of Betty Gohmert

Prentice-Hall, Inc.

THIRTY FROM THE 30's © 1974 by Tom Tierney. Currently available through Dover Publications

J. Pressman Toy Corporation

Courtesy of Ruth Garfinkel West

Courtesy of Virginia Crossley

5956 *MAGNETIC SMALL FRY FASHION SHOW* (not pictured)

1205 *STITCH AND SEW*. $6.00

1212 (Title not available). $6.00

Courtesy of Marilyn Johnson

1214 *SNOW WHITE*. $15.00

Courtesy of Betsy Slap

Title and stock number unknown

169

Progressive Toy Corporation

502 *PROGRESSIVE SEWING SET*, 1941. $15.00
Two paper dolls, cloth clothes

502 *PROGRESSIVE SEWING SET*
Box contents

G.P. PUTNAM'S SONS

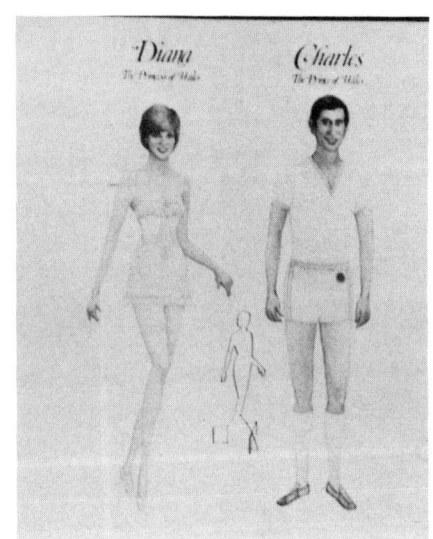

THE PRINCESS DIANA PAPER DOLL BOOK OF FASHION
By Clarissa Harlowe and Mary Anna Bedford, *A PERIGEE BOOK*, published by G.P. Putnam's Sons, © 1982 by Clarissa Harlowe and Mary Anna Bedford. Perigee Books is a division of The Putnam Publishing Group. Currently available

Grosset and Dunlap Publishers is now a division of the Putnam Publishing Group. Some years ago it published the following paper dolls.

Courtesy of Virginia Crossley

C2000 *THE BOBBSEY TWINS PLAY BOX*, 1950. $22.50

Courtesy of Betsy Slap

LITTLE FACES FROM FAR PLACES, 1933. $35.00

Rand McNally and Company

The Rand McNally company was established in 1856 in Chicago by William Rand and Andrew McNally. It became well known for its printing of railroad items such as time tables, passenger tickets and maps of rail routes. Today it is best known for printing road atlases.

The company also published a large amount of children's books, and for many years they produced the *Child Life Magazine*. In 1976 Rand McNally bought the Saalfield Publishing Co. Many of the more recent Saalfield books are being reprinted by Rand McNally including some paper doll books.

Pictured are the two paper doll books published by Rand McNally in the 1930's plus a book that contains one paper doll page from 1928.

RM 103 *THE MAKE-IT BOOK*, 1928. $3.00

186 *LITTLE FRIENDS FROM HISTORY*, 1936. $18.00

211 *LET'S PLAY ESKIMO*, 1937. $15.00

Rea-Harrison Company

Courtesy of Jean Woodcock
THE BETTY BELLE PAPER DOLLS. $25.00

Red Farm Studio

Red Farm Studio was founded in 1947 by a New England artist, Ellen Nelson. The company was located in Massachusetts at that time. The current owners of the company moved the organization to Pawtucket, R.I. when they purchased the company in 1958. The company is a privately-held, family-operated business serving several thousand retail shops and stores across the country.

Besides the two paper dolls pictured here (which are still available), the company publishes greeting cards, stationery, gift wrap and other paper goods including a complete line of Christmas paper items.

KIM'S PAPER DOLL COLORING BOOK
©1978 Red Farm Studio. Currently available

KIM'S COUSIN GINGER'S PAPER DOLL COLORING BOOK © 1982 Red Farm Studio

Reely-Trooly Company

These sets were sold around the time of World War I. The box set would seem to be the original of the two as it states "Patent Applied For", while the envelope states "Patented". In the box set, the dolls are made of cloth backing while the dolls in the envelope are of cardboard.

These paper dolls were also sold by the Rust Craft Co. of Boston, but there was a change: "Trooly" was spelled "Truly".

Courtesy of Rosalie Eppert
REELY-TROOLY DOLLS. $25.00
Box set

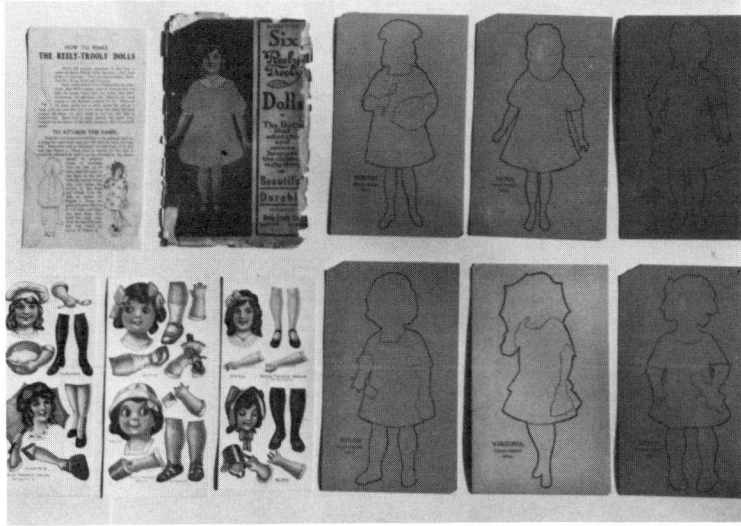

Courtesy of Katharine McIntire
REELY-TROOLY DOLLS. $25.00
Envelope

Percy Reeves

JUMBO MOVY-DOLS

MARGUERITE CLARK, 1920. $45.00

MARY MILES MINTER, 1920. $45.00

MARY PICKFORD, 1920. $45.00

Courtesy of Shirley Hedge

LILA LEE, 1920. $45.00

The Regensteiner Corporation

Courtesy of Audrey Sepponen

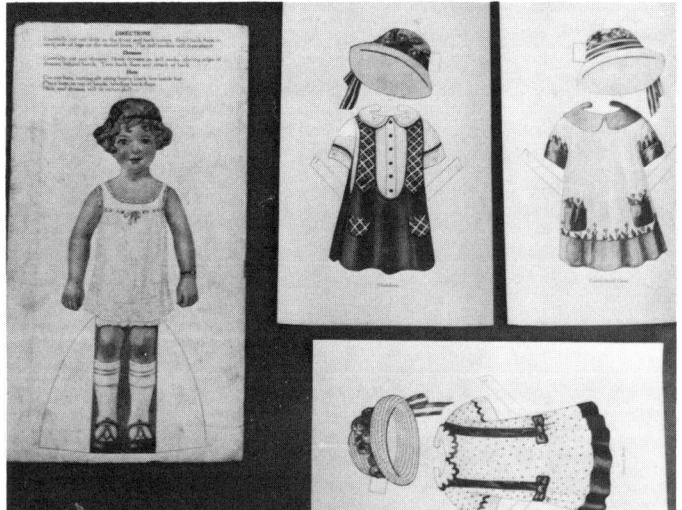

JANE AND JILL'S NEW FROCKS AND FRILLS, 1925. $30.00

The Reilly and Britton Company

In 1917 Will Pente designed and patented his "Fold-A-Way Toys". That year he designed four storybooks for the Reilly and Britton Co. which included paper dolls, outfits and stand-up figures. The books were small, only 5¼ x 7¼". The cut-outs were on the right side of the page and the story on the left so that the story would remain when the paper dolls were cut out. Will Pente designed at least two other books that year for Reilly and Britton of the stand-up toy variety.

The following is a list of the Reilly and Britton Co. paper doll and stand-up books that are known but not pictured:

THE STORY OF LITTLE BLACK SAMBO
THE STORY OF THE THREE BEARS
DOLLY BLOSSOM'S BUNGALOW, A BOOK OF FOLD-A-WAY TOYS, 1917

DOLLY'S BREAKFAST-THE FOLD AWAY CAN'T BREAK DISHES
THE OZ TOY BOOK, 1915 (Includes over 50 stand-up figures)

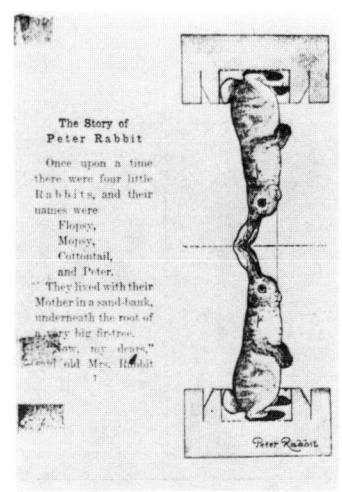

Courtesy of Richard Rusnock

THE STORY OF PETER RABBIT, 1917. $30.00

Courtesy of Jean Woodcock

THE STORY OF CINDERELLA, 1917. $30.00

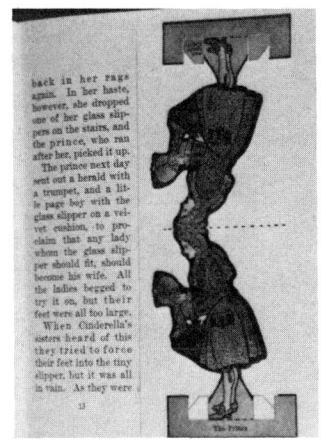 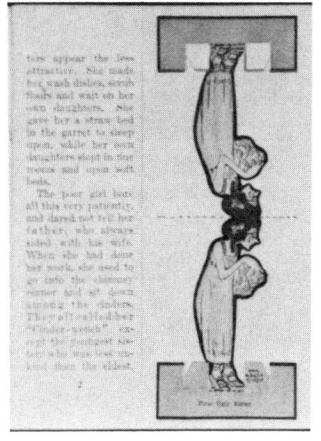 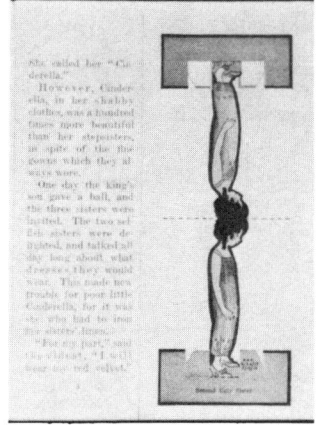 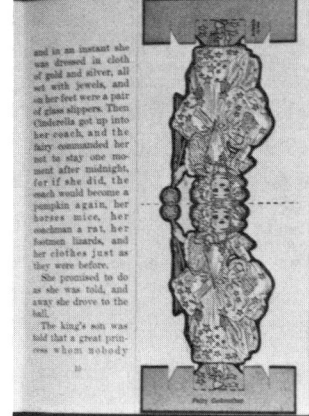

THE STORY OF CINDERELLA

Ritt-Miller Company

BETTY, COMPLETE WARDROBE AND TRUNK, 1932. $25.00

Courtesy of Carol Carey

Rogers, Kellogg, Stillson

Courtesy of Richard Rusnock

GLORIANA THE FAMOUS HOLLYWOOD STAR, 1932. $35.00

GLORIANA THE FAMOUS HOLLYWOOD STAR

Schattel's

Courtesy of Judy Curtis

MR. AND MRS. HAWAII, 1955. $10.00

Selchow and Righter Company

The Selchow and Righter Company is an off-shoot of a business started in 1867 by A.B. Swift. Mr. Swift ran a wholesale distributorship of toys and games on John Street in New York City. One of the games listed in his first catalog that year was Parchessi®. In 1870 the company was purchased by Mr. Elisha G. Selchow. Mr. Selchow hired a young man named John Harris Righter to help run the business. Righter did such a successful job, he was soon made manager and later became a partner of the firm. The company continued to sell large quantities of toys, games, baseball equipment and a large assortment of mechanical toy banks. Mr. Righter died in 1909 and Mr. Selchow in 1915, but the company continued to succeed under the name of Selchow and Righter. Like most other toy companies, they experienced only two major slowdowns during the years that followed: one during the Depression of the early Thirties and the other during World War II.

After the war, a crossword game was brought to Selchow and Righter for consideration but was turned down. It was not the first time the owner of the game had been turned down; so, he decided to set up his own factory and produce the game himself. The name of the game was Scrabble®, and the owner had the name trademarked. He asked Selchow and Righter if they would sell him a small quantity of playing boards which they agreed to do. A year later, a larger amount of playing boards was ordered and by 1952, the order was large enough to cause Selchow and Righter to wonder if they had done the right thing in turning down the game. The owner's little factory was beginning to swim in Scrabble tiles and new orders from customers made the owner realize he could no longer handle it alone. Hence, the game was licensed to Selchow and Righter. The game has now been translated into many foreign languages and also made in Braille.

For many years the Selchow and Righter Co. was the American distributor for J.W. Spear and Sons of London/Bavaria. They handled all types of Spear's games and toys including toy theaters and paper dolls. A "Little Red Riding Hood" theater with jointed figures was pictured in the 1924-1925 Selchow and Righter catalog. Spear's paper dolls were also featured in that catalog.

The following paper dolls of J.W. Spear and Sons of London/Bavaria were distributed in the United States by Selchow and Righter and are listed in their catalog of 1924-1925:

DAISY AND HER DRESSES-Box 7 x 7"
DOLLY DIMPLE-10" doll in box 11½" x 6½" with 4 costumes
DOLLY ROSYCHEEKS AND HER PRETTY DRESSES AND HATS-Box 11 x 14¼"
DOROTHY-Box 9¾ x 11" with 4 dresses, 4 hats and 5 playthings
JOAN-Box 11 x 14¼" with 4 dresses, 4 hats and 4 miscellaneous items
LITTLE DICK-7" doll in box 7 x 8"
LITTLE DICK-Same as above, only larger 9¾" doll
PEGGY-7" doll in box 7 x 8"
PEGGY-Same as above, only larger 9¾" doll
PEGGY AND HER NEW OUTFIT-Box 9¾ x 11", with 4 dresses, 4 hats, 5 playthings

The following are *SPEAR'S CHARACTER DOLLS* with removable heads:
JOAN-13" doll, box 11 x 14" complete outfit with several heads
OUR BABY-12½" doll, box 14 x 12" complete outfit with several heads
One Doll in 9¾ x 11¼" box with 4 dresses, 4 hats and 6 heads

The following are paper dolls published by Selchow and Righter, undated, which are not pictured.

Lady Alice
Lady Betty

Courtesy of Rosalie Eppert
DOLLY MAY. $50.00

Courtesy of Virginia Crossley
FAIR MARGARET. $50.00

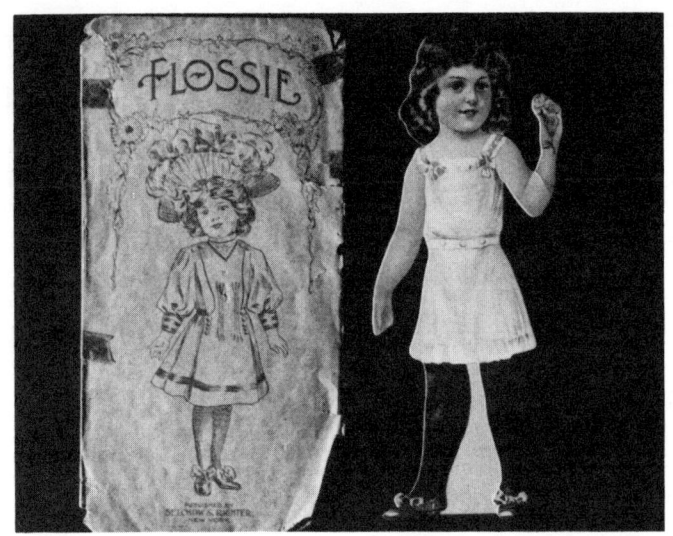

Courtesy of Maurine Popp

FLOSSIE. $50.00

Courtesy of Rosalie Eppert

LADY BELLE. $50.00

Courtesy of Rosalie Eppert

LITTLE LADDIE. $50.00

Courtesy of Virginia Crossley

MAMIE. $50.00

Courtesy of Maurine Popp

MAMIE. $50.00

TEDDY BEAR. $75.00

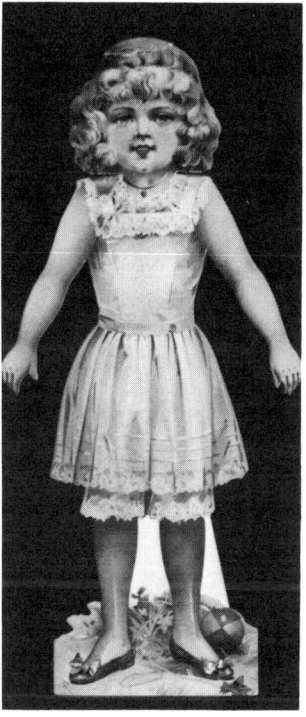

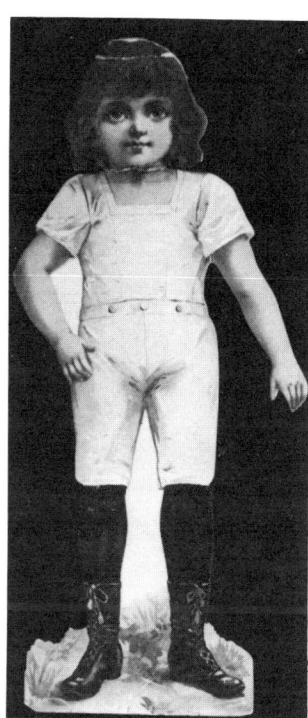

Courtesy of Rosalie Eppert

Courtesy of Virginia Crossley

OUR FAVORITE DOLLS. $50.00

OUR FAVORITE DOLLS. $50.00

Each of the folders are yellow, brown and white. The name Selchow and Righter appears on each, and down at the bottom of the folder in smaller print is American Litho. Co. The Amlico Co. also produced these dolls and it's more than likely that Amlico stands for American Litho. Co.

Simplex Toys

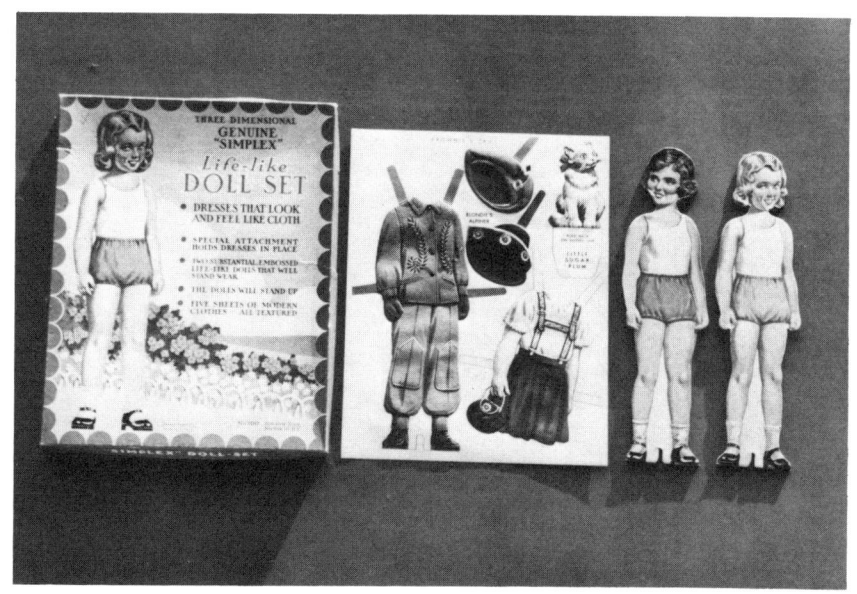

Courtesy of Audrey Sepponen

100 *LIFE-LIKE DOLL SET.* $15.00

J.V. Sloan and Company

DOLLS OF THE NATIONS, 1909 Courtesy of Rosalie Eppert

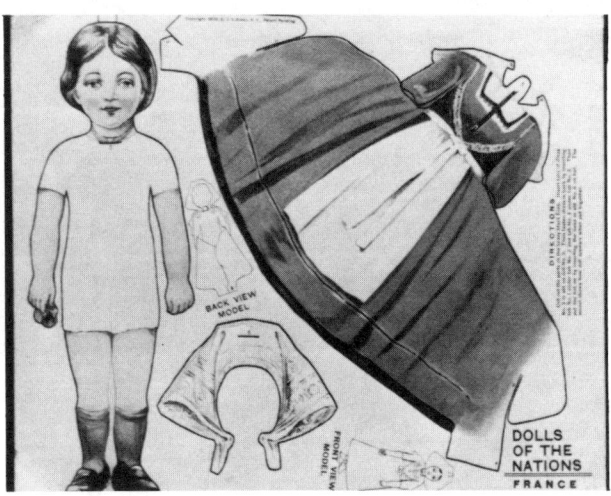

FRANCE. $10.00 a sheet

GERMANY. $10.00 a sheet

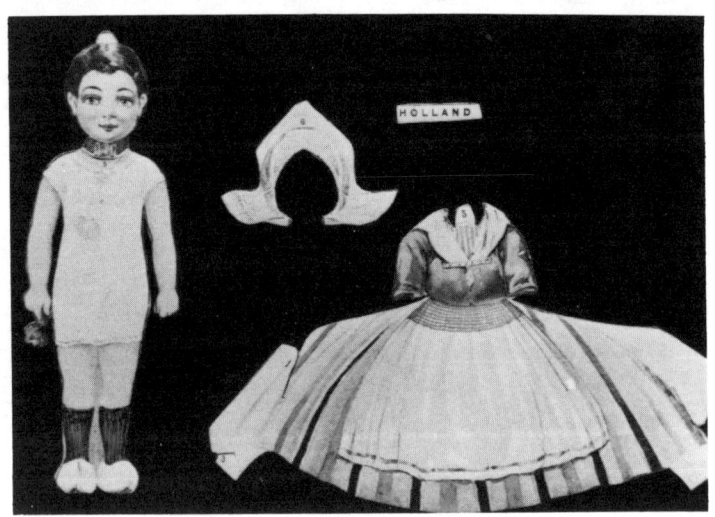

HOLLAND. $10.00 a sheet

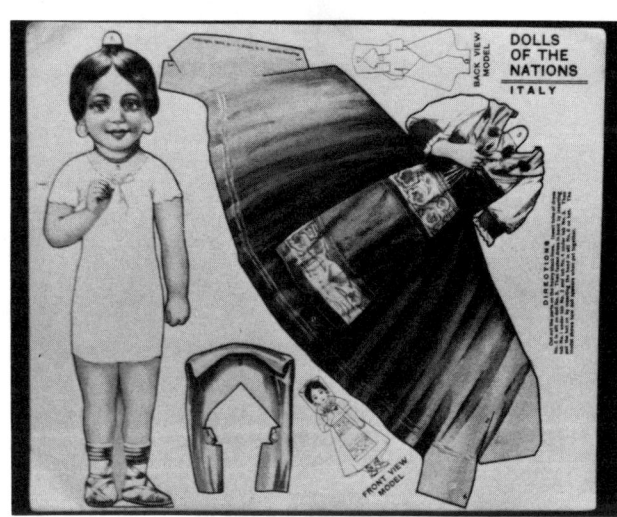

ITALY. $10.00 a sheet

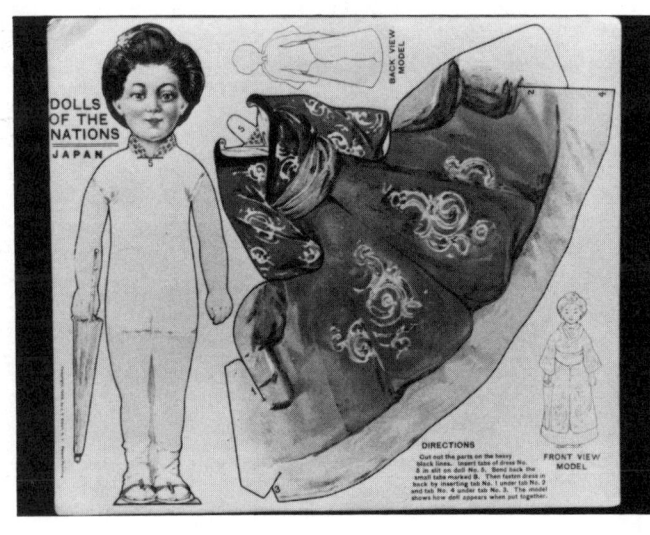

JAPAN. $10.00 a sheet

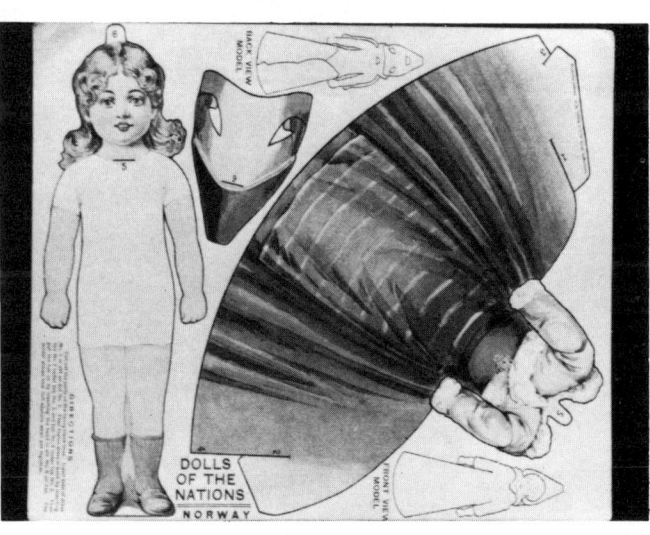

NORWAY. $10.00 a sheet

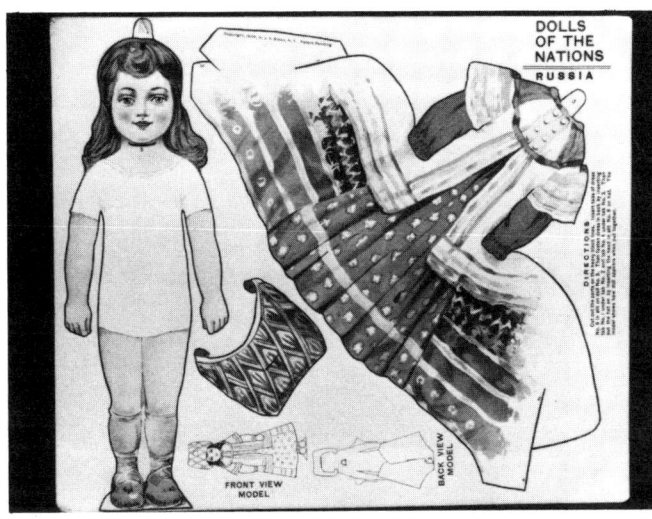
RUSSIA. $10.00 a sheet

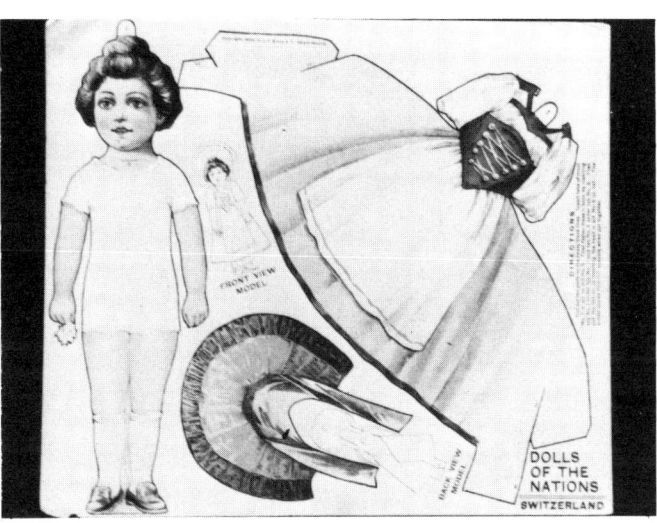
SWITZERLAND. $10.00 a sheet

Courtesy of Zelda Cushner
DANIEL BOONE AND KIT CARSON. $12.00 a sheet

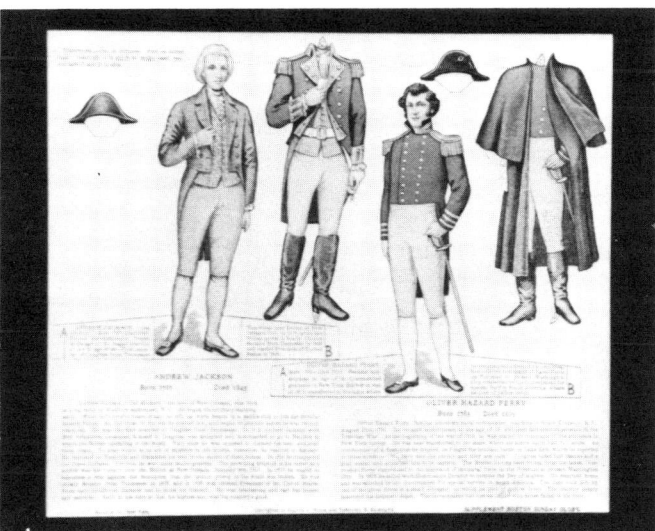
ANDREW JACKSON AND OLIVER HAZARD PERRY. $12.00 a sheet

Courtesy of Zelda Cushner
POCAHONTAS AND JOHN SMITH. $12.00 a sheet

Courtesy of Zelda Cushner
PRISCILLA AND JOHN ALDEN. $12.00 a sheet

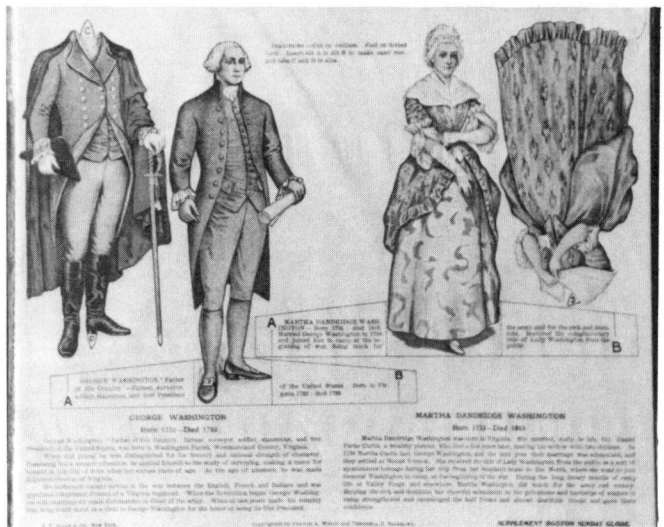

QUEEN ISABELLA OF SPAIN AND CHRISTOPHER COLUMBUS. $12.00 a sheet (Not pictured)

GEORGE WASHINGTON AND MARTHA DANDRIDGE WASHINGTON. $12.00 a sheet

Courtesy of Zelda Cushner

Smart Style Paper Doll Company

PATTY AND PAUL (not pictured)   *BOB AND BARBARA* (not pictured)

Smethport Specialty Company

53 *MAGNETIC MISSY.* $5.00

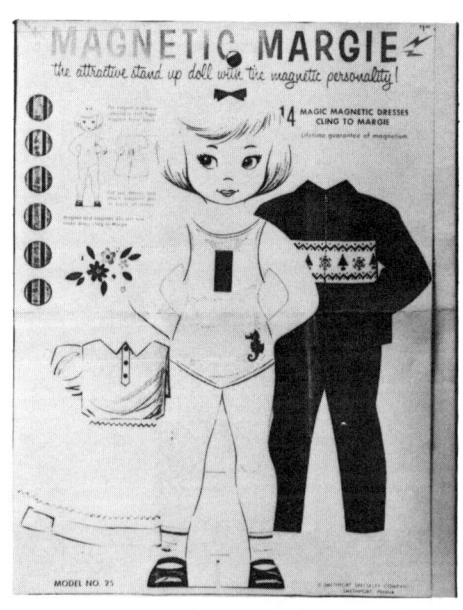

25 *MAGNETIC MARGIE.* $5.00

67 *MAGNETIC MARCIA.* $5.00

171 *COMBAT JOE,* 1965. $7.00
160 *COMBAT JIM,* 1965. $7.00

Courtesy of Virginia Crossley

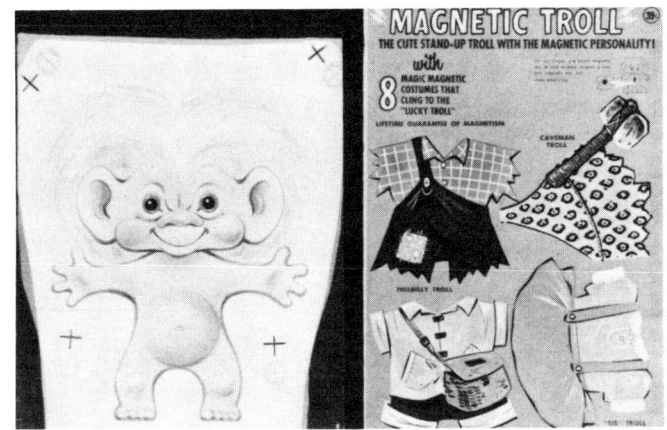

116 *MAGNETIC TROLL*, 1965. $5.00
© Uneeda Doll Company, Inc.

Spertus Publishing Co.

600 *NEW YORK WORLD'S FAIR "MAKE A MODEL"* (stand-ups) (not pictured)
700 *DRESS UP FOR THE NEW YORK WORLD'S FAIR*, 1963 (red cover on book) (not pictured)

700 *SINGER WORLD'S FAIR DRESS-UP BOOK*, 1961 (yellow cover on book) (not pictured)

Standard Publishing Company

2590 *BIBLE CHILDREN PAPER DOLLS*. $5.00

2591 *CHILDREN OF GOD'S WORLD*. $5.00

Stanton and Van Vliet Co.

This book contains eight movie star paper dolls in color and the same eight stars in black and white to be colored, for a total of 16 pages of paper dolls. The eight stars include May Allison, Douglas Fairbanks, Charlie Chaplin, Elsie Ferguson, Mary Pickford, Norma Talmadge (pictured on the cover of the book), Marguerite Clark and Geraldine Farrar.

PERCY REEVES MOVY-DOLS PAINTING BOOK I, 1919. $40.00

The Stecher Lithographic Company

In 1871 Frank A. Stecher and his partner John Mensing began the Lithographic and Chromo Company in Rochester, New York. In 1886 the firm was incorporated as The Stecher Lithographic Company. Mr. Stecher died in 1916, but the company continued to flourish and in 1933 it merged with Traung Label and Lithograph Co. In 1965 the company merged with Schmidt Lithograph Co. to form the Stecher-Traung-Schmidt Corporation. The headquarters for the firm was moved to Detroit, Michigan, in 1978 but an office is still maintained in Rochester.

100 *BETTINA AND HER PLAYMATE ROSALIE*. $30.00

Courtesy of Saalfield Archives

732 *BOY AND GIRL CUTOUT DOLL BOOK*, 1932. $25.00

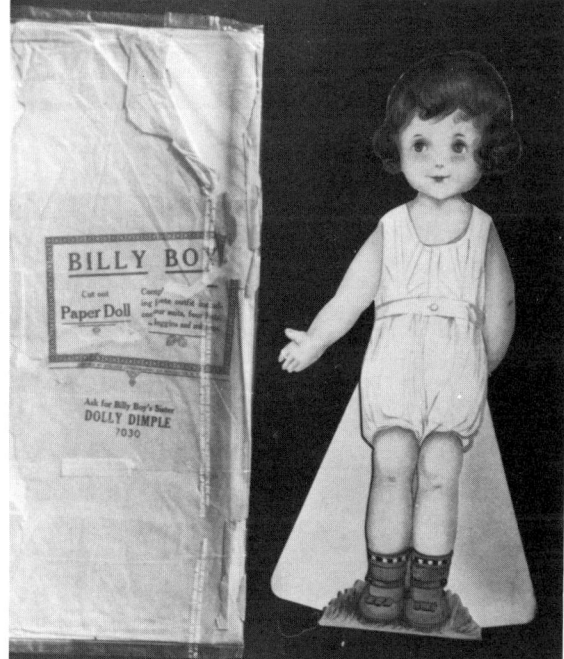

Courtesy of Virginia Crossley

7029 *BILLY BOY*. $35.00

38 *BETTY'S PAINTING AND CUT OUT BOOK*, 1926 (Not pictured; stand-ups)

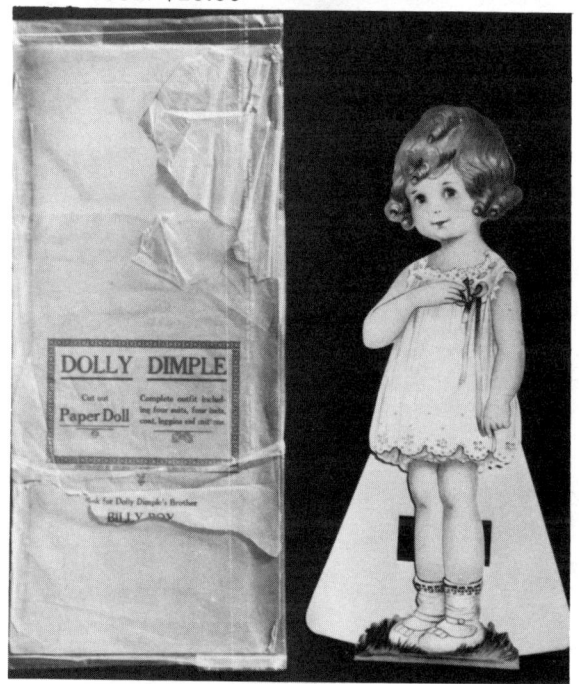

Courtesy of Virginia Crossley

7030 *DOLLY DIMPLE*. $35.00
(Some dolls of *DOLLY DIMPLE* have © 1915 Stecher Litho. Co. printed below the doll's feet)

Stephens Publishing Company

Courtesy of Virginia Crossley

135 *CIRCUS DAY,* 1946. $6.00

136 *JUNE BRIDE*, 1946. $7.00

137 *THE SCISSORS BIRD PAPER DOLLS.* $7.00

Courtesy of Edith Linn

155 *FILMLAND FASHIONS.* $10.00

Courtesy of Genie Kalb

156 *PLAYTIME FASHIONS.* $10.00

165 *PLAYHOUSE DOLLS,* 1949. $8.00

166 *SWEETIE-PIE TWINS*, 1949. $6.00

175 *PATTY'S PARTY*. $6.00

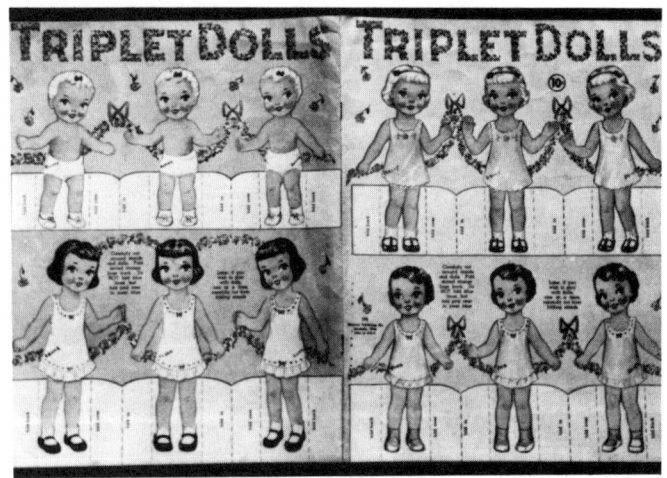

176 *TRIPLET DOLLS*. $6.00

177 *GLAMOUR MODELS*. $8.00

178 *MOVIE STARLETS*. $8.00

181 *LITTLE SWEETHEARTS*. $8.00

183 *6 GOOD LITTLE DOLLS.* $6.00

182 *CHEERLEADER TEEN-AGE DOLL CUT-OUTS.* $8.00

184 *GLAMOUR PARADE.* $6.00

Courtesy of Virginia Crossley

2129 *DOLL HOUSE CUT OUTS.* $8.00

2229 *PAJAMA PARTY.* $8.00

Frederick A. Stokes Company

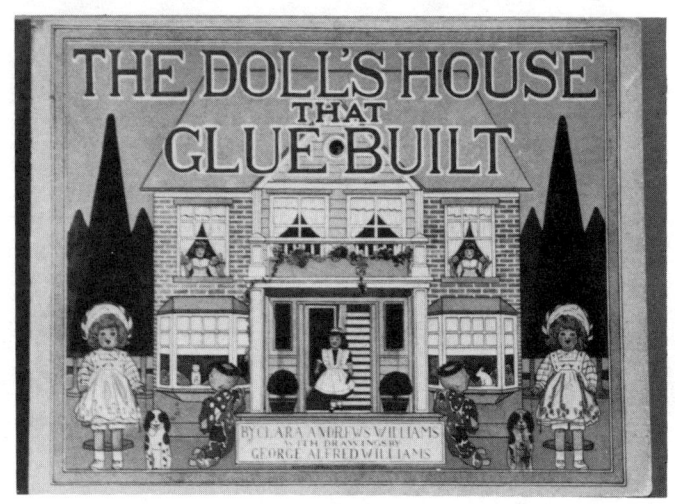

Courtesy of Audrey Sepponen

THE DOLL'S HOUSE THAT GLUE BUILT, 1910. $35.00

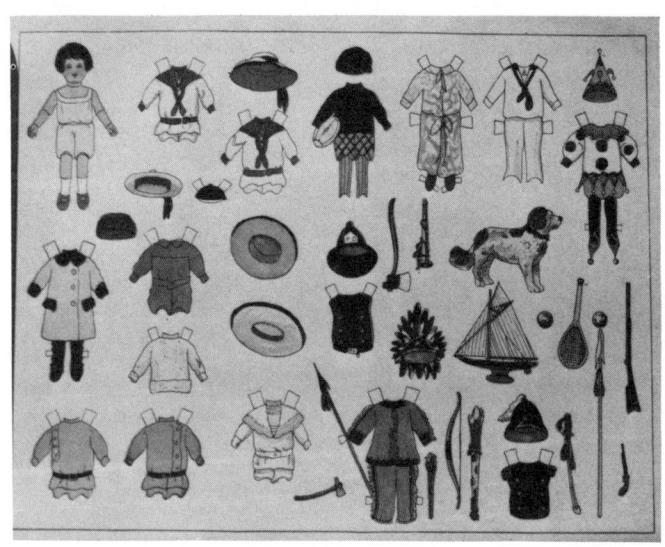

THE DOLL'S HOUSE THAT GLUE BUILT

A YEAR OF PAPER DOLLS, 1894 (not pictured)
THE CHILDREN'S STORE, 1910 (stand-ups) (not pictured)
FAMOUS QUEENS AND MARTHA WASHINGTON, 1895 (not pictured)

THE FUN THAT GLUE MADE, 1907 (cut and paste book) (not pictured)
PRINCE AND PRINCESS PAPER DOLLS, 1895 (not pictured)

Stoll and Edwards Co. Inc.

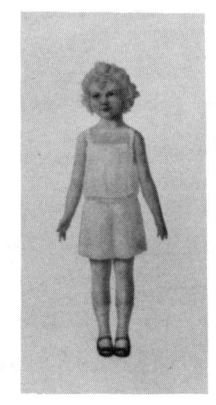
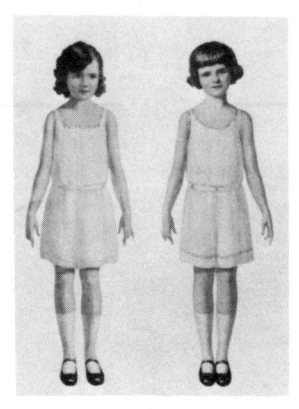

Courtesy of Grayce Piemontesi

WE ARE THE WARDROBE PAPER DOLLS, 1921. $30.00

SUNSHINE CUT-OUTS, 1926. $40.00
Every Day Series

SUNSHINE CUT-OUTS
Every day Series

SUNSHINE CUT-OUTS, 1926. $40.00
Sports Series

SUNSHINE CUT-OUTS
Sports Series

SUNSHINE CUT-OUTS, 1926. $40.00
Vacation Series

SUNSHINE CUT-OUTS
Vacation Series

BETTY BONNET 1915 (not pictured; originally appeared in *Ladies Home Journal*)
KITTY CLOVER 1918 (not pictured; originally Betty Bonnet in *Ladies Home Journal*)
POLLY PITCHER AND HER PLAYMATES SERIES ONE, 1917 (see Geo. W. Jacobs & Co.)
POLLY PITCHER AND HER PLAYMATES SERIES TWO, 1918 (see Geo. W. Jacobs & Co.)
JOLLY TIME SERIES (not pictured)
FAIRY FOLK SERIES (not pictured; originally published by Geo. W. Jacobs)

George Sully and Company

Courtesy of Audrey Sepponen
51 *DOLLS TO MAKE AND DRESS*, 1919. $40.00

51 *DOLLS TO MAKE AND DRESS*
Inside pages

50 *THE PLAY DAY BOOK*, 1919 (not pictured)
60 *THE BIRD-TOY BOOK* (not pictured)
61 *BIRD CUT OUTS* (series 1) (not pictured)
62 *BIRD CUT OUTS* (series 2) (not pictured)
70 *THE ANIMAL TOY BOOK* (not pictured)
71 *ANIMAL CUT OUTS*, 1919 (series 1) (not pictured)
72 *ANIMAL CUT OUTS*, 1919 (series 2) (not pictured)

The paper dolls in #50 *Play-Day Book* include the same dolls as those shown for #51 plus a doll named Sue (and her garden). She was also in the book *Play-Day Cut Outs* #52 and is pictured on the far left of the picture for #52.

52 *PLAY DAY CUT OUTS*
Partial cut set of some of the dolls

Suntex Corporation

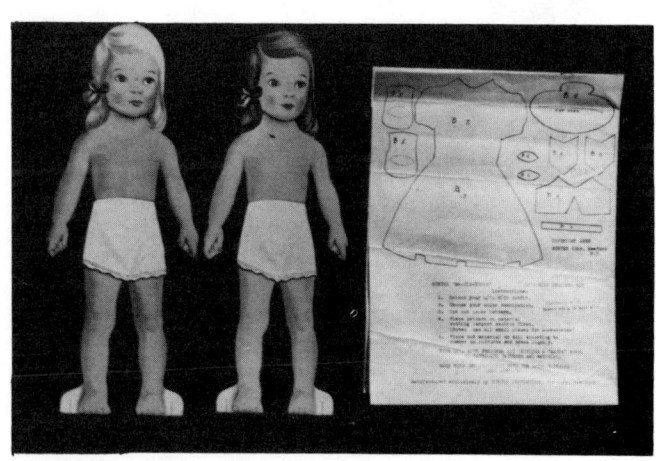

LI'L MISS DESIGNER KIT, 1953. $7.00
Dolls with Plastic Clothes

Charles Thompson Company

FORGET-ME-NOT PAPER DOLLS, 1912. $30.00

FORGET-ME-NOT PAPER DOLLS

FORGET-ME-NOT PAPER DOLLS

FORGET-ME-NOT PAPER DOLLS

FORGET-ME-NOT PAPER DOLLS

FORGET-ME-NOT PAPER DOLLS

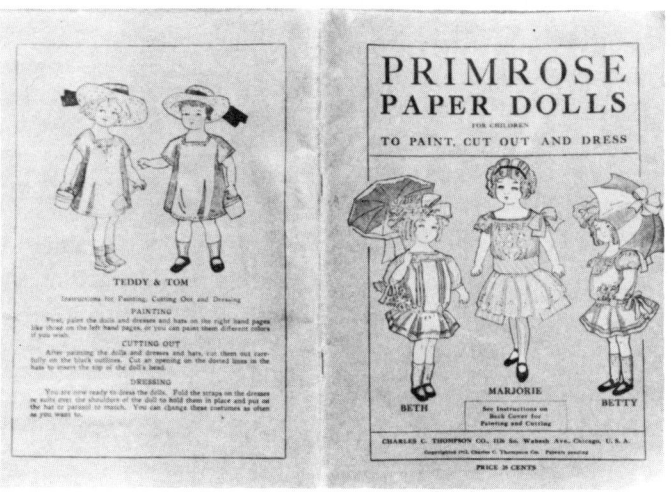

PRIMROSE PAPER DOLLS, 1912. $30.00

PRIMROSE PAPER DOLLS

PRIMROSE PAPER DOLLS

PRIMROSE PAPER DOLLS

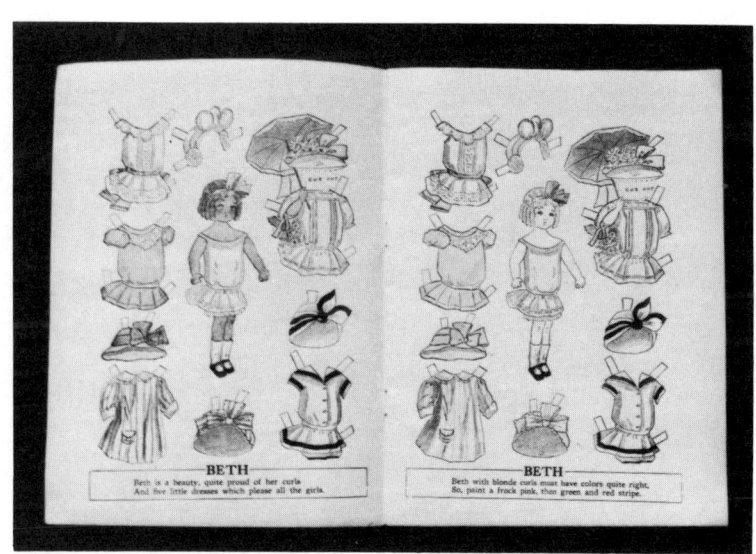

PRIMROSE PAPER DOLLS

REAL LIFE IN DOLLY LAND, 1913 (not pictured)

Toy Factory

This company evolved from the Magic Wand Company

The following paper doll box sets are not pictured:

101 *DENIM DOLLS*, 1974
102 *LORI*, 1974
103 *LITTLE DARLINGS*, 1974
104 *WIZARD OF OZ*, 1975
105 *FONZIE*, 1976
106 *KOTTER*, 1976
107 *BARBARINO*, 1976
108 *THE SWEATHOGS*, 1976
109 *AMY*
110 *JILL*, 1977
111 *SABRINA*, 1977
112 *KELLY*, 1977

Transogram Toy Company

1515 *DOLL HOUSE DRESS SHOP*, 1938/41. $8.00

Courtesy of Virginia Crossley

4101 5 *MODEL MISS CUTOUT DOLLS*, 1961. $15.00
The dolls in this set are identical to the five dolls in the Angela Cartwright set. The doll in the middle was Angela and is named Penny in this set.

4102 *PAM AND JEFF*, 1963. $10.00

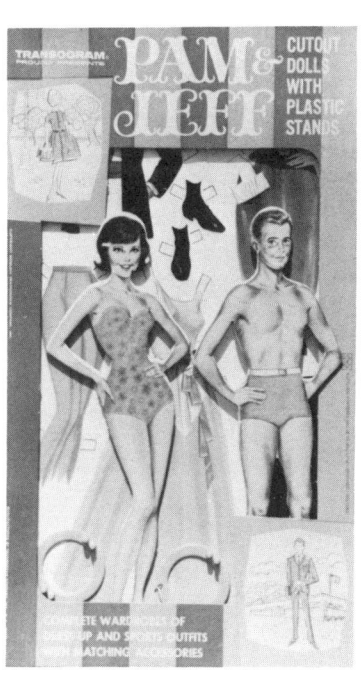

520W *DRESSES FOR DOLLS*, cloth dresses (not pictured)
2526 *PLAYTIME DRESSES FOR DOLLY* (not pictured)
4101 *ANGELA CARTWRIGHT*, 1960 (not pictured; same as Five Model Miss)
4101 *CUTIE CUT-UPS THAT STAND UP*, 1964 (not pictured same as Five Model Miss)
4106 *PAM AND JEFF*, 1964 (not pictured; same as 4102)

Treasure Books

Courtesy of Audrey Sepponen
T-153 *MY OWN DOLLS TO COLOR AND DRESS*, 1952. $7.00

T-167 *THE DRESS-UP DOLL BOOK*, 1953. $7.00

265 *DOLLS TO CUT OUT* (reprint of #T-153)
353 *DOLLS AROUND THE WORLD*, 1960
370 *PEGGY LEE*, 1961
2901 *DRESS-UP DOLLS*, 1960
2906 *SHARI LEWIS AND HER PUPPETS*, 1961 (not paper dolls)

2907 *DOLL HOUSE*, 1961, activity book with some pages from #T-153
3750 *DOLLS TO CUT OUT AND COLOR*, 1957 (reprint of #T-153)
9544 *SCISSORS AND COLORING FUN* (reprint of #T-153)

Trim Molded Products Company

Courtesy of Betsy Slap
B101 *CREATIVE CUT-OUTS, 5 STAND-UP PLASTIC BALLET GIRLS.* $5.00

Courtesy of Virginia Crossley
C102 *CREATIVE CUT-OUTS, THE DOLL HOUSE FAMILY.* $6.00

Troubador Press

Troubador Press was founded in 1959 in San Francisco. It began as a printer and manufacturer of a nationally distributed greeting card line. The company evolved into a publishing house and published its first book in 1967. The first paper doll book, "Fashion Kit Design and Color Paper Doll", was published in 1972. Currently the company has two paper doll books available, "Great Ballet Paper Dolls" and "Gorey Cats Paper Dolls", which are pictured.

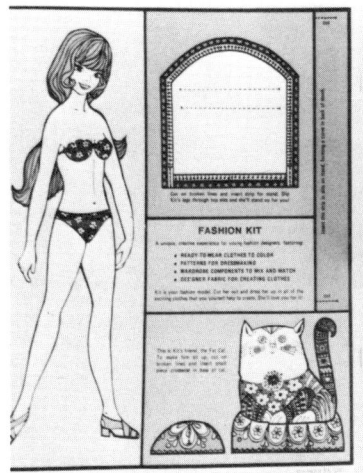

FASHION KIT DESIGN AND COLOR PAPER DOLL. $4.00
© 1972 by Troubador Press (out of print and unavailable)

GREAT BALLET PAPER DOLLS by Nancie Swanberg © 1981 Published by Troubador Press, 385 Fremont Street, San Francisco, California 94105. Currently available

GOREY CATS PAPER DOLLS
Published by Troubador Press © 1982
385 Fremont St. San Francisco, California 94105. Currently available

Ullman Mfg. Co., Art Publishers

PARADISE OF PAPER DOLLS. $27.00
Box Set with Five Sheets of Paper Dolls

Courtesy of Richard Rusnock

PARADISE OF PAPER DOLLS. $27.00

PARADISE OF PAPER DOLLS.

PARADISE OF PAPER DOLLS.

PARADISE OF PAPER DOLLS.

PARADISE OF PAPER DOLLS.

Universal Toy and Novelty Mfg. Co.

The trademark of Universal is a world globe with the company's name written on it. This trademark makes it easy to identify paper doll sheets by this company. Besides paper dolls the company also published sheets of paper furniture.

$10.00 each uncut sheet

Courtesy of Pam Hunter

DOTTY DOLLS

Courtesy of Pam Hunter

DOTTY DOLLS

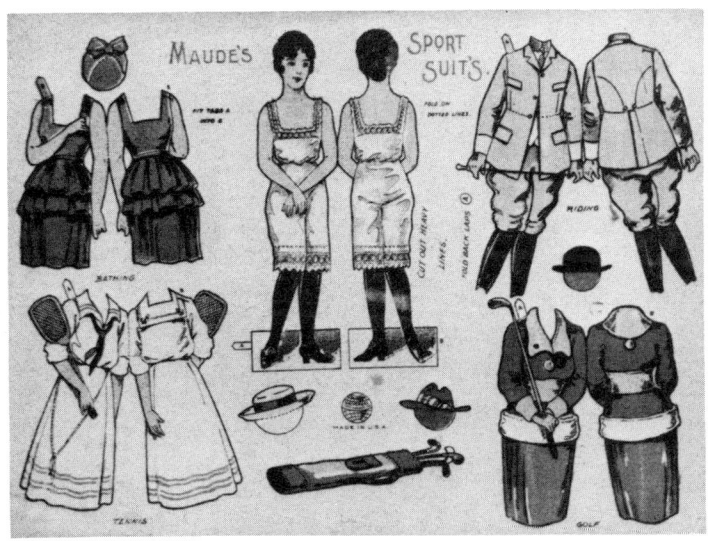

MAUDE'S SPORT SUITS

TOMMY TUCKER

197

Courtesy of Virginia Crossley

FLOSSIE'S ROBES

No title given

PAPER TOY DOLLS

Warren Paper Products

Built-Rite Division

Warren Paper Products was established in 1921 in Lafayette, Indiana. It began as a manufacturer of cardboard containers for items such as candy. In the early 1930's the company began producing doll houses of paper board. Toy forts and toy gas stations also were made at that time, and in the 1940's they added stations and towns for train sets, furniture for the doll houses and farm sets. All the sets were of paper board and were made to be put together easily. Paper dolls, doll houses and other toy sets were produced by the Built-Rite Division of Warren Paper Products. Paper dolls were introduced in the early 1950's and were produced up until 1970.

Currently the company produces a nice line of picture puzzles, games, children's educational products and playsets.

Following the list of the company's paper dolls is a list of their early toy sets and doll houses which have become quite collectable. Since the paper dolls were not dated, catalog dates are given when known.

15 *CINDY AND LINDY* (not pictured; 1955/56 catalogs, dolls same as #460)
15 *DEBBY AND DOTTY* (not pictured; 1955/56 catalogs)
33 *ANN AND PAM* (1953-1961 catalogs)
33 *JAN AND JEAN* (1953-1961 catalogs)
33 *MARGE AND MARY* (dolls same as *SANDY AND CANDY*)
33 *SANDY AND CANDY* (1953-1961 catalogs)
33 *TONI AND TERRY* (not pictured)
34 *JOAN AND BILL*

35 *JEAN AND JANET* (not pictured; dolls same as *ANN AND PAM*)
359 *TV PAPER DOLL SET, BARN DANCE JAMBOREE* (1957/58 catalogs) (not pictured)
359 *TV PAPER DOLL SET, TALENT SHOW* (1957/1958 catalog) (not pictured)
460 *MAGIC PRESS-ON PAPER DOLLS* (in small playing card size box, in 1961/62 catalog)
488 *COUNTRY AND WESTERN* (the dolls are the same as #359 *BARN DANCE JAMBOREE*)

847 *TWO BIG STAND-UP DOLLS, COLOR AND RE-COLOR* (1959/60 catalogs. Later in the 1963 catalog the name of set is changed to *COLOR BY NUMBER DOLL SET* and is listed in catalogs up to 1970.)
848 *FOUR MERRI-TIME DOLLS WITH LIFE LIKE FUR GARMENTS.* (1960-1968 catalogs)
867 *THE DRESS-UP GAME* (not pictured; 1963-1970 catalogs)
970 *FURRY GARMENTS* (not pictured; 1962 catalog)
2006 *JUNIOR MISS* (not pictured; game chest that includes #867 and #359 Talent Show. 1969/1970 catalogs)

Built-Rite Doll Houses, Toy Buildings and Stand-Ups
1 *TOY SOLDIERS*
2 *TRENCH SET*
7 *DOLL HOUSE MADE FOR LIFE MAGAZINE*
7 *TOY GARAGE*
8 *DOLL HOUSE*
9 *DOLL HOUSE*
10 *TWO STORY DOLL HOUSE*
10 *ONE ROOM FURNISHED DOLL HOUSE*
11 *PLAYTIME DOLL HOUSE STYLE* 4
12 *PLAYTIME DOLL SET*
14 *TRENCH AND SOLDIER SET*
14 *PLAY TIME DOLL HOUSE STYLE* 20
15 *TOY GARAGE*
16 *TOY FORT*
17 *GAS STATION*
18 *AIRPORT*
19 *RAILROAD STATION*
20 *MODEL STOCK FARM* (plastic animals)
20 *BATTERY SET*
20 *RAILROAD TUNNEL*
22 *ARMY OUTPOST*, 20 "action" soldiers
24 *TOY FORT SET*
25 *TOY FORT SET*
26 *UNITED AIRLINES AIRPORT HANGER*
27 *DOLL MANSION*
27 *BARN WITH ANIMALS*
28 *PLAYTIME DOLL HOUSE STYLE* 12
29 *THREE CAR SET*
33F *BUILT-RITE TOY HOUSE*
34 *DOLL HOUSE*
35 *MODERN DOLL HOUSE*
36F *THREE ROOM FURNISHED DOLL HOUSE*
36 *DOLL HOUSE*
37 *FARM MACHINERY SET*
40 *RAILROAD ACCESSORY SET, SUBURBAN*
41 *MINIATURE VILLAGE*, 11 buildings

45 *RAILROAD SET, PASSENGER & FREIGHT STATIONS*
46 *DINING ROOM FURNITURE*
47 *DOLLY'S ROOMETTE, PLAY HOUSE*
49 *KITCHEN FURNITURE*
51 *BEDROOM PLAYROOM SET*
52 *DINING ROOM PLAY ROOM SET*
53 *KITCHEN PLAY ROOM SET*
55 *MINIATURE HOUSES*
56 *MINIATURE BUILDINGS*
57M *MINIATURE FARM BUILDINGS*
66 *BUILD YOUR OWN KITCHEN*
75 *LIVING ROOM FURNITURE*
76 *DINING ROOM FURNITURE*
77 *BEDROOM FURNITURE*
78 *KITCHEN FURNITURE*
98 *MOTOR SET*
99 *GARAGE WITH 6 CARS*
99 *GARAGE WITH 3 CARS*
100 *FORTRESS*
105 *FARM SET, BARN ETC.* (plastic animals)
111 *TRAIN ACCESSORY SET*
112 *AMERICAN SOLDIERS*
115 *FURNISHED DOLL HOUSE WITH GARAGE*
119 *STOCK FARM DELUXE*
119 *BUILT-RITE FARM SET*
120 *FIVE ROOM SUBURBAN DOLL HOUSE*
127 *LARGE FARM*
128 *MINIATURE VILLAGE & SCENERY SET*
148 *TRAIN ACCESSORY SET*
156 *MINIATURE HOUSES AND BUILDINGS*
178 *TRAIN ACCESSORY SET*
201 *GUARDSMEN*
204F *DOLL HOUSE*
212 *STATION AND RAILROAD ACCESSORY SET*
245 *TRAIN ACCESSORY SET*
252 *26 PIECE FORT SET*
257 *FORT AND SOLDIERS SET*
298 *TRAIN ACCESSORY SET*
415 *DOLL HOUSE AND GARAGE*
459 *FIVE ROOMS OF TOY FURNITURE*
498 *TRAIN ACCESSORY SET*
556 *MINIATURE VILLAGE*
1033 *BUILT-RITE TOY HOUSE*
1422 *94 PIECE FORTRESS SET*
2050 *COUNTRY ESTATE DOLL HOUSE*
4132 *NATIVITY SET*

Courtesy of Virginia Crossley

33 *ANN AND PAM.* $6.00

Courtesy of Virginia Crossley

33 *JAN AND JEAN.* $6.00

33 *MARGE AND MARY.* $6.00

Courtesy of Virginia Crossley
33 *SANDY AND CANDY.* $6.00

34 *JOAN AND BILL.* $6.00

460 *MAGIC PRESS-ON PAPER DOLLS.* $3.50

488 *COUNTRY AND WESTERN PAPER DOLL SET.* $6.00

Courtesy of Audrey Sepponen
847 *2 BIG STAND-UP DOLLS.* $10.00

Courtesy of Audrey Sepponen
848 *4 MERRY-TIME DOLLS WITH LIFE LIKE FUR GARMENTS.* $12.00

Whitehall Publishing Company

Courtesy of Virginia Crossley

DRESS UP JUMBO AND BUNNY, 1950
DRESS UP PUSS AND CHICKY, 1950
$7.00 each

Courtesy of Virginia Crossley

Inside pages.

The doll of Jumbo was also published alone as *MUMBO THE ELEPHANT DRESS-UP* and Puss was done alone in *SHUFFLE ON CATSY DRESS-UP*

Albert Whitman and Company

Courtesy of Rosalie Eppert
BROWNIES FROM BINGO-LAND, 1922. $30.00

BROWNIES FROM BINGO-LAND
One page from the book

The John C. Winston Company

THE MARY FRANCES HOUSEKEEPER, ADVENTURES AMONG THE DOLL PEOPLE, 1914

This is a hard cover book with four color pages of paper dolls and four duplicate pages in black and white. There are also fourteen pages of paper furniture in color and again each of these is duplicated in black and white. This was done to allow removal of the color pages without breaking the continuity of the story book. The child was also encouraged to use the black and white pages for tracing, to make additional paper dolls and furniture. The story is about a family of paper dolls in need of a house in which to live. There are 253 pages in the book. The child reader learns the art of housekeeping in an enjoyable manner. Included in the book are detailed instructions for making a cardboard dollhouse for the paper dolls.

Other books in the series were *The Mary Frances Sewing Book*, *The Mary Frances Cook Book* and *The Mary Frances Garden Book*, but these books did not contain paper dolls.

There is a reprint of *The Mary Frances Housekeeper* entitled, *Easy Steps in Housekeeping*.

The book pictured is in mint condition with all paper doll and furniture pages intact, and includes the dust jacket on the book.

Courtesy of Rosalie Eppert

THE MARY FRANCES HOUSEKEEPER, 1914. $125.00 and up

THE MARY FRANCES HOUSEKEEPER
Inside page of paper dolls

FIRST DAYS IN SCHOOL, 1942.
$12.00

FIRST DAYS IN SCHOOL
Inside page

FIRST DAYS IN SCHOOL
Inside page

Winthrop-Atkins Co., Inc.

405 *TAMMY'S MAGIC MIRROR FASHION SHOW*.
$10.00

Courtesy of Virginia Crossley

6310 *MARTHA ANN*. $10.00

Wonder Books

These paper doll books are not pictured:
6685 *PEBBLES*, 1974
6686 *BAMM-BAMM*, 1974
6687 *PEBBLES AND BAMM-BAMM*, 1974
6688 *WILMA AND FRED*, 1974
6689 *BETTY AND BARNEY*, 1974
6690 *YOGI AND CINDY*, 1974

9600 *HEIDI*, 1971
9601 *ALICE IN WONDERLAND*, 1971
9602 *LITTLE RED RIDING HOOD*, 1971
9603 *CINDERELLA*, 1971
9604 *SNOW WHITE*, 1971
9605 *BRIDE AND GROOM*, 1971

The World Publishing Company

R-501 *THE WARDROBE BOOK*, 1952. $17.00

THE WARDROBE BOOK
Inside page of dolls

Additions to the Saalfield, Lowe and Merrill Collector's Guide

Saalfield Section:
On page 8 reference is made to *The Doll I Love Best*. Recently a box set has been found with the same doll on the box cover; however, the title reads *Dolls I Love Best* and the set contains two dolls instead of one. The number on the box is 2B and the dolls are Margaret-#203 and Alice-#204.

A small 6½ x 7½" Saalfield linen type book of paper dolls with no stock number has been found. The title is *Paper Dolls, Bob and Judy*. There is no date. It evidently came in a box with other activity books.

Another book to be added is #1170 *The Four Little Dolls*, Saalfield, 1920. This is a story book with four pages of paper dolls at the back of the book. One doll is named Gladys and is found in #1180 *Dollies to Paint, Cut-Out and Dress* published in 1918. (The doll is named Elizabeth in #1180.) Two other dolls named Rose and Violet are missing from the book. They may have been in #1180 also, under different names. The last doll is Saraphine. She has never appeared before now and may have been drawn especially for this story book.

Additions to the Saalfield List of Paper Dolls:
1170 *THE FOUR LITTLE DOLLS*, 1920
3827 *MY THREE SONS*-coloring/paper doll book (3927)
3843 *WEDDING DAY*-coloring/paper doll book (9619)
5144 *DARLING PAPER DOLLS*, 1966/1969/1972 (4452 Sugar Plum Pals)
6050 *SHARI LEWIS AND HER PUPPETS* (activity box)

Courtesy of Verlee Waterman

1170 *THE FOUR LITTLE DOLLS*, 1920. $30.00

PAPER DOLLS, BOB AND JUDY. $5.00

Addition to the Lowe List of Paper Dolls:
1353 *THE LOLLYPOP CROWD* (1049)

Correction to the Merrill List of Paper Dolls:
3457 *Angel Babies*, 1953 (4853) This is wrong and should read-
3457 *ANGEL BABIES*, 1953 (1553 Heavenly Twins)

PHOTO INDEX

ALL MY DOLLIES.....76
AMERICAN BEAUTIES.....106, 108
AMERICAN COLONIAL BRIDES.....94
AMERICAN FAMILY.....90
AMERICAN MISS.....150
ANN AND JOE.....51
ANN AND PAM.....199
ANTIQUE DOLLS GO TO A PAPER DOLL WEDDING.....22
ANTIQUE FRENCH DOLL PAPER DOLLS.....21, 22
ANTONY, MARK.....27
AROUND THE WORLD WITH BOB AND BARBARA.....31, 108
AROUND THE WORLD WITH DOROTHY DOT.....34
AT HOME-ABROAD DOLLS.....162
BABY BETTY.....68
BABY JANE.....28
BABY MERRY.....125
BABYLAND - BOBBY, PEGGY.....73
BEAUTIFUL BRIDE.....102
BEAUTIFUL DOLLS FOR CHILDREN TO DRESS.....166
BEAUTY DOLLS TO DRESS.....89
BECKY.....41
BETSY BALLERINA.....45
BETSY MCCALL.....23, 25, 66
BETTINA AND HER PLAYMATE ROSALIE.....184
BETTY AND DICK TOUR THE U.S.A......23
BETTY AND JACK DOLLS TO DRESS.....166
BETTY AND PEGGY.....161
BETTY ANN AND AUDREY.....157
BETTY ANN AND HER FRIENDS.....157, 160
BETTY BELLE PAPER DOLLS.....172
BETTY, COMPLETE WARDROBE AND TRUNK.....175
BETTY IS GOING AWAY TO BOARDING SCHOOL.....74
BETTY JANE.....68
BETTY LOU, JANE.....7
BETTY MARIE.....109
BEWITCHED.....112
BIBLE CHILDREN PAPER DOLLS.....183
BIBLE LAND CHILDREN.....143
BIBLE THINK AND DO.....85
BIG GIRL.....119
BIG SISTER.....109, 119
BILD-A-SET, 10 BEAUTIFUL JUNIOR GIRLS IN UNIFORMS.....155
BILLY BOB, GEORGIE.....7
BILLY BOY.....184
BIRTHDAY PARTY.....142
BLACK IS BEAUTIFUL.....112
BLONDIE.....38
BOB AND JUDY.....205
BOB AND NAN.....50
BOBBIE GIRLS.....40
BOBBSEY TWINS PLAY BOX.....170
BOBBY, DOLL TO DRESS.....110
BOONE, DANIEL AND KIT CARSON.....181
BOY AND GIRL CUTOUT DOLL BOOK.....184
BRADLEY'S TRU-LIFE PAPER DOLLS.....136
BRIDAL PARTY.....77
BRIDE.....39, 121
BRIDE AND GROOM.....111, 112
BRIDE DOLL.....63
BRIDE OF FRANKENSTEIN.....126
BRIGHT EYES.....39
BRONCO BESS.....133
BROTHER BOB.....66
BROWNIE SCOUT PAPER DOLLS.....43
BROWNIES FROM BINGO-LAND.....201
BUSTER BROWN AND TIGE.....148
CAROL AND HER DRESSES.....70
CAROLINE.....111
CELIE.....123
CENTURY DOLLS.....164
CHANTICLEER PAPER DOLL.....148
CHEERLEADER TEEN-AGE DOLL CUT OUTS.....187
CHILDREN OF GOD'S WORLD.....183
CHILDREN OF THE WAR ZONE.....30
CHRISTINA FROM SWEDEN.....21
CHUBBY CUBBY.....15
CINDERELLA.....99, 133, 175
CIRCUS DAY.....185
CIRCUS TWINS.....141
CLAIRE.....39
CLARK, MARGUERITE.....173
CLEOPATRA.....27
COLONIAL DOLLS.....163
COMBAT JIM, COMBAT JOE.....182
CONNIE.....25, 167

CORINNE.....10
COSTUME DOLLS.....160
COSTUME PARTY.....77, 108
COUNTRY AND WESTERN PAPER DOLL SET.....200
COUNTRY WEEK END WITH KATHY AND JILL.....31, 108
COUSIN KATE.....65
CREATIVE CUT-OUTS.....194
CUDDLY DOLLS.....88
CURLY LOCKS.....89
CURLY TOP.....44
CUTIE PAPER DOLLS.....134, 138, 139
DAINTEE DOLL.....20
DAINTY DOLLIES.....59, 81
DAISY DOLLY.....85, 86
DANCING PRISCILLA.....27
DANDY DOGGIE.....15
DEARIE DOLLS.....87, 89
DEBBIE.....24
DEBBIE DOLLS.....116, 118
DEBBY DOLLS.....102, 103
DEBUTANTES.....75
DENNISON PAPER DOLLS.....47, 48, 49
DIMPLE DOLL FAMILY.....73
DOLL CUT OUTS.....7, 36
DOLL DRESSES TO COLOR.....68
DOLL HOUSE CUT OUTS.....187
DOLL HOUSE DRESS SHOP.....193
DOLLIES A'LA MODE.....83
DOLLIES DRESSES.....138
DOLLIES TO DRESS LIKE FATHER AND MOTHER.....159
DOLLS ACROSS THE SEA.....160
DOLLS FROM FAIRYLAND.....146
DOLLS FROM THE LAND OF MOTHER GOOSE.....158
DOLLS'S HOUSE THAT GLUE BUILT.....188
DOLLS OF ALL NATIONS.....144
DOLLS OF FAR-OFF LANDS.....160
DOLLS OF THE NATIONS.....180, 181
DOLLS' OPEN HOUSE.....158
DOLLS THAT YOU LOVE.....92
DOLLS TO CUT-OUT AND DRESS.....121
DOLLS TO MAKE AND DRESS.....190
DOLLS WITH WILLIAMSBURG COLONIAL DRESS.....77
DOLLY DARLING.....58, 65
DOLLY DELIGHT.....84
DOLLY DIMPLE.....184
DOLLY MAY.....177
DOLLY SHEETS.....84
DOLLY TWINS.....40
DOLLYLAND.....71, 72
DOLLY'S HOME.....14
DOLLY'S KUT-OUT KLOTHES.....18
DOROTHY.....167
DOROTHY AND RUTH DOLLS TO DRESS.....166
DOROTHY DIMPLE AND HER FRIENDS.....97
DOTTIE DRESS-UP.....56
DOTTIE WITH THE SNAP-ON DRESSES.....42
DOTTY AND DANNY ON PARADE.....28
DOTTY DOLLS.....197
DOTTY DRESS DOLL.....30
DRESS A DAY.....6
DRESS ME BOOK.....83
DRESS OUR DOLLS.....79
DRESS-UP.....107, 194
DRESS UP JUMBO AND BUNNY, PUSS AND CHICKY.....201
DRESS-UPS.....147
EARLY AMERICAN DOLLS.....158
EFFANBEE PRESENTS _____.....93, 94
EIGHTEEN LITTLE MOVIE STAR PAPER DOLLS.....119
EMBROIDERY DOLLS.....104
EVER-NEW DOLL.....69
EVERY DAY PLAY SET.....18
FAIR MARGARET.....177
FAIRY FAVORITE.....52
FAIRY-TALE AND FLOWER PAPER DOLLS.....52, 53, 54
FAIRY TALE CUT OUT DOLLS AND FURNITURE.....168
FANCY DRESS DOLLS.....84
FASHION KIT DESIGN AND COLOR PAPER DOLL.....195
FASHION MODEL.....70
FESTIVAL FUN.....45
FILMLAND FASHIONS.....185
FIRST DAYS IN SCHOOL.....202, 203
FIRST LADY.....112
FIVE FLYING AMERICANS.....90
FIVE MODEL MISS CUTOUT DOLLS.....193
FLOSSIE.....178
FLOSSIE'S ROBES.....198

Title	Page
FLUFFY RUFFLES	148
FOLLIES GIRL, JACKIE	155
FOREIGN DOLLS	163
FORGET-ME-NOT PAPER DOLLS	191
FOUR LITTLE DOLLS	205
FOUR MERRI-TIME DOLLS	200
FOUR SNAP-IN-PLACE STAND-UP DOLLS	101
FRANCES AND HER FROCKS	73
FRIEND PAPER DOLL	50
FRIENDSHIP PAPER DOLLS	63
FROGGIE WENT A COURTING	38
FUN FARM FROLICS	96
FUNNY BUNNIES	117
GAY DOLLS	159
GINA	39
GINGHAM GIRL	45
GLAMOROUS MOVIE STARS OF THE THIRTIES	57
GLAMOUR MODELS	186
GLAMOUR PARADE	187
GLENDORA	42
GLENN	101
GLITTER DOLLS	168
GLORIANA THE FAMOUS HOLLYWOOD STAR	176
GOING ABROAD DOLLS	161
GOLDILOCKS	39, 134
GOREY CATS PAPER DOLLS	195
GRANDMOTHERS DOLLS	63
GRANNY	112
GREAT BALLET PAPER DOLLS	195
HANSEL AND GRETEL	42
HAPPI TIME DRESSMAKER KIT	29
HEIDI	40
HELLO, I'M ADELINE	19
HISTORICAL DOLLS	160
HONEY BUN	38, 102
I WISH I WERE	140
I'M GROWING UP DOLLS	162
IMPROVED PAPER DOLL OUTFIT	151
IRENE	167
IVY	101
JACK AND JANET PAPER DOLLS	106
JACKIE AND CAROLINE	111
JACK-O'-LANTERN CUT-OUT PAPER DOLLS	100
JACKSON, ANDREW AND OLIVER HAZARD PERRY	181
JAN AND JEAN	199
JANE AND JILL'S NEW FROCKS AND FRILLS	174
JANET AND DICK	158
JANET AND JEANNE	161
JAUNTY JUNIORS	107
JEAN AND TOMMY	157
JEANS' AND THINGS	135
JET AIRLINE STEWARDESS	102
JILL	41
JIMMY, JACK	8
JOAN AND BILL	200
JODI	126
JOHNNY JONES	85, 86
JUDY	110
JUNE BRIDE	185
JUNIOR FASHIONS	71
JUNIOR MISS DOLLS	161
JUNIOR SHOP	67
JUVENILE ARTIST	62
KATIE	123
KATRINE FROM HOLLAND	21
KIM'S PAPER DOLL	172
KITTY AND DOGGIE	156
LACE-ME-UPS	35
LACEY DAISY	105
LADY BELLE	178
LEE, BRENDA	125
LEE, LILA	174
LET'S BUILD OUR CAMP	78
LET'S PLAY ESKIMO	171
LET'S PLAY PAPER DOLLS	117
LET'S TELL OTHERS ABOUT JESUS	85
LETTIE LANE PAPER FAMILY	99
LIFE-LIKE DOLL SET	179
LIFE SIZE DOLL	37
LI'L MISS DESIGNER KIT	190
LIL' PEARL	89
LINDA B.	126
LINDA THE BALLERINA	24, 25
LISA YOUR PAPER DOLL PLAYMATE	49
LITTLE ALICE BUSY BEE	10
LITTLE AMERICANS FROM MANY LANDS	79, 80
LITTLE AUDREY	80
LITTLE BETTY GAD-ABOUT	9
LITTLE BO PEEP	42, 58
LITTLE BOY BLUE	165
LITTLE BUNTINGS	165
LITTLE CHERUBS	165
LITTLE DARLING DRESSING DOLLS	14
LITTLE DOCTOR	108
LITTLE FACES FROM FAR PLACES	171
LITTLE FOLKS CREPE PAPER DOLL OUTFIT	18
LITTLE FOLKS DOLL'S SET	139
LITTLE FRIENDS FROM HISTORY	171
LITTLE KITTY CUT-UP AND HER PLAYMATES	15
LITTLE LADDIE	178
LITTLE MISS UP-TO-DATE	9
LITTLE NEDDIE NEVER-STILL	10
LITTLE NURSE	108
LITTLE ORPHAN ANNIE	68
LITTLE PET'S PLAY HOUSE	79
LITTLE POLLY DRESS-UP	10
LITTLE RED RIDING HOOD	41
LITTLE RED SCHOOL HOUSE KINDERGARTEN	117
LITTLE SISTER	36
LITTLE SWEETHEARTS	186
LITTLE WILLIE WIDE-AWAKE	10
LITTLEST DARLING	40
LIZZIE	124
LOOK WHO I AM!	92
LOVE PAPER DOLL	50
LOVEY AND DOVEY MAGIC DOLLS	151
LULA-BYE-BYE	89
LULLABY TWINS	141
LYNDA-LOU DOLL	105
MABEL	85
MADAME HATTIE	108
MAGIC DOLL	95, 152, 153
MAGIC LOCKET PAPER DOLL	25
MAGIC MARY PAPER DOLLS	129-133
MAGIC PRESS-ON PAPER DOLLS	200
MAGIC PRINCESS	112
MAGIC TOUCH PAPER DOLL	25
MAGNA MAGIC SUE	31
MAGNETIC PAPER DOLLS	31, 129-133, 140, 182, 183
MAKE-IT BOOK	171
MAMIE	123, 178
MAMMY AND KINKY-TOP	46
MARCELLA'S RAGGEDY ANN DOLL BOOK	116
MARDI GRAS	59
MARGARET EVANS PRICE PAPER DOLLS	60, 61
MARGE AND MARY	200
MARGIE	26
MARGY, MILDRED	7
MARIE, PATSY ANN	7
MARTHA WASHINGTON DOLL BOOK	95
MARY ALICE	68
MARY ANN GOES TO MEXICO	108
MARY FRANCES HOUSEKEEPER	202
MARY LOU AND HER FRIENDS	162
MARTHA ANN	203
MAUDES' SPORT SUITS	197
MERRIE WITH THE GO-ROUND DRESSES	140
MERRY MERMAIDS	108
MIMI, THE FRENCH MODEL	42
MINI-MODS	112
MINTER, MARY MILES	173
MISS AIRLINES, PAT KENNELLY OF TWA	32
MISS AMERICA	106, 153
MISS HOLLY DAY	42
MISS HOLLYWOOD	107
MISS NURSE DRESS-UP KIT	33
MISS SILVER SCREEN	107
MODERN DOLLS	83, 157, 162
MODERNE SEWING FOR LITTLE GIRLS	17
MOTHER AND DAUGHTER	90, 108
MOTHER AND DAUGHTER DRESSES	56
MOTHER DAUGHTER DOLLS	38
MOTHER GOOSE CUT-OUT PICTURE BOOK	141
MOVIE STARLETS	186
MOVIELAND	107
MOVING EYE DOLLY	68
MR. AND MRS. HAWAII	176
MULTI-HEAD PAPER DOLLS	116
MY BABY	33, 44
MY BOOK OF DARLING DOLLIES	82
MY BOOK OF DARLING DOLLS	82
MY COMPLETE SEW-DRESS BOX	69
MY DOLL JACK	65
MY DOLL JILL	65
MY DOLLIES PASTIME CUT OUT SHEETS	79
MY DOLLY'S CRAYON BOOK	81
MY FAIR LADY	24
MY LADY FAIRE DOLL	140
MY NAME IS MARION	39
MY OWN DOLLS TO COLOR AND DRESS	194
MY PAPER DOLL'S SEWING KIT	91
MY WARDROBE DOLLS	66

Title	Page
NANCY	48, 167
NANCY AND JANE	95
NAYAN DOLLS NO. 1	145
NELLIE	123
NEW JUDY	6
NEW LAURIE	6
NEW MODEL BOOK OF DOLLS	114
NURSE AND TWINS	89
NURSERY FAVORITE	52
NURSERY RHYME PARTY DOLLS IN COSTUME	115
NURSERY RHYMES	31, 134
OLD FASHIONED DOLL	33
OLD DEERFIELD DOLLS	147
OUR AMERICA	69
OUR DOLLIES MODEL BOOK	115
OUR FAVORITE DOLLS	5, 19, 179
OUR HAPPY FAMILY	78
OUR SAMMY	11
OUR WORLD CUT-OUT OF THE MONTH	61, 62
OUTDOOR FUN	109
PAINT ME PRETTY	113
PAJAMA PARTY	187
PAM AND JEFF	193
PANSY PRATTLE	86
PAPER DOLL BAZAAR	70
PAPER DOLL OUTFIT	17, 154
PAPER DOLLS	108
PAPER DOLLS OF THE WORLD	98
PAPER TOY DOLLS	198
PARADISE OF PAPER DOLLS	195, 196
PARTY DOLLS	159
PARTY OF THE PAPER DOLLS	118
PATSY	31, 108
PATTY'S PARTY	186
PEGGY	167
PENNY AND HER DOLLY	39
PERCY REEVES MOVY-DOLS PAINTING BOOK I	183
PETER RABBIT	175
PETTICOAT JUNCTION	24
PICKFORD, MARY	174
PLAY DAY CUT OUTS	190
PLAY PAPER DOLLS	67
PLAYHOUSE DOLLS	185
PLAYMATE	41
PLAYTIME DOLLS	160
PLAYTIME FASHIONS	185
PLAYTIME PALS	35
POCAHONTAS AND JOHN SMITH	181
POKY-HONTAS	45
POLLY ANN	100
POLLY DOLLY	105
POLLY PERT	66
POLLY PITCHER AND HER PLAYMATES	99
PONY TAIL	71
PRETTY DOLLS	159, 165
PRETTY KITTY	15
PRETTY PAPER PETS	59
PRETTY PENNY AND HER PAL	109
PRIMROSE PAPER DOLLS	192
PRINCESS DIANA PAPER DOLL BOOK OF FASHION	170
PRINCESS ELIZABETH MAGIC DOLL	154
PRINCESS MARGARET ROSE MAGIC DOLL	154
PRISCILLA AND JOHN ALDEN	181
PROGRESSIVE SEWING SET	170
PUSS IN BOOTS	94
QUEEN ELIZABETH I	26
RAG DOLL SUE	93
RAGGEDY ANN CUT OUT DOLLS	134
REAL SLEEPING DOLL	119
REED, DONNA	126
REELY-TROOLY DOLLS	173
ROSEMARY THE ROUND ABOUT DOLL	59
ROSETTA FROM MEXICO	20
ROSS, BETSY	158
ROUND ABOUT DOLLS	116, 117, 119, 120, 136, 137, 138
ROYAL FAMILY	26
SALLY DIMPLE	28
SALLY, JANET	7
SANDRA THE BRIDE	25
SANDY AND CANDY	200
SAPPHIRE, QUEEN OF THE NIGHT CLUB	107
SCHOOL DAYS	71, 142
SCHOOL MATES	68
SCISSORS BIRD PAPER DOLLS	185
SEVEN DOLLS IN ONE	41
SEW-EASY DOLL	73
SEWING SET, DOLLS TO DRESS	30
SHIPMATES	91
SHIRLEY	167
SHOO-SHOO SHIRLEY	38
SISTER NAN	66
SISTERS	76
SIX GOOD LITTLE DOLLS	187
SIX PLAYTIME DOLLS	90
SLEEPING BEAUTY AND PRINCE CHARMING	43
SLEEPY TIME GIRL	139
SMART FASHIONS	82
SMILE DRESS-UP KIT	33
SNOW WHITE	169
SNUGGLY DOLLS	89
STAND-UP CUT OUT DOLLS WEDDING BOOK	142
STAND-UP DOLLS	142
STITCH AND SEW	169
SUE AND SAL, THE SNAP-ON SISTERS	146
SUNNY THE WONDER DOLL	135
SUNSHINE CUT-OUTS	189
SUPER MARKET	91
SUSAN	84
SUSIE, JUDY, LAURA AND ANNIE	6
SUZIE SWEET	66, 92
SWEET SUE	111
SWEETIE-PIE TWINS	186
TAMMY'S MAGIC MIRROR FASHION SHOW	203
TED AND BOB	51
TEDDY BEAR	146, 148, 156, 178
TEEN-AGE TRAVEL FUN	109
TEENA THE TEENAGER	24
TEENEY WEENY PRETTY DOLLIES	87
TELEVISION DOLLS	136
TEMPLE, SHIRLEY	80, 81
THREE BEARS' HOME	114
THREE BIG DOLLS	40
THREE HIGH FASHION MODELS	113
THIRTY FROM THE 30's	169
TINA THE TALKING PAPER DOLL	33
TINY DOLLS	88
TINY TEARS	111
TINY TIPTOE	51
TINY TWINKLE	88
TODDLER TWINS	76
TODDLING TOM	68
TOMMY TOM	96
TOMMY TUCKER	197
TONI	126
TOWN AND COUNTRY	36, 82
TRESSY	111
TRIPLE-JOY-BOOK	155
TRIPLET DOLLS	186
TUBBY TWINKLE	88
TURN AND TURN ABOUT DOLLIES	74
TWINKLEY EYES	139
TWINNIES	67, 69, 75
TWINS TRAVELOGUES	5
TWO BIG STAND-UP DOLLS	200
TWO-GUN PETE	133
VALENTINO, RUDOLPH	57
VELVA DOLL	104
VICKI VELCRO PAPER DOLL	75
VICTORIA	149
WARDROBE BOOK	204
WARDROBE DOLLS	29
WASHINGTON, GEORGE AND MARTHA WASHINGTON	182
WE ARE THE WARDROBE PAPER DOLLS	188
WE THREE	109
WEDDING BELLES	56
WEDDING PARTY	75
WENDY AND HER MOMMY	110
WENDY WALKS	126
WENDY'S WARDROBE	100
WHEN I GROW UP	35
WIDE AWAKE AND FAST ASLEEP DOLL	73
WILDWEST TWINS	141
WILLIAMSBURG COLONIAL DOLLS	164
WINKLE FAMILY	74
WINKY WINNIE	102
WINNIE AND HER WARDROBE	118
WINNIE WINKLE	70
WOOD DOLLS WITH ROUND ABOUT DRESSES	137
YOUNG AMERICAN DESIGNER	55
YOUNG MISS DOLLS	159
YOUR OWN QUINTUPLETS	28